Mystic Mountain Memories

– A Mother-Son Cookbook

Written and Compiled by
JOSIE and JERRY MINERICH

Illustrated by
COLETTE B. McLAUGHLIN

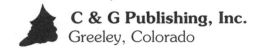

C & G Publishing, Inc.
Greeley, Colorado

MYSTIC MOUNTAIN MEMORIES

By Josie and Jerry Minerich

Published by:

C & G Publishing, Inc.
2702 19th Street Road
Greeley, CO 80631
1-800-925-3172

Copyright © 1990, 1993 by Josie and Jerry Minerich
First printing: 1001 copies, April 1990
Second printing: 1001 copies, Sept. 1990
C & G Publishing, Inc.:
Third printing: 5000 copies, Nov. 1993, completely revised
Printed in the United States of America

Library of Congress Catalog Card Number: 93-73836
ISBN 0-9626355-3-4

INTRODUCTION

We have created this cookbook to be much more than just a collection of recipes. We have gone to extra expense and effort to make this an educational book that will teach you about being creative and economical. Our special section, "Lessons and hints on Eating, Cooking and Living Better", will give you hints on how to create your own recipes, change recipes by deleting, substituting or adding ingredients. Besides the hints, you will find "ideas" at the end of several recipes for suggestions.

We GUARANTEE you will save enough money to pay for this book several times over in just the first year. By simply going through your newspaper ads and planning your menu around the specials instead of planning a menu and then buying, you will save more than enough in one week to cover the cost of this book.

As a creative cook, you'll save even more. You will be able to open your refrigerator or cabinet and use what's there instead of going out and buying more while what you already have sits in the corner of the refrigerator until it starts to mold.

Being creative will also help you prepare fresh meals every meal without having leftovers, even if you're by yourself or just 2 of you. By making up your own recipe, you can make up just the amount you want instead of eating leftovers 4 nights in a row. You will impress friends and who knows, you might even invent a recipe that could win you a contest.

OTHER FEATURES:

1. A separate division for fresh fruits, so that you may take advantage of fruit in season without having to jump all over the book.
2. Cross referencing in the index. Several items may be listed more than once. Example, most of the pies will be found in the fruit section according to the filling, but you will find all the pies, cakes, cookies and candies listed together in the index under their category as well as under the name.
3. A special page to tell you "What to do with the Rest of It" (last page, just prior to the index) such as leftover egg whites or yolks, sour cream, etc.
4. ** on both sides of the title indicates an impressive item such as **German Chocolate Cake**.
5. EZ marked on the right of the title, indicates an easy recipe.
6. Besides "HEALTHY" being printed on the right of healthier recipes, we have also given you hints throughout as to how to make any recipe healthier.
7. Quantities, especially on cookies, are more honestly appraised. I often wonder how small the cookies must be in most other recipes. I normally get about 70% of what they usually say.
8. All recipes have been tested. We have selected all the most popular. If you have any special recipe requests or ideas for our next book, please let us know.
9. All ingredients are readily available in supermarkets.

DEDICATION

I dedicate this book to my parents. To my mother who co-wrote this book with me, I thank you for the childhood memories of fresh baked bread, cookies, cakes and pies. No matter how lean the year, there was always dessert and after school snacks. Mom, I don't know how you ever got so much done. I still look back on those times when I need some inspiration.

And to my dad, a dreamer like myself with dreams of a successful farm. Although you never made it quite like you wanted to, you have taught me that there is no failure in trying but rather in failing to try.

I look back now with appreciation. We were poor in finances but the richest family in love.

Secondly, I'd like to dedicate this book to all the great people volunteering and working to make the world a little bit better place. Hopefully, we will be able to help a little through the sales of this book.

Sincerely,

Jerry Minerich

Appetizers
Beverages

TEMPURA BATTER

This is a recipe a friend gave me from a popular restaurant he used to work at (Chinese)

1 c. corn starch
1 c. flour
12 oz. beer
Dash of garlic powder
2 drops of Tabasco
  sauce
Dash of white pepper
Drop of Worcestershire
  sauce

Combine all dry ingredients; mix well. Add beer, Tabasco sauce and Worcestershire sauce and mix well with a wire whisk. Don't overbeat. Preheat vegetable oil or shortening to 375°. Oil should be about 2 inches deep in large pan or wok. Dip desired food (any vegetables, shrimp, pork, chicken, etc.) into batter and drop into hot oil. Brown on both sides. Remove from oil and drain on paper towel. Eat while hot. Dip in your favorite sauce (sweet and sour, Ranch, etc.)

"Idea:" Use mushrooms, following directions. When fried and drained, place on ovenproof dish. Add grated Cheddar; place under broiler until cheese is melted. *Superb!*

COLD PIZZA

Take this one to a party. It's an instant hit!

2 large size pkg.
  refrigerated crescent
  rolls dough
2 (8 oz.) pkg. cream
  cheese, softened
1 Tbsp. dill
Dash of garlic salt
Dash of seasoning salt
2/3 c. mayonnaise
2 medium size tomatoes,
  thinly sliced
1/2 lb. fresh mushrooms,
  thinly sliced
10 black olives, thinly
  sliced
2 or 3 scallions, thinly
  sliced
Alfalfa sprouts

Preheat oven to 400°. Unroll crescent rolls into large pizza pan and press seams together. Bake in oven for 10 minutes until lightly browned. Remove and cool completely.

In a small bowl, blend together the cream cheese and seasonings until mixture is well blended. Add mayonnaise and mix well. Spread cream cheese mixture over the top of the crust. Add vegetables, adding the sprouts last. Refrigerate 4 to 6 hours.

BEEF JERKY

Mom always doubles this recipe or more. It's great to take on hikes or for after school snacks. It lasts a long time, and since it takes a while to make, make a bunch!

Marinade:
4 Tbsp. soy sauce
4 Tbsp. Worcestershire
sauce
1 Tbsp. ketchup
1/4 tsp. pepper
1/4 tsp. garlic powder
1/4 tsp. onion salt
1/2 tsp. salt

Use either 1 pound very lean round steak or flank steak (Mom prefers flank). While partially frozen, cut meat into 3/8 to 1/4 inch strips. (It is easier to cut meat while partially frozen.) Cut against the grain for more tender jerky. Marinate meat for 1 hour.

For dehydrator, go by directions. For oven, temperature should be 140° to 160° for the first 3 1/2 hours. Lower temperature to 130° until jerky is dry. Place meat on wire racks with foil or baking pan underneath the drying tray to catch the drippings.

ORIGINAL CRISPIX MIX - EZ

3 Tbsp. butter or
margarine
1/4 tsp. garlic salt
1/4 tsp. onion salt
2 tsp. lemon juice
4 tsp. Worcestershire
sauce
7 c. Crispix cereal
1 c. salted mixed nuts
1 c. pretzels

Melt butter in 13x9 inch pan in oven at 250°. Remove from oven. Stir in garlic salt, onion salt, lemon juice, and Worcestershire sauce. Add cereal, nuts and pretzels, stirring until coated. Return to oven for another 45 minutes, stirring every 15 minutes. Spread on absorbent paper to cool. Yield: About 9 cups.

COCOA MIX - EZ

This cold weather drink is great for a family or after a sledding party or around the holidays. Add peppermint Schnapps or Amaretto and whipped cream.

1 (8 qt.) box dry milk
1 (6 oz.) jar dairy creamer
1 c. powdered sugar
1 lb. instant cocoa

Mix all together and store in covered container. To use, place 1/3 cup mix for 1 cup boiling water. If cocoa isn't as hot as you'd like after mixing, pop it in the microwave.

DO-AHEAD HOT BUTTERED RUM

Holidays.

1 pt. French vanilla ice
  cream
1 c. butter
3 c. brown sugar, packed
3 1/2 c. powdered sugar
1 tsp. nutmeg
1 tsp. cinnamon
Rum
Boiling water
Cinnamon sticks

Put ice cream and butter into a bowl and let soften. Add sugars and spices. Stir until smooth. Freeze. At serving time, place 3 tablespoons of the mix into a mug. Add 3 tablespoons rum. Fill with boiling water. Garnish with cinnamon sticks.

PINA COLADA SLUSH

Summer drink.

1 (20 oz.) can crushed
  pineapple (undrained)
2 (15 oz.) cans cream of
  coconut
1 (6 oz.) can pineapple
  juice
1 1/2 c. rum (optional)
1 (32 oz.) bottle club
  soda

In blender, combine crushed pineapple and cream of coconut; blend until smooth. In a large freezer-safe bowl, combine coconut mixture, pineapple and rum (if used). Cover; freeze overnight. Remove from freezer 30 minutes before serving. When mixture is slushy, spoon into a large punch bowl. Gradually add club soda. Garnish with pineapple tidbits and maraschino cherries if desired. Makes 4 quarts.

CHRISTMAS PUNCH - EZ

Christmas or St. "Paddy's" Day.

2 small pkg. lemon-lime
  Kool-Aid
1/2 c. sugar
1 qt. cold milk
1 pt. vanilla ice cream
2 (7 oz.) bottles 7-Up
Vodka (optional)

Mix sugar, milk and Kool-Aid. Add ice cream and stir until melted. Just before serving, add 7-Up and vodka.

Very good, with or without vodka. Good any season.

REFRESHING SLUSH

Outdoor drink for a bunch.

1 c. water
2 c. sugar
2 c. boiling water
4 bags green tea
1 (12 oz.) can frozen lemonade
1 (12 oz.) can frozen orange juice
2 c. brandy or gin
7-up

Mix water and sugar together in small saucepan and bring to a boil until sugar is dissolved. Set aside to cool.

Meanwhile, pour 2 cup of boiling water over tea and allow to steep. Remove tea bags and allow tea to cool. Mix syrup and tea together. Add lemonade and orange juice. Stir in gin or brandy. Put in covered containers and freeze. To use, put 1 tablespoon of slush in 1 tall glass and fill with 7-up. Serves a lot.

Liquor content in each glass will be very small.

STRAWBERRY-PINEAPPLE COOLER

Outdoor drink.

2 (10 oz.) pkg. frozen strawberries in syrup, thawed
1 (8 oz.) can crushed pineapple
1 1/2 c. pineapple juice, chilled
3/4 c. cream of coconut
2 (12 oz.) bottles club soda, chilled
Pineapple sherbet or sorbet

In a blender, combine strawberries and pineapple; blend until smooth. In a pitcher, combine strawberry puree, pineaple juice and cream of coconut. Just before serving, add club soda. Scoop sherbet into glasses; pour in juice mixture. Garnish with pineapple chunks and strawberries if desired. Makes about 7 cups.

"Idea:" Why not add rum or vodka? Maybe throw in a banana? Use a different flavor sherbet.

Soups
Sandwiches
Salads
Vegetables

TURKEY STOCK - HEALTHY

A good way to finish off that turkey carcass left from the holidays. With the freezer, it is not necessary to eat turkey leftovers day after day after day. Freeze it in sections for use later on.

**1 turkey carcass with
  some meat
4 qt. water
2 carrots, sliced
2 celery stalks, sliced
1 medium onion, sliced
1 large clove garlic,
  sliced
1 large sprig parsley
1 bay leaf
2 tsp. leaf basil,
  crumbled
1 tsp. thyme**

Cut turkey into pieces and place in a large kettle or Dutch oven. Add water, carrots, celery, onion, garlic, parsley, bay leaf, basil and thyme. Bring to boiling over high heat. Reduce heat to low. Simmer the stock, partially covered, for 3 to 4 hours, skimming and discarding any foam from the surface as it forms.

Cool stock slightly and then carefully strain it through colander lined with double thickness of dampened cheesecloth. Discard solids. Chill stock and remove fat from the top if you wish. Freeze extra stock in plastic freezer bags or glass jar (leave room at the top for freezer expansion).

TACO BEEF SOUP

**1/2 lb. ground beef or
  turkey
1/4 c. chopped onion
1 1/2 c. water
1 (16 oz.) can stewed
  tomatoes, cut up
1 (16 oz.) can kidney
  beans
1 (8 oz.) can tomato sauce
1/2 env. (2 Tbsp.) taco
  seasoning
1 small avocado, peeled,
  seeded and chopped
Shredded Cheddar
  cheese
Corn chips
Dairy sour cream**

In large saucepan, cook ground beef and onion until meat is browned; drain off excess fat. Add water, undrained tomatoes, undrained kidney beans, tomato sauce and taco seasoning mix. Simmer, covered, 15 minutes.   Add avocado. Pass cheese, corn chips and sour cream to top each serving. Serves 6.

HEALTHY AND HEARTY PEA SOUP

This is a very filling and healthy soup, also inexpensive and easy.

2 stalks celery, chopped
2 large carrots, grated
1 medium onion, finely
   chopped
2 Tbsp. olive oil
8 c. water
1 lb dry green split peas
1/2 tsp. salt
1 tsp. dried thyme
1/2 tsp. pepper
1/4 c. chopped parsley
   or 2 Tbsp. dried
   parsley

In Dutch oven, cook celery, onion and carrots in olive oil until crisp tender. Stir in water, peas, salt, thyme and pepper. Cover and bring to a boil. Reduce heat. Simmer, covered, for 50 minutes or until peas are tender. Add parsley. Simmer, uncovered, for 50 minutes or until thick. Serves 8 (1 cup).

CREAM OF TOMATO SOUP - HEALTHY

Mom makes this soup with ripe tomatoes from her garden, then freezes it for cold winter days.

4 c. peeled and chopped
   ripe tomatoes
1/4 c. chopped onion
6 Tbsp. margarine
1/4 c. flour
1 tsp. salt
1/4 tsp. pepper
1/2 tsp. baking soda
2 c. half & half
2 c. milk

Simmer tomatoes and onion in margarine over low heat. Put in blender until well mixed. Put in freezer container, cool and freeze. To make soup, thaw and heat, adding the flour, salt and pepper, blended together. Add baking soda, half and half and milk; mix well. Heat. Serve with crackers and cheese.

You may substitute 1% milk for the half & half and milk for a good and lowfat meal.

ITALIAN TOMATO AND RICE SOUP - HEALTHY

2 c. water
1 (12 oz.) jar mild chunky
  salsa
1 c. tomato juice
1/3 c. quick cooking brown
  rice
1 Tbsp. dried minced
  onion
1 tsp. Italian seasonings,
  crushed
1/2 tsp. instant chicken
  bouillon granules
1/8 tsp. dried minced
  garlic
1/8 tsp. pepper
1 (16 oz.) pkg. loose
  pack frozen zucchini,
  carrots, cauliflower,
  lima beans and
  Italian bean mix
1/3 c. grated Parmesan
  cheese

In a large saucepan, combine water, salsa, tomato juice, rice, onion, Italian seasoning, bouillon granules, garlic and pepper. Bring mixture to boiling; reduce heat. Cover and simmer for 10 minutes.

Meanwhile, place vegetables in colander. Run cold water over vegetables until thawed. Stir into rice mixture. Return to boiling; reduce heat. Cover and simmer until vegetables and rice are tender, about 10 minutes. Top each serving with cheese. Serves 6.

EASY GREEN ONION POTATO SOUP -HEALTHY

1 c. sliced green onions
  with tops
1 medium clove garlic,
  crushed
1 Tbsp. vegetable oil
4 c. chicken broth
1 c. milk or half & half
1 (4 serving) pkg.
  instant mashed
  potatoes
1 medium carrot,
  shredded
Fresh ground pepper to
  taste
Minced parsley

In medium saucepan over medium heat, saute onions and garlic in oil, stirring occasionally, about 5 minutes. Add broth; bring to rolling boil. Remove from heat and stir in potatoes, milk and carrots. Cook just until thoroughly heated. Season with pepper; sprinkle wit' parsley. Serves 4.

SOUPER GOMER'S

Combination of cream of potato, Cheddar and mushrooms. I created this soup for my restaurant. It's simple and very popular. Here again, the measurements are approximate, as I never measure them.

**2 medium size red
   potatoes
3 to 4 c. milk
1 can cream of mushroom
   soup
1/2 lb. Cheddar cheese,
   diced
1/2 tsp. garlic salt
1/2 tsp. seasoning salt
1/2 tsp. salt
1/2 tsp pepper
2 tsp. parsley flakes
Dash of nutmeg**

Scrub or peel potatoes (I personally prefer to leave the skins on). Cut into pieces and boil, only until potatoes are tender. Drain and mash slightly with a fork, leaving chunky. In the same pan, add the milk, soup and all of the seasonings, stirring well until heated thoroughly. Do not boil. Stir in cheese until melted. Taste it and add more cheese or seasonings if desired.

"Idea:" Use roux instead of potatoes, chicken bouillon instead of milk, eliminate salts and add cooked, pureed broccoli for a Cheddar broccoli soup. See how easy it is to vary a recipe? Exact measurements are necessary only in baking. It's great! It's up to you whether you want a thick soup or a thin one, a little more or less cheese, etc.

CREAMY TUNA 'N BROCCOLI SOUP - HEALTHY/EZ

Sounds a little strange, but it is delicious!

**1/4 c. butter or margarine
3 Tbsp. minced onion
3 Tbsp. flour
1 tsp. salt
1/2 tsp. celery salt
1/2 tsp. ground sage
1/4 tsp. pepper
Few grains of cayenne
   pepper
1 qt. milk
1 (10 oz.) pkg. frozen
   chopped broccoli
1 (6 1/2 oz.) tuna fish,
   drained and flaked**

Melt butter in large heavy saucepan over low heat. Add onion and cook until tender. Blend in flour, salt, celery salt, sage, pepper and cayenne pepper. Heat until mixture bubbles. Gradually add milk, stirring constantly. Bring to a boil. Stir in broccoli. Cook over low heat, stirring occasionally, 10 to 12 minutes. Mix in tuna and heat about 3 minutes. Serves 6.

NEW ENGLAND CLAM CHOWDER

3 doz. fresh small, hard
shelled clams, scrubbed,
or 4 (6 1/2 oz.) minced
clams, drained (reserve
clam broth)
2 slices bacon, diced
1 c. finely chopped onions
3 c. diced potatoes
2 c. half & half
1/8 tsp. ground thyme
Freshly ground pepper

To cook fresh clams: In large kettle, steam clams in 1 inch of water. When opened, remove them from the kettle. Strain clam broth through cheesecloth line strainer. Reserve 2 cups of broth; discard remaining. Remove clams from shells and chop finely.

For chowder: In a saucepot or large frying pan, cook bacon until crisp. Remove with slotted spoon and drain on paper towels. To drippings in pot, add onions; cook about 5 minutes until soft. Stir in reserved clam broth and potatoes. Reduce heat; simmer, covered, for 25 minutes until potatoes are fork tender. Stir in clams.

Meanwhile, in small saucepan, warm half & half over medium heat until there are bubbles around edge. Pour hot half & half into simmering clam mixture. Taste for seasonings. Makes 7 1/2 cups.

Note: If you use canned clams and don't have 2 cups of clam broth, finish filling cup with water.

CHICKEN AND HAM SALAD

2 c. mayonnaise
1/4 c. half & half
2 Tbsp. lemon juice
1 Tbsp. wine vinegar
1 tsp. dry mustard
1 tsp. salt
3 hard-boiled eggs,
shelled and chopped
1/4 c. chopped dill
pickles
2 Tbsp. finely chopped
chives
1 head iceberg lettuce
3 c. chopped cooked
chicken
3 c. chopped cooked ham
3 large tomatoes, cut in
wedges

Blend mayonnaise with half & half, lemon juice, vinegar, mustard, and salt in a medium size bowl; fold in eggs, pickles and chives. Cut lettuce in 12 thin wedges; arrange 2 each in 6 individual salad bowls. Top with chicken and ham; spoon 1/2 cup dressing mix over each. Garnish with tomato wedges. Serves 6.

CHICKEN SALAD DELUX

1 (3 lb.) fryer chicken
4 c. water
1 small onion, sliced
Few celery tops
1/4 tsp. salt
1/3 c. mayonnaise
1/3 c. sour cream
1 Tbsp. lemon juice
1/4 tsp. pepper
3/4 c. chopped celery
1 medium size onion,
    chopped fine
1/4 c. chopped dill
    pickle
Lettuce
Ripe olives
Paprika

Combine chicken with water, sliced onion, celery tops, and salt in a kettle or large pot. Bring to boil and reduce to simmer. Cover and cook for about 40 minutes or until tender. Remove from broth and cool until easy to handle. (Save broth for soup.) Skin chicken and take meat from bones. Cut meat into bite-size pieces; put in medium size bowl.

Blend mayonnaise, sour cream, lemon juice, and pepper in a small bowl. Combine celery, onion and dill pickles with chicken. Add dressing and toss until evenly coated. Cover and chill for at least 1 hour to season and blend flavors. Line a salad bowl with lettuce. Spoon salad into bowl and sprinkle with paprika. Garnish with olives.

MACARONI-TUNA SALAD - EZ

This is one of my favorite items for company, especially in the summertime. You can clean up the mess ahead of time and also you don't have to worry about what time they're going to arrive; it's ready when they are.

1/2 lb. shell macaroni
3 hard-boiled eggs,
    shelled and diced
3 medium size sweet
    pickles, diced
1/4 c. diced red onion
1 (6 1/2 oz.) can tuna,
    drained
1 (17 oz.) can sweet
    green peas, drained
1 c. mayonnaise
1/2 tsp. dried mustard
Dash of garlic powder
Dash of celery salt

Cook macaroni according to package directions. Drain and run cold water over shells. Drain thoroughly; cool. Add remainder of ingredients and stir well. Chill for at least 1 hour before serving.

Serve with bread sticks or crackers and cheese and you have a complete meal. Serves 6 to 8.

SHRIMP LOUIS SALAD - HEALTHY/EZ

Hot weather seafood.

1/2 lb. cooked salad
  shrimp
1/4 c. mayonnaise
1/4 c. sour cream
2 Tbsp. chili sauce
1 tsp. lime juice
1/2 tsp. sugar
1/2 tsp. grated onion
1/4 tsp. seasoned salt
1 large head iceberg
  lettuce, broken into bite-
  size pieces
Sliced fresh tomatoes
Sliced hard-boiled eggs

Combine shrimp with all remaining ingredients except lettuce, tomatoes and eggs. Cover and chill at least 30 minutes before serving.

Fill large bowl with lettuce and toss shrimp dressing over top. Toss well until greens are well coated. Add tomatoes and eggs over top. Serves 4 as a dinner entree. Serve with crackers and your favorite cheese.

TWENTY-FOUR HOUR SLAW - HEALTHY

1 head cabbage,
  chopped fine
1 medium onion,
  chopped
3 carrots, peeled and
  shredded
1/2 c. sugar
1 tsp. salt
1/2 tsp. dried mustard
2 tsp. sugar
1/2 c. vinegar
1/2 c. olive oil

Layer cabbage, onion and carrots in a large bowl with a lid. Sprinkle the 1/2 cup sugar over the mixture. Mix salt, mustard and the 2 teaspoons sugar in saucepan. Add vinegar and bring to a rolling boil. Add oil and pour over slaw. *Do not stir.* Cover and let stand in refrigerator 24 hours. Stir and enjoy.

This will keep in refrigerator up to 3 weeks.

SPINACH SALAD

1 egg
3/4 c. sugar
1/2 c. vinegar
1 tsp. salt
1/8 tsp. Worcestershire
  sauce
1/2 tsp. dry mustard
1 medium onion, chopped
2 lb. fresh spinach,
  cleaned and torn in
  large bite-size pieces
1/4 lb. bacon, fried,
  drained and crumbled
Plus whatever you would
  like to add (hardboiled
  egg, fresh mushrooms,
  sunflower seeds, water
  chestnuts, shrimp, bean
  or alfalfa sprouts)

Lightly beat egg in saucepan. Add sugar, vinegar and salt. Mix well. Cook over moderate heat, stirring frequently, just until mixture reaches boiling point and is thickened. (It won't become real thick.) Add onion, mustard and Worcestershire sauce. Transfer mixture to a bowl; cool slightly. Refrigerate until chilled. Makes about 3/4 cup dressing.

Just before serving, toss together spinach, bacon and whatever else you would like to add. Add desired amount of dressing. Lightly, but thoroughly, toss together again. Serves 4.

ZESTY FRENCH DRESSING

1 can tomato soup
1/2 tsp. salt
1/2 c. sugar
1/2 tsp. garlic powder
1/2 tsp. paprika
1 Tbsp. prepared mustard
1 Tbsp. prepared
  horseradish
1/3 c. vinegar
1/2 c. salad or olive oil
1 Tbsp. Worcestershire
  sauce

Mix ingredients thoroughly. Dressing is ready to use. Refrigerate leftovers.

EXCELLENT BLEU CHEESE DRESSING - EZ

3/4 c. sour cream
1/2 tsp. dry mustard
1/2 tsp. black pepper
1/2 tsp. salt
1/3 tsp. garlic powder
1 tsp. Worcestershire
  sauce
1 1/3 c. mayonnaise
4 oz. Bleu cheese,
  crumbled

Blend the sour cream, mustard, pepper, salt, garlic powder, and Worcestershire sauce together in a mixing bowl and beat on low speed 2 minutes. Add the mayonnaise and blend another 1/2 minute at low speed, then blend an additional 2 minutes at medium speed. Add the Bleu cheese and blend on low speed for an additional 4 minutes. Let set, refrigerated 24 hours, before using. Makes approximately 2 1/2 cups.

POPPY SEED DRESSING - EZ

5 Tbsp. sugar
3 Tbsp. white wine
  vinegar
1/2 c. vegetable oil
1 tsp. minced onion
1/2 tsp. salt
1/4 tsp. dry mustard
1/4 tsp. poppy seed

Mix sugar, vinegar and oil in blender; blend 1 minute. Add onion, salt, mustard, and mix 1 minute. Stir in poppy seed.

RHUBARB SALAD - HEALTHY

2 c. rhubarb, finely cut
1/2 c. sugar
1/2 c. water
1 (3 oz.) box strawberry
  jello
1 c. boiling water
1/2 c. well drained crushed
  pineapple
2 c. finely chopped, peeled
  apples
1/4 c. finely chopped nuts.

Combine rhubarb, sugar and 1/2 cup water in saucepan. Cook, covered, until soft over low heat; cool. Dissolve jello in 1 cup boiling water. Cool until it just begins to set. Add to rhubarb. Add pineapple, apples and nuts. Chill and serve.

CINNAMON SWIRL SALAD

Good fall time jello salad.

2 (3 oz.) pkg. lemon jello
1/2 c. red cinnamon
candies
3 c. boiling water
2 c. applesauce
1 Tbsp. lemon juice
1/2 c. coarsely chopped
walnuts

Topping:
2 (8 oz.) pkg. cream
cheese, softened
1/4 c. milk
2 Tbsp. mayonnaise

Dissolve jello and candies in boiling water. Stir in applesauce and lemon juice. Chill until partially set. Fold in nuts. Turn into 8x8x2 inch pan.

Topping: Beat together cream cheese, milk and mayonnaise. Spoon atop salad; swirl through to marble. Chill until firm. Cut in 9 squares.

APPLESAUCE-PEACH SALAD - HEALTHY/EZ

1 (3 oz.) pkg. lemon jello
1 1/2 c. boiling water
1 c. applesauce
1/2 c. chopped pecans
1 large peach, peeled
and sliced, or 1
(12 oz.) pkg. frozen
sliced peaches*

Dissolve gelatin in the boiling water. Chill until partially set. Stir in applesauce, pecans and peach slices. Turn mixture into 8 inch square baking dish; chill until set, 3 to 4 hours. To serve, cut in squares. If desired, garnish with additional peach slices; pass mayonnaise. Serves 6.

*If using frozen peaches, thaw and drain, reserving 1/2 cup syrup. Dissolve gelatin in 1 cup boiling water instead of 1 1/2 cups. Add reserved peach syrup.

EASY FRUIT SALAD - HEALTHY

**2 (8 oz.) cans chunk
  pineapple, drained
  (reserve juice)
3 bananas, peeled and
  diced
3 apples, peeled and
  diced
2 (11 oz.) cans
  mandarin oranges,
  drained (reserve juice)
1 (3 oz.) pkg. instant
  vanilla pudding
2 Tbsp. Tang
1 c. reserved pineapple
  and mandarin orange
  juice, mixed**

Mix pineapple, bananas, apples, and mandarin oranges. Set aside. Beat pudding, Tang and reserved fruit juice together until mixture thickens. Stir into fruit, mixing well.

FIVE CUP SALAD - EZ

**1 c. pineapple tidbits,
  drained
1 c. flaked coconut
1 c. mandarin oranges,
  well drained
1 c. miniature
  marshmallows
1 c. sour cream
1 c. chopped pecans
Maraschino cherries for
  garnish**

Mix all ingredients. Chill several hours or overnight. Garnish with cherries. Serves 6.

"Idea:"   While this salad is great for winter, try substituting fresh fruit when available. You may have to add lemon juice if you use peaches, apples or bananas to keep them from turning brown.

WINNIE'S LIME OR LEMON PARTY SALAD - HEALTHY

**2 (3 oz.) pkg. lime or
  lemon jello
2 Tbsp. cider vinegar
Pinch of salt
2 c. shredded cabbage
1 c. shredded carrots
1 c. diced celery
3/4 c. chopped almonds**

Dissolve jello in 1 1/2 cups boiling water. Add 1 1/2 cups cold water. Add vinegar and salt. Chill until partially set. Add cabbage, carrots, celery, and almonds.   Refrigerate until set. Serve with 1 teaspoon mayonnaise on each serving. Makes 8 to 10 servings.

SEVEN-UP SALAD

2 c. boiling water
1 (6 oz.) pkg. lemon jello
2 c. 7-up
2 large bananas, peeled
  and diced
1 c. miniature marsh-
  mallows
1 (20 oz.) can crushed
  pineapple, drained
  (reserve juice)

Topping:
2 Tbsp. flour
1/2 c. sugar
2 Tbsp. butter or
  margarine
1 (8 oz.) tub whipped
  topping
1 egg, beaten
1 c. pineapple juice,
  reserved from
  pineapple

Add boiling water to Jello; stir until dissolved. Add 7-Up. Chill until partially set; stir in bananas, marshmallows and drained pineapple. Chill until firm. In medium sized saucepan, combine all topping ingredients except the whipped topping. Cook over medium heat, stirring constantly until thickened, about 6 minutes. Cool. Fold in whipped toping. Spread on top of jello mixture.

FRUITED COTTAGE CHEESE SALAD - EZ

1 (3 oz.) pkg. jello (flavor)
1 (32 oz.) ctn. creamed
  cottage cheese
1 lb. fruit (your choice)
1 (9 oz.) ctn. non-dairy
  topping

Sprinkle dry gelatin over cottage cheese. Mix well. Mix together fruit and topping. Fold topping mixture into cottage cheese. Refrigerate, covered, overnight or longer. Serve as a salad or dessert. Serves 8.

Possible combinations: Strawberry or raspberry jello with pineapple, bananas or fruit cocktail. Orange jello with mandarin oranges and miniature marshmallows. Black cherry jello with black sweet cherries and miniature marshmallows.

ORANGE LIME SALAD

Impressive looking and tastes great!

1 (3 oz.) pkg. lime jello
1 c. chopped apples
1 c. nuts, chopped
1/3 c. pineapple,
drained
1 stalk celery, finely
chopped
1 (3 oz.) pkg. orange
jello
1 Tbsp. mayonnaise
1 (3 oz.) pkg. cream
cheese, softened

Prepare lime jello according to directions. Mix apples, nuts, pineapple, and celery; add to lime gelatin. Chill until firm. Prepare orange gelatin according to directions. Mix mayonnaise and cream cheese into orange jello with electric mixer. Pour on top of lime layer. Chill.

BROILED TUNA SANDWICHES - HEALTHY/EZ

1 (7 oz.) can flaked tuna,
drained
1 c. chopped celery
1/4 c. mayonnaise
1 tsp. dried onion flakes
1 1/2 tsp. prepared
mustard
1/4 tsp. salt (optional)
1/8 tsp. pepper
4 hamburger rolls,
split and toasted
Grated Parmesan
cheese to taste

In a bowl, mix all ingredients except rolls and cheese. Place toasted roll bottoms on cookie sheet; divide tuna mixture to cover. Sprinkle with Parmesan cheese. Broil until bubbly, about 5 minutes. Cover with roll top. Serves 4.

OPEN FACE CRAB SANDWICH - EZ

4 English muffins, toasted
2 cans (8oz.) crabmeat
or imitation crab flakes
1/2 c. mayonnaise
1 Tbsp. Dijon mustard
1 tsp. Worcestershire
sauce
1 c. shredded Swiss cheese

Mix mayonnaise and mustard. Spread, dividing evenly on muffins. Stir crab and Worcestershire sauce together and divide evenly on top of muffins. Top with shredded Swiss cheese. Broil until hot and cheese is melted.

CHICKEN LIVER LOVER'S SANDWICH

This sandwich was a hit in my restaurant. One customer told me, "I hate chicken livers, but I love this sandwich".

6 slices bacon
1 lb. chicken livers
2 Tbsp. flour
1/4 tsp. seasoned salt
1 (4 oz.) can chopped mushrooms
3 large tomatoes, each cut in 6 slices
3 split large hamburger buns

Saute bacon just until crisp in a large frying pan; drain on paper toweling, then crumble. Drain off all drippings, then measure 2 tablespoons and return to pan. (Set bacon aside.)

Wash and clean out veiny parts of the chicken livers. Shake livers with flour and seasoned salt in a paper bag to coat. Brown slowly in drippings in frying pan until almost cooked. Stir in mushrooms and liquid. Heat, stirring constantly, to boiling. Cover and simmer 3 minutes, or until livers lose their pink color.

While livers cook, place tomato slices and bun halves in a single layer on rack in broiler pan. Broil 3 to 4 minutes, or until tomatoes are heated through and buns are toasted. Top with chicken liver mixture and top all with fresh tomato slices.

TURKEY REUBEN SANDWICH - HEALTHY/EZ

1 Tbsp. Thousand Island dressing
2 slices rye bread
2 oz. thinly sliced cooked turkey breast
1/3 c. canned shredded sweet-sour red cabbage, drained
1 1/2 oz. sliced Monterey Jack cheese

Spread dressing on both slices of bread. Place sliced turkey on 1 of the bread slices; top with cabbage. Place sliced cheese on the cabbage, then top with remaining slice of bread, dressing side down. Serves 1.

MOLLY BROWN

This was probably the most popular item in the restaurant I once owned. We also did a version with roast beef, turkey and Cheddar cheese, we called the Horace Tabor.

1 wide size loaf
    sourdough bread
    (unsliced)
1/3 c. mayonnaise
2 tsp. Dijon style
    mustard
1 tsp lemon juice
1 tsp. Worcestershire
    sauce
1/4 tsp. white pepper
6 oz. thinly sliced ham
6 oz. thinly sliced
    turkey
6 slices Swiss cheese
Melted butter

Slice bread lengthwise; trim crust from the slices. (Save top and bottom pieces; they are great for garlic toast or croutons.) Flatten each slice with a rolling pin. Combine mayonnaise, mustard, lemon juice, Worcestershire sauce, and pepper. Spread mayonnaise mixture on each slice of bread. Layer ham, turkey and cheese on each slice. (Use amounts of ham, turkey and cheese as needed, not necessarily the amounts mentioned.) Roll up sandwich; secure with toothpick. Brush with melted butter and place on baking sheet. Bake in preheated oven at 375° for 12 to 15 minutes or until golden brown. Serves 5 or 6

SPICY BEEF SANDWICH - EZ

1 lb. ground beef or
    turkey
1/2 c. chopped onion
1 clove garlic, minced
1 (8 oz.) can tomato
    sauce
1/4 c. ketchup
1 tsp. oregano
1 tsp. sugar
1 (3 oz.) pkg. cream
    cheese
1/3 c. Parmesan cheese
Hero sandwich loaves
    of bread or 1 loaf
    French bread

Saute ground beef or turkey with onion and garlic on medium high in large skillet until the onion is tender. (If you're using turkey, add 2 tablespoons shortening, as there is no fat in the turkey.) Drain the excess fat. Stir in tomato sauce, ketchup, oregano, and sugar. Cover and simmer about 15 minutes until mixture is thickened, stirring occasionally. Add cheeses and stir until they melt. Slice the bread in half lengthwise and again into serving size pieces. Spoon the meat onto one bread half and cover with the other.

"Idea:" This is great for the single person, as the mixture freezes well. Don't freeze it on the bread; do that when you're ready to eat it. This mixture is also good with sour cream dopped on top. It is also a good filling for an omelet with sour cream on top and sliced avocados.

SLOPPY JOE HAMBURGERS - EZ

1 lb. lean ground beef
1/4 c. chopped onion
2 Tbsp. brown sugar
1 tsp. salt
1 1/2 c. tomato juice
2 Tbsp. flour
1 Tbsp. Worcestershire
sauce
1/2 tsp. chili powder

Brown meat and onion until meat is brown. Mix the 2 tablespoons of flour into meat. Add rest of ingredients and simmer about 20 minutes or until thickened.

Kids and adults love these and they are great to take outdoors.

ITALIAN SAUSAGE HEROES - EZ

8 sweet Italian sausages
(about 1 1/4 lb. or
use bulk sausage)
1 Bermuda onion,
peeled and chopped
2 large green peppers,
quartered, seeded and
sliced
1 tsp. salt
1 tsp. sugar
1 tsp. Italian seasoning
2 large tomatoes,
chopped
2 large hero rolls
Butter or margarine
8 slices Mozzarella
cheese

Score sausages every 1/2 inch; saute slowly in a large frying pan 15 minutes, or until cooked through. Drain on paper toweling. Pour off all drippings, then measure 3 tablespoons and return to pan. Stir in onion and saute until soft. Stir in peppers, salt, sugar, and Italian seasoning. Cover and cook 5 minutes. Stir in tomatoes; place sausages on top. Cover and steam 5 minutes, or until mixture is bubbly hot.

While vegetables cook, split hero rolls; cut out center of each half to make a boat shape shell. Spread insides of rolls with butter or margarine; place on a cookie sheet. Heat in a 350° oven 10 minutes or until crispy hot. Place on serving plates; spoon vegetable mixture into hollows. Top each with 2 sausages. Top each with 2 slices of Mozzarella cheese and return to oven long enough for cheese to melt.

"Idea:" I prefer making this sandwich with bulk sausage and stuffing it in a pita pocket, placing the 2 halves together and then topping with the cheese.

ARTICHOKE WITH ARTICHOKE BUTTER - EZ

Artichoke Butter:
1/2 c. butter
1/8 c. lemon juice
1/2 tsp. salt
Dash of parsley
1/4 tsp. dry mustard
Dash of Tabasco

Melt butter in a small saucepan. Stir in other ingredients.

Fill medium size saucepan 1/2 full of water. Add a small handful of peppercorns, 1 bay leaf and a clove of garlic. Steam artichoke over medium heat with lid on for 45 minutes to an hour, until outside leaves are tender. (You may have to add more water; keep an eye out.) Remove and eat, pulling the leaves off, dipping them in butter and pulling the tender center flesh off with your teeth, eating down to the heart. Peel the fuzzy stuff off in the center before eating the heart.

BEET JELLY

This is different and delicious. Fun to have everyone guess what the ingredients are, also very colorful. Everyone wants this recipe!

4 c. strained beet juice*
1/2 c. fresh lemon juice
1 small pkg. raspberry jello
1 pkg. Sure-Jell
6 c. sugar

Mix beet juice, lemon juice and Sure-Jell in medium saucepan. Bring to a full boil. Add sugar and gelatin and boil hard for 10 minutes. Ladle into prepared jelly glasses and cover with 1/8 inch melted paraffin.

*To get beet juice, scrub fresh beets and cover with boiling water. Boil until beets are tender. Remove beets and use the water they have been cooked in. Save beets to eat later. (You can have your beets and eat them too!)

BROCCOLI SOUFFLE - EZ

2 pkg. frozen chopped broccoli
1 (10 oz.) can cream of mushroom soup
1 c. shredded Cheddar cheese
1/4 c. milk
1/2 c. mayonnaise
1 egg, beaten
2 Tbsp. butter
1 c. bread crumbs

Cook and drain broccoli and place in bottom of casserole dish. Mix together soup, cheese, milk, mayonnaise, and egg. Pour this mixture over the broccoli. Do not mix together. Melt butter and combine with bread crumbs. Sprinkle on top. Bake at 350° for 45 minutes. Serves 6 to 8.

BARBEQUE GREEN BEANS

This is my youngest brother's favorite vegetable.

2 cans French cut green
    beans or fresh geen
    beans, cooked
4 slices bacon, diced
1 small onion, diced
1/2 c. catsup
1 Tbsp. Worcestershire
    sauce
1/4 c. brown sugar

Fry bacon and onion until bacon is slightly browned. Add the rest of ingredients except the beans. Mix well and bring to boil. Reduce heat. Add beans and cook until beans are warmed.

APPLE ORANGE CARROTS - HEALTHY

4 large or 6 miedium
    carrots, peeled and
    cut in 1/2 inch slices
3 Tbsp. butter or
    margarine
2 Tbsp. frozen orange juice
    concentrate, thawed
1/2 c. natural applesauce
1/4 tsp. salt
1/2 tsp. cloves

Cook carrots in a small amount of water until almost tender. Add all the other ingredients and heat through.

CALICO BEANS - EZ

For a crowd.

1 lb. hamburger
1 lb. bacon, diced
1 medium onion, chopped
1 (24 oz.) can pork and
    beans
1 (15 oz.) can red kidney
    beans
1 small can lima beans
1 c. brown sugar
1 c. catsup
2 Tbsp. dried mustard
Salt and pepper to taste

Fry hamburger, bacon and onion; drain fat. Add remaining ingredients. Bake at 350° for 1 1/2 hours.

This is a large recipe, but leftovers freeze very well.

ONION PATTIES

A great alternative to onion rings and a lot simpler.

3/4 c. flour
2 tsp. baking powder
1 Tbsp. sugar
1/2 tsp. salt
1 Tbsp. corn meal
1/2 c. dry milk
2 1/2 c. onions, finely
chopped

Stir all ingredients, except onions, together in a mixing bowl. Stir in enough cold water for a thick batter. Mix onions into batter. Drop by teaspoonfuls into hot oil in a large skillet until browned on edges. Turn over and finish cooking other side. Drain on paper towels.

CANNED SWEET PEPPER RINGS

Very pretty for holiday meals. Another old family recipe.

10 red and green sweet
peppers

7 pint canning jars,
washed and scalded

Syrup:
1 qt. vinegar
2 qt. sugar (this is
correct)

Cut red and green sweet peppers into rings. Cover with boiling water and simmer for 2 minutes. Drain and put in ice water. Let stand 10 minutes and drain.   Pack in scalded jars and cover with syrup which has been boiled for 10 minutes. Fill jars with syrup to overflowing and seal. Makes about 7 pints.

EASY AND DELICIOUS POTATOES

6 potatoes (baking size),
washed
1/2 c. margarine
3/4 c. water
1 pkg. dry onion soup
mix

Cut unpeeled potatoes into 1/4 inch slices. Melt margarine in water; add dry onion soup mix. Layer potatoes and liquid into a 2 quart casserole dish. Bake, covered, in a 350° oven for 1 hour.

These are very good warmed over the next day.

MOM'S OWN EASY DELICIOUS SCALLOPED POTATOES

**5 c. sliced potatoes
 (about 4 large-peeling
 optional)
1 c. diced cheese
3 tsp. dried onions
1 (10 1/2 oz.) can cream
 of mushroom soup
3/4 soup can of milk**

Spray a 2 quart casserole with vegetable spray. Put a layer of potatoes, 1 teaspoon of the onions and 1/2 cup of the cheese. Make another layer of potatoes, onions and cheese. Cover with a few potato slices. Mix soup and milk. Pour over potatoes. Cover and bake at 350° for 1 1/2 hours.

"Idea:" For a large group, double the recipe and use 1 can each of cream of mushroom and cream of celery soup.

SKILLET POTATOES

**1/4 c. margarine
1/2 c. chopped onions
1 (10 1/2 oz.) can cream
 of mushroom soup
1/2 soup can of milk
1 c. grated Cheddar cheese
1 c. cheese flavored
 cracker crumbs
1/8 tsp. ground black
 pepper
6 boiled medium potatoes,
 washed and diced
 (peeling optional)
1 small green bell pepper,
 diced
2 Tbsp. chopped pimento
 (optional)**

Melt margarine; add onions.   Saute until onions are soft. Combine mushroom soup with milk, mixing until smooth.   Stir soup mixture into sauteed onions, mixing well. Add grated cheese, cracker crumbs and pepper. Add potatoes, green pepper and pimento.   Mix thoroughly over medium heat, stirring occasionally, until potatoes are heated. Serves 6.

This dish can be prepared in advance. Cover and refrigerate if prepared in advance. Serve eggs with this for a great breakfast!

TOMATO JUICE COCKTAIL - HEALTHY

8 1/2 lb. (about 24
    medium) tomatoes
1 c. chopped celery
1 c. chopped onion
1 medium green
    pepper, chopped
1/4 c. snipped parsley
    (fresh)
1/4 c. snipped fresh
    basil or 4 tsp. dried
    basil
1/4 c. fresh snipped
    thyme or 4 tsp. dried
    thyme
2 bay leaves
1 tsp. salt
1/2 tsp. pepper

Wash tomatoes, remove stems and chop. In 10 quart Dutch oven, combine all ingredients. Simmer, uncovered, for 1 3/4 to 2 hours. Press tomato mixture through food mill to extract juice. Discard seeds and skins. Pour mixture into hot, clean pint jars, leaving 1 inch head space. Wipe jar rims; adjust lids. Process in pressure canner at 15 pounds for 40 minutes. Makes 4 pints.

CHOCOLATE ZUCCHINI CAKE

The frosting on this cake is chocolate chips.

1/2 c. margarine,
    softened
1/2 c. vegetable oil
1 3/4 c. sugar
2 eggs
1 tsp. vanilla
1/2 c. sour milk (add 1
    tsp. vinegar to
    regular milk and stir)
2 1/2 c. flour
4 Tbsp. cocoa
1/2 tsp. baking powder
1 tsp. baking soda
1/2 tsp. cinnamon
1/2 tsp. cloves
2 c. peeled, shredded
    zucchini
1 1/4 c. chocolate chips

Preheat oven to 325°. Cream margarine, oil and sugar until light and fluffy. Add eggs, vanilla and sour milk; beat until well mixed. Stir together all the dry ingredients, except the chocolate chips and zucchini, and add to cream mixture until well blended. Stir in zucchini and pour into greased and floured 9x13 inch cake pan. Sprinkle chocolate chips over top of cake. Bake about 40 to 50 minutes, until tested done.

LEMON ZUCCHINI COOKIES

2 c. flour
1 tsp. baking powder
1/2 tsp. salt
3/4 c. margarine or
   butter, softened
3/4 c. sugar
1 egg, beaten
1 tsp. or more grated
   lemon peel
1 c. shredded, peeled
   zucchini
1 c. chopped walnuts

Lemon Frost:
1 c. powdered sugar
1 1/2 Tbsp. fresh lemon
   juice

Cream butter and sugar together until light and fluffy. Add egg, blending well. Stir in flour, baking powder and salt until well mixed. Add lemon peel, zucchini and walnuts; mix well. Drop dough onto lightly greased cookie sheets by the teaspoonfuls, about 2 inches apart, and bake at 375° about 15 minutes, until lightly browned. Let cookies cool on cookie sheet about 5 minutes before removing to wire racks. While warm, drizzle lightly with Lemon Frost.

Lemon Frost: Stir together powdered sugar and fresh lemon juice until smooth. If too thick, slowly add a little hot water until desired thickness is achieved.

"Idea:"   Why not substitute orange for the lemon?

ZUCCHINI AND CARROTS - HEALTHY/EZ

1 lb. small carrots
1 lb. small zucchini
1 c. water
1/2 tsp. salt
3 Tbsp. butter or
   margarine
1/2 tsp. dried marjoram

Wash carrots and zucchini. Peel carrots and cut diagonally into 1/8 inch pieces. Do not peel zucchini; cut it in 1/2 inch slices. Bring water and salt to a boil. Add carrots and cook, covered, over low heat for 10 minutes. Add zucchini and continue cooking, covered, an additional 10 minutes. Remove cover and cook a few minutes longer until most of the water has evaporated. Add butter and marjoram; toss lightly. Serves 6.

Entrees

Poultry
Beef
Seafood
Ethnic
Old-Timers

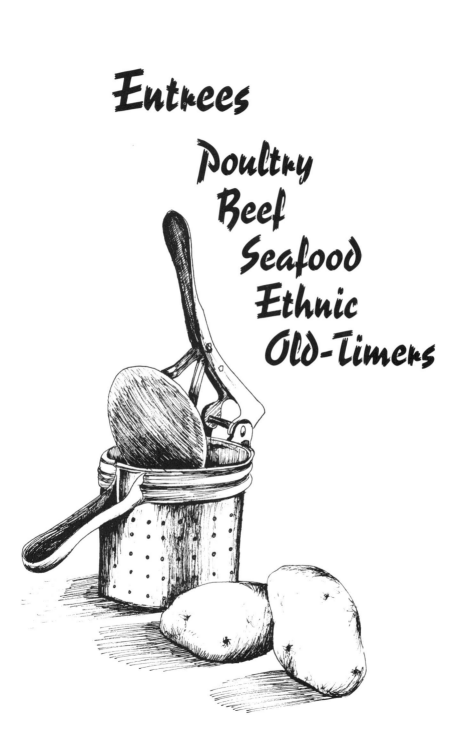

ROCK CORNISH HENS VIN' ROSE - HEALTHY

4 to 6 Cornish game
  hens
1/2 tsp. dried rosemary
  leaves
1 c. rose wine
1/2 c. butter
1 tsp salt
1/2 tsp. black pepper
1 lb. fresh mushrooms
1 lb. pearl onions,
  peeled

Wash thawed hens; pat dry. Add rosemary leaves to wine and set aside to steep. Make paste of softened butter, salt and pepper; brush well over birds. Stuff, if you wish, with your choice of dressing (not necessary) and truss lightly. Surround birds with onions, breast side down. Pour wine mixture over all, reserving 1/2 cup for later basting during cooking. Roast approximately 1 hour in a 350° oven until done. Add mushrooms about 20 minutes before bird is done. Serves 4 to 6 (more if you serve half of a hen).

CHICKEN A L'ORANGE - HEALTHY

1/2 c. flour
2 tsp. grated orange rind
1 tsp. paprika
3/4 tsp. black pepper
3 lb. chicken breasts or
  parts
1 Tbsp. vegetable oil
1/2 c. water
1 1/2 c. orange juice
1/4 c. chopped pecans
2 Tbsp. light brown
  sugar
3/4 tsp. cinnamon
1/4 tsp. ginger
Orange slices for garnish

Remove skin from chicken. In a paper or plastic bag, combine flour, orange rind, paprika, and 1/2 teaspoon of the black pepper. Set aside 2 tablespoons of the mixture. Add a few pieces of chicken to the bag at a time. Coat well, shaking off excess flour. In a large skillet, heat oil until moderately hot. Add chicken. Brown on all sides. Add water. Bring to boil. Reduce heat and simmer, covered, until chicken is tender, about 30 minutes.

Remove chicken to a serving platter; keep warm. Stir 2 reserved tablespoons , flour mixture into chicken drippings. Add orange juice, pecans, brown sugar, cinnamon, ginger, and remaining 1/4 teaspoon black pepper. Cook over moderate heat, stirring until thickened. Spoon sauce over chicken. Garnish with orange slices. Serves 4.

CHICKEN CORDON BLEU

4 half chicken breasts,
  boned
4 slices Swiss cheese
4 thin slices ham
1 (10 1/2 oz.) can cream
  of mushroom soup
1/4 c. chopped, fresh
  mushrooms
1/4 c. Bleu cheese,
  crumbled
2 Tbsp. sherry (optional)
1 Tbsp. chopped parsley

Pound chicken breasts as thin as possible. Remove skin if you wish. Place a slice of Swiss cheese and a slice of ham on each chicken breast. Roll each chicken breast around cheese and ham, securing with a round toothpick. Place in a buttered 9x9 inch square glass baking dish. Cover and bake 30 minutes at 350°

Meanwhile, combine remaining ingredients to small saucepan and heat either on stove top or in microwave; do not boil. When chicken is cooked, remove top and add soup mixture. Return to oven without cover for an additional 5 minutes.

FRIED-IN-THE-OVEN CHICKEN - EZ

3 lb. frying chicken, cut
  in pieces
1 c. packaged biscuit mix
1/2 tsp. paprika
1/2 tsp. baking powder
1/3 c. vegetable oil or
  melted margarine
1/2 tsp. poultry
  seasoning
1/4 tsp. garlic powder
3/4 tsp. salt
1/4 tsp. pepper

Pour oil or margarine in a shallow baking dish. Mix biscuit mix, paprika, baking powder, poultry seasoning, garlic powder, salt, and pepper together. Roll chicken pieces in dry ingredients. Arrange on baking dish. Preheat oven to 350°. Bake 30 minutes. Turn chicken over and bake another 30 minutes.

Add a baked potato for an easy meal.

HERB FRIED CHICKEN

Outdoor eating.

1/2 tsp. dried thyme
1/2 tsp. crushed
marjoram
1/2 tsp. garlic powder
1/2 tsp. paprika
1 tsp. salt
1/4 tsp. pepper
1 (2 1/2 to 3 1/2 lb.)
broiler-fryer chicken,
cut in pieces
1/3 c. all-purpose flour
3 Tbsp. vegetable oil

Combine all seasonings and sprinkle over chicken, then roll chicken in flour. Slowly brown chicken in hot oil, being careful not to crowd pieces. Reduce heat; cover. Cook until tender, 30 to 40 minutes, uncovering skillet the last 10 minutes. Drain on paper towel.

To make gravy, reserve about 3 tablespoons of the oil, scraping bottom of pan. Add 3 table-spoons flour and brown flour over medium heat in the same skillet the chicken was cooked in. Slowly add 1 1/2 cups milk, stirring constantly. Bring gravy to a boil; turn down heat. Cook until desired consistency is reached.

And, of course, what's better on a picnic than cold chicken and potato salad?

CRISPY BAKED CHICKEN - HEALTHY/EZ

An original by "Mom". Delicious, easy and lowfat!

1 c. whole wheat
crackers, crushed
1 Tbsp. chopped
parsley
1/2 c. oat bran
1/4 tsp. poultry
seasoning
1/2 tsp. paprika
1/4 tsp. garlic powder
3/4 c. 1% milk
1 Tbsp. olive oil
1 (2 1/2 lb.) fryer, cut in
quarters, or 6 chicken
thighs (skinless)

Blend crackers, oat bran, parsley, poultry seasoning, paprika, and garlic powder in a blender or food processor until ground fine. Spray nonvegetable spray in a 9x13 inch baking dish. Dip chicken in milk and then in crumb mixture. Place in pan. Sprinkle olive oil over chicken. Bake in preheated oven at 400° for 40 minutes or until tender. Do not turn.

HERBED CHICKEN STRIPS - HEALTHY

1 1/4 c. Quaker Oats
1 1/4 tsp. basil
1 tsp. paprika
1/2 tsp. oregano
1/2 tsp. thyme
1/4 tsp. garlic powder
2 whole chicken breasts,
  skinned, boned and
  cut in 1 inch strips
1/4 c. milk (regular or
  skim)
1/4 c. margarine,
  melted
1 (8 oz.) can tomato
  sauce
1/2 c. sliced green onions

Heat oven to 425°. Place oats in blender or food processor bowl. Cover and blend 1 minute. Add 1 teaspoon basil and other spices. Blend 1/2 minute more. Coat chicken strips in oatmeal mixture. Place on 15x10 inch cookie sheet (lined with foil for easy cleaning). Drizzle with margarine. Bake 25 to 30 minutes, until tender.

Combine tomato sauce, onions and remaining basil. Heat through, stirring occasionally. Dip chicken in sauce. Serves 4 as a dinner item, more as an appetizer.

BROCCOLI CHICKEN CASSEROLE - EZ

2 (10 oz.) pkg. frozen
  chopped broccoli,
  cooked according to
  directions
3 c. diced cooked
  chicken
1 egg, beaten
1 (10 1/2 oz.) can cream
  of chicken soup
1 (10 1/2 oz.) can cream
  of celery soup
2/3 c. mayonnaise
1 tsp. lemon juice
1/2 c. shredded Cheddar
  cheese
1/2 c. margarine
1 (6 oz.) pkg. stuffing
  mix

Place cooked broccoli on the bottom of a greased casserole dish. Place cooked chicken on top. Combine egg, soups, mayonnaise, and juice in a bowl and pour over chicken. Sprinkle shredded cheese on top. Melt margarine and add to dressing. Mix well. Spread over the top. Bake at 350° for 1 hour. Serves 4 to 6.

CHICKEN AND DUMPLINGS - HEALTHY

**2 large broiler-fryer
   chickens, cut up and
   skin removed
2 sprigs fresh parsley
4 celery ribs with leaves
1 carrot, pared and
   sliced
1 small onion, chopped
2 tsp. salt
1/4 tsp. pepper
1 bay leaf**

**Dumplings:
1 c. flour
2 tsp. baking powder
1/2 tsp. salt
1/2 c. milk
2 Tbsp. vegetable oil
2 Tbsp. snipped parsley**

**Gravy:
1 qt. broth
1/2 c. flour
1 c. cold water
1 tsp. salt
1/4 tsp. pepper**

In large kettle, add enough water to cover chicken. Add parsley, celery, carrot, onion, salt, pepper, and bay leaf. Cover and bring to a boil. Simmer about 1 1/2 hours or until meat is tender. Cool and remove chicken from bones, discarding bones and skin. Reserve liquid and degrease by placing ice cubes on top. Let set for about 10 minutes. Grease will adhere to cubes, then you can remove. Add chicken back to kettle.

Dumplings: Sift together dry ingredients. Combine milk and oil; add with parsley to dry ingredients. Stir just to moisten. Drop from tablespoon directly into chicken in boiling stock. Cover tightly; return to boiling. Reduce heat.. (Don't lift cover.) Simmer 14 minutes. Remove chicken and dumplings to hot platter; keep hot.

For gravy, strain broth; measure 1 quart broth in saucepan. Heat to boiling. Combine flour with cold water; gradually add to broth, mixing well. Cook, stirring constantly, until mixture thickens. Add salt and pepper. Pour over chicken and dumplings and serve. Makes 6 to 8 servings.

CHICKEN BREASTS AND RICE - EZ

A good recipe to put on while you're out for a couple of hours.

**1 c. uncooked rice
   (regular)
1 pkg. dry onion soup
   mix
4 chicken breasts with
   bones, skinned
Pepper to taste
1 (10 1/2 oz.) can cream
   of mushroom soup
1 can chicken broth
Paprika**

Spray a 13x9 inch baking dish with nonstick spray. Distribute rice evenly over the bottom. Sprinkle soup mix over rice. Lay chicken breasts on rice. Add pepper. Mix mushroom soup and chicken broth together and pour over chicken. Sprinkle paprika over all. Cover and bake at 325° for 2 hours.

CHICKEN-BROCCOLI CREPES

2 c. diced cooked chicken
1/2 lb. cooked broccoli,
cut up
1 tsp. pepper
1/2 lb. shredded Cheddar
cheese
Crepes (page 128)
Creamy Veloute Sauce
(page 46, Seafood
Crepes)

Prepare sauce and crepes as directed. Add broccoli, chicken, and pepper to the sauce. Place 2 tablespoons sauce in each crepe. Fold over and sprinkle with Cheddar cheese.

SCALLOPED CHICKEN

An impressive casserole for a potluck.

5 lb. stewing hen
2 tsp. salt
4 c. bread crumbs
1/2 tsp. celery salt
1/4 tsp. sage
1/8 tsp. pepper
6 Tbsp. melted margarine
6 c. broth (from chicken)
1/3 c. margarine
1/3 c. flour
6 eggs, beaten

Cover hen with water in a large cooking pan. Add salt and cook until tender. Cool. Remove meat from bones. Cut in bite-size pieces and set aside. Strain broth and save.

Meanwhile, stir bread crumbs, celery salt, sage, pepper, and margarine together, mixing well. Place this mixture in a greased 9x13 inch pan. Put chicken pieces over the dressing.

In a large saucepan, melt the 1/3 c. margarine. Add flour and stir until well blended over low heat. Add broth and cook over medium high heat until slightly thickened, about 6 minutes. Add this gravy to beaten eggs very slowly, stirring constantly, to keep the eggs from curdling. Pour this mixture over chicken and dressing. Sprinkle bread crumbs on top. Bake at 325° for 1 hour. Serves 6 to 8.

CHICKEN SPAGHETTI

Mom often makes this for families in need. She put instructions on top of casserole for baking.

1 large hen
2 large onions, diced
2 Tbsp. olive oil
2 bell peppers, diced
1 c. diced celery
1 (16 oz.) pkg. spaghetti
2 oz. pimentos (optional)
1 lb. Cheddar cheese,
  grated
1/2 tsp. garlic salt
1 (4 oz.) can mushroom
  slices
1 (2 oz.) can chopped
  green olives
Salt and pepper to taste
1 (10 1/2 oz.) can cream
  of mushroom soup

Boil hen until tender. Set aside and cool. Skim off fat. Saute onions, peppers and celery in olive oil until tender. Bone chicken and cut in pieces. *Save the broth.* Cook spaghetti in *chicken broth* for 15 minutes. *Do not drain.* Add the rest of the ingredients and stir well. Divide between a greased 9x13 inch pan and a 9x9 inch pan. Bake at 350° for 25 minutes. Serves 12 to 14.

If you would like, freeze one pan before or after baking for use at another time.

EASY TURKEY A LA KING

1/4 c. finely chopped
  onion
1/4 c. butter
2 c. milk
2 (10 1/2 oz.) cans cream
  of chicken soup
1 (10 oz.) pkg. egg
  noodles, cooked, 6
  patty shells or bisquits
1 (10 oz.) pkg. frozen
  peas
2 c. cubed·cooked turkey
2 Tbsp. chopped pimento
  optional)
1/4 tsp. pepper

In large saucepan, cook onion in butter over medium heat until tender. Stir in milk, soup and peas; bring to boil, stirring constantly. Cook over medium heat, stirring occasionally, for 5 minutes. Stir in turkey, pimento and pepper and cook until heated through. Serve over egg noodles, patty shells, or my favorite, home-made biscuits.

STUFFING FOR TURKEY

This one of my favorite memories of the holidays. Mom always makes the best stuffing and gravy. I always like to open the oven when the turkey is almost cooked and sneak out some of the dressing.

2 Tbsp. margarine
4 Tbsp. chopped onion
1/2 c. chopped celery
8 c. dry bread cubes
1/2 tsp. salt
1/2 tsp. pepper
1 tsp. poultry seasoning
1/2 tsp. ground sage
1 can chichen broth
1 egg, beaten

Cook onion and celery in margarine until tender. Combine bread with seasonings. Add beaten egg and chicken broth. Toss lightly until well mixed. Makes about 6 cups of stuffing or enough for about a 10 pound turkey. If too soft, add more bread cubes.

This can be mixed the night before and refrigerated. After stuffing the turkey, use a slice of bread to keep stuffing from falling out. Also remember to remove all the stuffing from turkey before storing in the refrigerator to prevent salmonella. You may also add the giblets and meat boiled off the neck. Save some for the gravy though.

HOT AND SPICY TURKEY CHILE - HEALTHY

2 Tbsp. olive oil
1 bell pepper, diced
1 small onion, diced
2 tsp. chili powder
1 (16 oz.) can tomatoes, crushed
1/2 c. water
1 (15 1/2 oz.) and 1 (10oz.) can red kidney beans
2 c. diced cooked turkey
1 tsp. sugar
1/2 tsp. salt
1/2 tsp. crushed red pepper
3/4 c. Monterey Jack cheese, shredded
Corn chips

In large skillet over medium heat, saute green pepper and onion in olive oil until tender, stirring occasionally. Stir in chili powder and cook 1 minute. Stir in tomatoes with liquid, kidney beans (undrained), turkey, sugar, salt, red pepper, and 1/2 cup water over high heat. Heat to boiling. Reduce heat to low and simmer 10 minutes to blend flavors, stirring occasionally. Spoon chile into soup bowls and serve   with shredded cheese and chips.. Serves 8.

Good one to make and freeze in portions for a later day.

TURKEY TACOS

1 tsp. vegetable oil
1 medium onion
2 cloves garlic, minced
2 tsp. chili powder
1 (16 oz.) can tomatoes,
   drained
1 (4 oz.) can mild chopped
   green chiles, drained
1 tsp. cider vinegar
1/2 tsp. salt
3/4 lb. cooked turkey,
   julienned
8 taco shells
Shredded iceberg lettuce
1 c. shredded Cheddar
   cheese
1 small onion, chopped
Avocado slices for garnish

In large skillet, heat oil over medium high heat. Saute onion 5 minutes until tender. Add garlic and chili powder; cook, stirring 1 minute. Add tomatoes, green chiles, vinegar, and salt. Reduce heat to medium low; cook, stirring to break up tomatoes, 5 minutes or until sauce thickens. Add turkey and heat through.

To serve, heat taco shells according to package directions. Fill shells with turkey mixture. Top with lettuce, cheese and onion. Garnish with avocado slices if desired.

TACO STYLE POTATO AND TURKEY SKILLET - HEALTHY

4 medium potatoes,
   peeled and quartered
1/2 tsp. salt
3 to 4 Tbsp. skim milk
1 lb. ground turkey
1/2 c. shredded carrot
1/2 c. chopped onion
1 c. water
1 (6 oz.) can tomato paste
2 tsp. chili powder
1/4 tsp. salt
1/4 tsp. oregano
1/8 tsp. garlic powder
Hot pepper sauce to taste
1 (10 oz.) pkg. frozen
   green beans
1/4 c. shredded Cheddar
   cheese

In medium saucepan, boil potatoes in a small amount of water, covered, until tender. Drain and mash potatoes, adding 1/4 teaspoon salt and the milk. Cover to keep warm.

Meanwhile, in large skillet, cook turkey, carrot and onion until turkey is browned. Drain off any fat. Stir in water, tomato paste, chili powder, salt, oregano, garlic powder, and hot pepper sauce. Add green beans, stirring to separate. Bring to a boil. Reduce heat and simmer about 7 minutes. Spoon potatoes on turkey mixture. Sprinkle cheese over the potatoes. Cover and cook 2 or 3 minutes, until cheese melts. Serves 6.

TURKEY STROGANOFF - HEALTHY

1 (16 oz.) pkg. wide
noodles
1/4 c. margarine
1 c. chopped onion
1 lb. fresh mushrooms,
sliced
1 clove garlic, minced
2 lb. ground turkey
2 Tbsp. dry sherry
1 tsp. dill weed
1 tsp. paprika
1 tsp. salt
1/8 tsp. ground red
pepper
2 (10 1/2 oz) cans cream
of celery soup
1 (12 oz.) can evaporated
milk
2 c. plain yogurt

Cook noodles according to package directions; drain. In large skillet, melt margarine. Add onion, mushrooms and garlic; saute about 5 minutes or until onion is tender. With slotted spoon, remove mixture. Add turkey to skillet and cook until browned. Spoon off extra fat and discard. Add sherry, dill weed, salt, paprika, and pepper. Return onion and mushroom mixture to skillet; cook 2 minutes. Stir in soup and milk and simmer 5 minutes, stirring occasionally. Fold in yogurt. Mix with noodles. Serves 8.

STUFFED TURKEY PATTIES WITH TOMATO SAUCE - HEALTHY

1 lb. ground turkey
1/2 c. finely chopped
onion
1/4 c. dry bread crumbs
1 tsp. Worcestershire
sauce
1/2 c. shredded
Mozzarella cheese
1 (4 1/2 oz.) jar sliced
mushrooms, drained
1 (8 oz.) can tomato sauce
1/2 tsp. basil

In medium bowl, combine turkey, onion, bread crumbs, Worcestershire sauce, and garlic. Shape into 8 thin patties. Combine cheese and 1 tablespoon mushrooms and divide mixture equally onto the centers of 4 of the patties. (Reserve remaining mushrooms for sauce.) Cover with remaining patties; press edges to seal. Broil 3 to 4 inches from heat 12 to 16 minutes or until browned, turning once. *These can also be barbecued.*

Meanwhile, combine tomato sauce, basil and reserved mushrooms; heat until bubbly. Serve over turkey patties. Serves 4.

TURKEY BURGERS - HEALTHY/EZ

1 lb. ground turkey
1 tsp. dried onion flakes
1/2 tsp. Mrs. Dash

Mix well and shape into 4 patties. Spray frying pan with butter flavored nonstick spray. Heat pan and fry patties as you would hamburgers, about 6 to 8 minutes on each side over medium heat. Serve on whole wheat buns as you would hamburgers, but try with Thousand Island dressing or a Ranch dressing. *These may also be barbecued.*

GROUND TURKEY AND HOMEMADE NOODLES - EZ

Noodles
1 tsp. salt
1/4 tsp. pepper
1 lb. ground turkey
1 (10 1/2 oz.) can cream
   of chicken or mushroom
   soup
1/2 c. milk

Brown turkey in a large skillet (sprayed with nonstick vegetable spray). Add salt and pepper. Set aside.

Cook noodles according to directions; drain. Add to turkey. Add soup and milk. Cook, covered, for 30 minutes, stirring occasionally over low heat. If it is too thick, thin down with more milk.

HOMEMADE EGG NOODLES - HEALTHY

1 c. flour
2 eggs (or 5 egg whites)
1 tsp. salt

Mix all together. Knead on floured board until dough is stiff. Roll very thin and cut into strips, about 1/4 inch thick. Spread on towel and separate to allow them to dry. Keep refrigerated in plastic wrap until ready to use. Cook as you would any pasta. Drop into boiling water with 1/2 teaspoon salt and a few drops of vegetable oil. Stir them occasionally to keep them from sticking together until noodles are tender.

Use for Ground Turkey and Homemade Noodles and any other purpose.

CREAMED TURKEY PATTIES - HEALTHY/EZ

1 1/2 lb. ground, raw
  turkey
1/2 c. chopped onions
2 slices fresh bread
  crumbs
1/2 tsp. salt
1 egg, beaten
1 (10 1/2 oz.) can cream
  of mushroom soup
3/4 "soup can full" of
  milk
2 Tbsp. chopped parsley

Mix turkey, onions, bread crumbs, salt, and beaten egg. Shape patties and put in buttered baking dish. Stir soup, milk and parsley together and pour over patties. Bake in a 350° oven, covered, for 25 minutes. Uncover and bake 10 minutes more. Serves 4.

ONION PEEK-A-BOO CASSEROLE - EZ

1 lb. ground turkey
1 tsp. salt
1/8 tsp. pepper
1 egg, beaten
1/4 c. fresh bread
  crumbs
8 small cooked onions
2 Tbsp. parsley
1 (10 1/2 oz.) cream of
  chicken soup

Combine turkey, seasonings, egg and bread crumbs, Divide into 8 portions, placing one onion in middle of each ball. Place balls in oiled 1 1/2 quart casserole. Stir parsley into soup and pour over balls. Cover and bake in a 350° oven for 20 minutes. Remove cover and continue baking 10 minutes. Serves 4.

TURKEY LOAF - HEALTHY/EZ

1 lb. ground raw turkey
1 c. herb seasoned
  stuffing mix
1/2 c. finely chopped
  parsley
2 stalks celery, chopped
1 large carrot, grated
1 small onion, finely
  chopped
1 clove garlic, minced
1/2 tsp. salt
1/4 tsp. pepper
1/4 tsp. poultry
  seasoning
1 egg, slightly beaten

Mix all ingredients together until well blended (by hand is the best way). Turn into foil lined loaf pan (8 1/2 x 4 1/2 x 2 5/8 inches). Allow foil to overhang. Bake in preheated oven at 350° for 40 to 45 minutes or until firm in the middle. Serve hot.

Leftovers can be served cold in sandwiches or party snacks. *Delicious!*

TURKEY-POPPY SEED CASSEROLE - HEALTHY

Mom's favorite ground turkey recipe. Is there any reason you can't use cooked, cubed turkey, using about 3 cups, only don't saute the turkey, just the vegetables. Neufchatel cheese is found next to the cream cheese in your supermarket.

1 1/2 lb. ground raw turkey
1/3 c. chopped onion
1/3 c. chopped green pepper
1 (15 oz.) can tomato sauce
1/2 tsp. salt
1/4 tsp. pepper
1 (8oz.) pkg. wide noodles
1 (8oz.) pkg. Neufchatel cheese, cubed
1 c. lowfat cottage cheese
1/2 c. plain lowfat yogurt
1 Tbsp. poppy seed

In a large skillet, cook the turkey, onion and green pepper until the meat is no longer pink and the vegetables are tender. Drain off liquid. Stir in tomato sauce, salt and pepper.

Meanwhile, cook the noodles according to package directions, but eliminate salt; drain. In a small mixing bowl, combine the cheeses, yogurt and poppy seed; toss the cheese   mixture with the hot noodles. Layer 3/4 of the noodle mixture in a 13x9 inch baking dish. Spoon the meat mixture over the center of the noodles, leaving a 1 to 2 inch border of uncovered noodles.   Layer the remaining noodle mixture over the center of the meat mixture, leaving 1 to 2 inch meat border. Bake, covered, in a 375° oven for 30 minutes. Uncover the casserole and bake an additional 10 to 15 minutes more, until casserole is heated through. Serves 8.

HOT FRANKFURTER POTATO SALAD - EZ

1 (10 1/2 oz.) can cream of celery soup
1/3 c. milk
3 Tbsp. sweet pickle relish
2 Tbsp. cider vinegar
2 Tbsp. chopped parsley (optional)
5 small potatoes (l lb.) cooked, peeled (if desired) and sliced
8 oz. chicken or turkey franks, cut diagonally in 1 inch pieces

In medium skillet or saucepan, bring undiluted soup, milk, relish, and vinegar just to a boil. Gently stir in potatoes and franks. Cook until heated through. Sprinkle with parsley. Serves 4.

VEAL PARMIGIANA - HEALTHY

Italian.

1/4 c. flour
1 tsp. salt
1/2 tsp. garlic powder
Dash of pepper
4 veal chops, tenderized
1/2 c. bread crumbs
1/4 c. grated Parmesan
  cheese
1 egg, beaten
2 Tbsp. olive oil
4 thin slices Mozzarella
  cheese
8 oz. tomato sauce
1 1/2 Tbsp. oregano

Mix flour and seasoning in one bowl; beat egg in another. In a third bowl or plate, mix bread crumbs and Parmesan cheese. Dip chops in egg, then in flour. Dip in egg again and finally in the crumbs. Brown chops in large skillet in oil on both sides on medium high heat. Remove skillet from stove and place a slice of Mozzarella cheese on each chop. Stir oregano into tomato sauce and pour over chops. Return to stove, covered, and cook over medium low heat 40 minutes. Uncover and cook an additional 10 minutes. Serves 4.

Traditionally served with spaghetti and garlic bread.

BARBEQUED SPARERIBS - EZ

Have extra napkins and enjoy! Everyone will ask for a copy of this recipe.

4 lb. spareribs
1/3 c. brown sugar
1 c. catsup
1/3 c. vinegar
1/3 c. molasses
2 tsp. salt
2 tsp. dry mustard
1/2 tsp. pepper
1/3 tsp. paprika

Trim fat from ribs. Brown ribs on both sales in large skillet with 2 tablespoons shortening over medium high heat. Place ribs in roaster. Mix all other ingredients and pour over ribs. Bake in a 300° oven for 2 hours. Baste with sauce once in a while.

OVEN BEEF STEW - EZ

This is so easy and so delicious!

3 lb. lean beef, cut in small
  pieces
6 carrots, sliced
6 stalks celery, sliced
1 large onion, diced
2 Tbsp. tapioca
2 tsp. salt
2 tsp. sugar
2 c. V-8 juice
3 large potatoes, cut in
  chunks
Pepper to taste

Brown beef in small amount of olive oil in large skillet, ovenproof or roasting pan. Add rest of ingredients. Cover and cook in a 275° oven for 4 hours. Serves 4 to 6.

BRAISED BEEF IN BEER

For a bunch.

2 Tbsp. salad oil
4 to 5 lb. beef cross rib
   pot roast
2 large onions, diced
1 c. beer
1 Tbsp. salt
2 tsp. dry mustard
1/4 tsp. pepper
1/4 c. flour

In Dutch oven in hot oil, cook pot roast until browned on all sides; remove meat from Dutch oven. Pour off all but 1 tablespoon drippings. In remaining drippings, cook onions 5 minutes, stirring occasionally, or until tender crisp. Return meat to Dutch oven; add all remaining ingredients except flour. Heat to boiling. Reduce heat to low; cover dutch oven. Simmer for 4 hours until meat is fork tender, turning meat occasionally, and adding more beer, if necessary.

Place meat on platter. If necessary, skim fat from pan liquid. In a cup, blend flour and 1/2 cup of *cold* water until smooth. Gradually stir into hot liquid in Dutch oven, stirring constantly, until mixture is thickened. Serve gravy with meat. Serves 10 to 14.

SWISS STEAK

1/4 c. flour
2 lb. round steak (1 inch
   thick)
3 Tbsp. olive oil
1/2 c. chopped celery
1 tsp. salt
1/2 tsp. pepper
1/2 c. chopped onions
1/2 c. chopped green
   peppers
1 can cream of
   mushroom soup
1 pkg. gravy mix,
   prepared according to
   directions

Combine flour, salt and pepper; pound into meat. In a large skillet, brown meat on both sides in hot olive oil. Remove meat. Saute onions, celery and green peppers in same skillet, adding a little more oil if necessary. Add soup to prepared beef gravy. Return steaks to skillet and pour gravy mixture over all. Bake, covered, in a 350° oven for 1 1/2 hours. Serves 6 to 8.

DEVILED STEAK

1 Tbsp. dry mustard
1/2 c. flour
1 1/2 lb. round steak
Salt and pepper to taste
1 c. sliced onions
1 1/2 c. carrots, diced
1 1/2 c. canned tomatoes,
   crushed
2 Tbsp. Worcestershire
   sauce
1 Tbsp. brown sugar

Mix dry mustard with flour and pound into round steak. Season with salt and pepper. Brown with a little fat in a hot large skillet. Place in small roaster or other pan (possibly the skillet). Pour the onions, carrots, tomatoes, Worcestershire sauce, and brown sugar over the steak. Cover and bake at 350° about 1 1/2 hours. Serves 4.

BEEF STROGANOFF - EZ

Good and easy dish for company or family.

1 lb. round steak, cut in
   thin strips
1/2 c. chopped onion
2 Tbsp. butter or
   margarine
1 (10 1/2 oz.) can golden
   mushroom soup
1/2 c. sour cream
1/3 c. water
Hot buttered noodles

In large skillet, brown meat and cook onion in butter until onion is tender. Stir in soup, sour cream and water. Cover; cook over low heat 45 minutes or until tender. Stir occasionally. Serve over noodles. Serves 4.

"Idea:" Try some other cream soup for a totally different meal, like cream of Cheddar, cream of celery or try a seafood stroganoff with cream of shrimp and substitute shrimp and crab for the beef. Go to it! Remove those cobwebs from the brain.

BEEF SALAMI - EZ

This is great for snacks or sandwiches.

2 lb. lean ground beef
1/2 tsp. pepper
1/2 tsp. dry mustard
1/2 tsp. minced garlic
4 tsp. tenderizer salt

Mix all ingredients together. Make a roll and wrap in foil. Refrigerate for 24 hours. Bake in preheated 325° oven for 1 hour; cool. Keep refrigerated.

CRAB-ARTICHOKE BAKE

1/4 c. butter or margarine
1/4 lb. fresh mushrooms,
  sliced
1/4 c. flour
1 tsp paprika
1/2 tsp. salt
1/4 tsp. pepper
2 1/2 c. milk
1 c. shredded Cheddar
  cheese
1/3 c. dry white wine
1 Tbsp. lemon juice
1 (6 to 8 oz.) pkg. frozen
  crab, thawed, drained
  and flaked or 1 (7oz.)
  can crab, drained and
  flaked
1 1/2 c. shell macaroni,
  cooked according to
  directions and drained
1 (14 oz.) can artichoke
  hearts, drained and
  halved.

Melt butter in a large skillet over moderate heat. Add mushrooms. Saute a few minutes over moderate heat, stirring. Stir in flour, paprika, salt, and pepper. Add milk. Cook over moderate heat, stirring constantly, until thickened and smooth. Add cheese. Stir until cheese melts. Stir in wine and lemon juice. Gently, but thoroughly, blend sauce with crab, macaroni and artichoke hearts. Turn mixture into greased 2 quart casserole. Bake, uncovered, in oven preheated to 350° about 20 minutes or until bubbly. Makes 4 to 6 servings.

I especially like this, because it's impressive and you can clean up most of the mess before guests arrive. Also you can stop the recipe after stirring in the wine and lemon juice and have an excellent mushroom and cheese soup.

SEAFOOD RICE CASSEROLE - HEALTHY/EZ

Good casserole for company as well as family.

1/2 c. green peppers,
  diced
1 c. chopped celery
1/2 c. finely chopped
  onion
2 c. cooked rice
1/2 lb. salad shrimp
6 oz. crab or imitation crab
1 c. mayonnaise
1/2 tsp. salt
1/4 tsp. black pepper
2 tsp. Worcestershire
  sauce
1/2 c. shredded Cheddar
  cheeee
1/2 c. toasted sliced
  almonds

Steam green pepper, celery and onion in a small saucepan with 2 tablespoons water for 2 to 3 minutes or until tender crisp. Mix with rice, seafood, mayonnaise, and seasonings. Mix well. Turn into buttered, shallow 2 quart baking dish. Sprinkle with cheese and almonds. Bake in a 350° oven for 25 minutes. Serves 6.

SEAFOOD CREPES

Creamy Veloute Sauce
**1/2 lb. cooked salad
  shrimp**
**1/2 lb. crabmeat or
  imitation crab**
**1/2 lb. fresh mushrooms,
  sliced**
**1/2 lb. Swiss cheese,
  shredded**
Crepes (see page 128)

Veloute Sauce:
**2 Tbsp. butter or
  margarine**
3 Tbsp. flour
1 c. chicken broth
1/3 c. light cream

Prepare Veloute Sauce and crepes according to instructions. Saute mushrooms in separate pan. Stir in crab, shrimp and mushrooms into the Veloute Sauce and heat until thoroughly hot. Place 2 tablespoons of the filling in each crepe, fold over and sprinkle the cheese over the top. Place under broiler until cheese is melted. Serves 4.

Veloute Sauce: In saucepan, melt butter; blend in flour. Add broth and cream all at once. Cook and stir until thickened and bubbly. Makes 1 1/2 cups.

"Idea:" This is an excellent sauce to use in all sorts of crepes, such as the Seafood Crepes and Chicken-Broccoli Crepes. This is also very good to use with pasta, rice or potatoes.

SHRIMP CREOLE - HEALTHY

**1 lb. large shrimp,
  cleaned and cooked**
3 Tbsp. butter
1 c. chopped onion
**3/4 c. chopped green
  pepper**
1/2 c. diced celery
1 clove garlic, fine cut
1 tsp. salt
1/4 tsp. pepper
Pinch of rosemary
Pinch of paprika
Pinch of thyme
Small bay leaf
1/2 Tbsp. dried parsley
1 Tbsp. sugar
**1/4 tsp. crushed red
  pepper**
**2 c. canned tomatoes,
  crushed**
3 c. hot cooked rice

Saute pepper, onion, garlic, and celery in melted butter until tender. Add seasonings, sugar, parsley, hot pepper, and tomatoes. Bring to boil; reduce heat. Simmer for 15 to 18 minutes. Add shrimp; heat thoroughly. Serve on hot rice. Serves 4.

SALMON LOAF WITH SHRIMP SAUCE

2 (1 lb.) cans salmon
1/4 c. finely chopped
  onions
1/4 c. chopped
  parsley
1/4 c. lemon juice
1/2 tsp. salt
1/2 tsp. pepper
1/2 tsp. thyme
2 c. coarse cracker
  crumbs
1/2 c. milk
4 eggs, well beaten
1/4 c. margarine or
  butter
Shrimp Sauce

Drain salmon; save liquid. Set aside. Flake salmon in a large bowl; add onion, parsley, lemon juice, seasonings, and cracker crumbs. Stir lightly. Add reserved salmon liquid plus enough milk to make 1 cup. Add eggs and melted butter. Mix lightly. Spoon into a greased 2 quart loaf pan or casserole. Bake in a 350° oven for 1 hour or until loaf is set in center. Remove and prepare Shrimp Sauce.

Shrimp Sauce: Heat 1 can of frozen shrimp soup according to directions. Add 1/4 cup milk. Stir until smooth., Slice salmon loaf and top with sauce.

SALMON SQUARES WITH MUSHROOM PEA SAUCE - HEALTHY/EZ

2 c. cooked rice
2 eggs, beaten
2 c. cottage cheese
  (16 oz.)
1 (1 lb.) can salmon
  drained and flaked
1 small onion, finely
  chopped
1/4 c. chopped green
  pepper
2 tsp. soy sauce
1 c. soda cracker crumbs

Mushroom Pea Sauce:
3 Tbsp. butter or
  margarine
1 (4 oz.) can sliced
  mushrooms, drained
3 Tbsp. flour
2 Tbsp. chopped
  pimentos
1 tsp. seasoned salt
1 1/2 c. milk
1 1/2 c. cooked peas
  (canned or frozen),
  drained

Combine all ingredients except cracker crumbs. Spoon into a buttered 12x7 1/2 x 2 inch baking pan. Sprinkle cracker crumbs over top. Bake at 350° for 40 minutes or until firm in center. Cut into squares. Serve with Mushroom Pea Sauce. Serves 8.

Mushroom Pea Sauce: Saute mushrooms in butter for 5 minutes. Stir in flour and salt. Gradually add milk. Cook until smooth and thick, stirring constantly. Stir in peas and pimentos. Spoon over salmon squares.

SALMON-STUFFED SHELLS

Lite meal.

3 Tbsp. chopped green
  onions
1/3 c. chopped bell
  pepper
1/3 c. thinly sliced and
  diced celery
1 (7 3/4 oz.) can pink
  salmon
3 Tbsp. tartar sauce
6 jumbo cooked pasta
  shells

Sauce:
2 slices bacon
1 1/2 Tbsp.bacon grease
1 1/2 Tbsp. flour
1/3 c. grated Cheddar
3/4 c. milk

In a small bowl, combine the green onions, bell pepper, celery, and salmon. Mix lightly with the tartar sauce. Fill cooked jumbo shells and place shells in a well greased small casserole dish. Cover and bake at 350° for about 25 minutes.

Sauce: Fry bacon in small saucepan until crisp and set aside. Discard all but 1 1/2 tablespoons bacon grease. Add flour and combine. Add cheese and milk and cook until creamy and thickened. To serve, place baked shells on serving plate and top with sauce. Garnish with crumbled crisp bacon. Serves 2.

POACHED FISH - HEALTHY/EZ

1 medium onion, sliced
3 thin slices lemon
3 sprigs fresh parsley,
  chopped
1 bay leaf
1 tsp. salt
2 peppercorns
1 lb. fish fillets such as
  halibut, cod or
  swordfish

Pour 1 1/2 inches of water in large skillet; add onion, lemon slices, parsley, bay leaf, salt, and peppercorns. Heat to boiling. Arrange fish in a single layer in skillet. Cover tightly; simmer 4 to 6 minutes or until fish flakes easily with a fork. Serves 3 (140 calories each).

OVEN FRIED FLOUNDER - HEALTHY

1/2 c. whole wheat bread
  crumbs
1/2 tsp. paprika
1/2 tsp. onion powder
1/4 tsp. dried thyme
  leaves
1 large egg white
1 Tbsp. water
1 lb. fresh or frozen
  (thawed and drained)
  flounder fillets, cut in 4
  portions
1 Tbsp. olive oil

Line a jelly roll pan with foil. Spray with vegetable cooking spray and the olive oil. Mix bread crumbs and seasonings in one dish. Beat egg white and water in another dish. Dip fish in egg white and then in crumbs. Place on cookie sheet. Bake at 450° for 10 minutes. Serves 4.

FLOUNDER WITH DILL-LEMON SAUCE - HEALTHY/EZ

2 1/2 Tbsp. margarine
  or butter
1 Tbsp. chopped fresh
  dill or 3/4 tsp. dill
  weed
1 Tbsp. fresh lemon juice
2 green onions, sliced
1 lb. flounder or other
  fish fillets

Saute first 4 ingredients over low heat until margarine is melted and onions are soft. Add flounder to mixture in skillet. Cover and cook about 7 to 10 minutes, depending on thickness. Baste fish occasionally with mixture in skillet. *Do not overcook.* Serves 4 (only 170 calories per serving).

CRISPY FLOUNDER FISH - HEALTHY

1/2 c. sesame seeds
1/3 c. unseasoned dried
  bread crumbs
1/4 c. finely chopped
  parsley
1/4 tsp. salt
1/4 tsp. ground red
  pepper
1 large egg white, lightly
  beaten
1 Tbsp. water
4 (6 oz.) flounder fillets
  or other firm fish
3 Tbsp. peanut oil

Combine sesame seeds, bread crumbs, parsley, salt, and red pepper in shallow dish. Combine egg white and water in pie pan. Dip fish pieces in egg white mixture, then into sesame seed mixture, Place on wax paper. (This can be done 1 hour ahead of time.)

Pan-fry fish in large skillet in peanut oil. If you can't get all the fish in pan, use 1 1/2 table-spoons peanut oil for each batch of fish. Fry over high heat, 3 minutes on each side. Turn and cook 2 minutes more on the other. Clean skillet with paper towel before frying second batch.

BEST TUNA CASSEROLE - EZ

This has been a family favorite for years. Easy and economical!

1/2 c. chopped onion
2 Tbsp. butter or
  margarine
1 (10 1/2 oz.) can cream
  of mushroom soup
1/2 c. milk
1 c. sharp Cheddar
  cheese, shredded
2 c. cooked macaroni
1 (7 oz.) can tuna, drained
2 Tbsp. buttered bread
  crumbs

Saute onion in margarine until tender. Stir in soup, milk, 3/4 cup of the cheese, tuna fish, and macaroni. Pour into greased 1 1/2 quart casserole dish. Top with remaining cheese and bread crumbs. Bake at 350° for 30 minutes or until lightly browned. Serves 4.

It is also good with fresh tomatoes, cut up, or crumble crackers or potato chips over the top.

CHINESE-TUNA CASSEROLE - EZ

1 (6 1/2 oz.) can tuna,
  drained
1 (16 oz.) can Chinese
  vegetables
1 (10 1/2 oz.) can cream
  of celery soup
1 (5 oz.) can chow mein
  noodles
1 (10 1/2 oz.) can cream
  of mushroom soup

Mix and put in greased casserole. Bake at 350° for 40 minutes.

You may also use frozen vegetables.

GINGER CHICKEN WITH PEANUTS - HEALTHY/EZ

1/2 to 3/4 lb. chicken
  breast, skinned, boned
  and cut in strips
1 Tbsp. soy sauce
1 tsp. cornstarch
2 Tbsp. peanut oil
1 (10 oz.) pkg. Japanese
  or Chinese style
  vegetables
1/4 c. water
1/2 tsp. ginger
2 Tbsp. salted peanuts

Combine chicken and soy sauce in bowl; stir in cornstarch. Saute chicken in hot oil in skillet just until tender, about 3 or 4 minutes. Remove from pan. Add vegetables, water and ginger to skillet. Bring to a full boil over medium heat, separating vegetables with a fork and stirring frequently. Reduce heat; cover and simmer 2 minutes. Add chicken and heat. Sprinkle with peanuts. Serves 3.

SIMPLE SWEET AND SOUR SAUCE - EZ

Chinese.

**1/4 inch thick slice fresh
    ginger root, chopped or
    1 tsp. ground ginger
1/2 c. sugar
1/2 c. vinegar
6 Tbsp. pineapple juice
1 Tbsp. sherry
1 1/2 Tbsp. cornstarch,
    dissolved in 4 Tbsp.
    water**

Using a garlic press, squeeze the ginger juice into a heavy saucepan, or use the ground ginger. Add the sugar, vinegar, pineapple juice, and sherry. Bring the sauce to a boil and stir in the cornstarch mixture to thicken. Use as directed in recipes.

This is one sauce I use for dipping batter fried items, such as pork, shrimp or chicken strips. Several of these items you can already buy prebreaded, but believe it or not, one of my favorites is Sweet and Sour Spam (no breading is necessary). (See tempura recipe under appetizers.)

SWEET AND SOUR SPAM - EZ

**1 medium green bell
    pepper, seeded and
    sliced
1 medium Bermuda
    onion, diced
1 large can Spam, diced
1 small can pineapple
    chunks, undrained
1 batch sweet and sour
    sauce
2 Tbsp. butter or
    margarine**

Saute onion and pepper in butter in large skillet until vegetables are slightly tender and browned. Add Spam and continue until meat is browned. Stir in sauce and pineapple and heat until warmed thoroughly. Serve over rice.

FRIED RICE - EZ

Chinese.

**2 to 4 Tbsp. peanut or
    vegetable oil
4 c. cooked rice
2 Tbsp. chopped green
    onion
1 tsp. salt
1/4 tsp. pepper
1/2 c. cooked pork, diced
2 eggs, beaten
2 Tbsp. soy sauce**

Stir-fry cooked rice in 2 tablespoons oil until lightly browned. Add more oil as needed to prevent sticking. Add onion, salt, pepper, and pork. Continue cooking until onion is soft. Add eggs, stirring rapidly, then soy sauce.

Other vegetables, such as fresh mushrooms or snow peas, may be added as well or even small, cut up shrimp.

CHINESE SUPPER - EZ

1 lb. ground hamburger or
  turkey
1 c. chopped celery
1 small onion, chopped
2 (10 1/2 oz.) cans cream
  of chicken or celery soup
  or one of each
1/4 lb. fresh bean sprouts
1/2 c. water
1/2 c. quick rice
2 Tbsp. soy sauce
Chow mein noodles

In large skillet, brown hamburger or turkey, celery and onion. Add the soups, sprouts, water, rice, and soy sauce. Place in lightly greased 2 quart casserole dish and bake at 350° for 45 to 55 minutes. Top with a small can of chow mein noodles before serving.

FAVORITE SPAGHETTI WITH MEATBALLS

Italian.

12 oz. spaghetti, cooked
  and drained
1/4 c. minced onion
2 cloves garlic, peeled
  and minced
1/4 c. olive oil
3 1/2 c. canned tomatoes
  or 3 c. fresh tomatoes,
  steamed, peeled and
  crushed
1 (6oz.) can tomato paste
3 c. hot water
3 tsp. salt
1/4 tsp. powdered cloves,
  (optional)
1/4 tsp. pepper
1 tsp. sage

Saute onion and garlic golden brown in hot oil in skillet. Add tomatoes, tomato paste, hot water, salt, cloves, pepper, and sage. Simmer 1 1/2 hours, uncovered, stirring often.

Meatballs: Combine all ingredients except olive oil. Shape into 8 balls, 2 inches in diameter. Brown on all sides quickly in hot olive oil in skillet. Add with drippings to sauce 1/2 hour before sauce is done. Cook 1/2 hour. Serve over cooked spaghetti. Top with grated Parmesan cheese. Serves 6.

Meatballs:
1 lb. ground chuck beef
2 garlic cloves, peeled
  and minced
1 egg, beaten
1 tsp. salt
1 Tbsp. minced parsley
1 c. soft bread crumbs
1/2 tsp. pepper
1/2 c. grated Parmesan
  cheese
2 Tbsp. olive oil

TURKEY SPAGHETTI - HEALTHY/EZ

Italian

1 small onion, chopped
fine
1 clove garlic, crushed
2 Tbsp. olive oil
1 (28 oz.) tomatoes,
crushed
1 1/2 c. water
1 tsp. basil
1 tsp. salt
Pepper to taste
2 c. chopped cooked
turkey
1/2 c. dry white wine
(optional)
1 lb. spaghetti or
macaroni, cooked

In medium saucepan, saute onion and garlic in oil until lightly browned. Stir in tomatoes and water, then basil, salt, pepper, turkey, and wine. Simmer 45 minutes. Serve on hot cooked spaghetti. Serves 4.

SPAGHETTI PIE

Italian.

8 oz. spaghetti
3 Tbsp. butter
2 eggs, lightly beaten
1/3 c. grated Parmesan
cheese
1 1/2 lb. ground beef
1 small onion, chopped
1 small green pepper,
chopped
1 (8 oz.) can tomatoes,
chopped
1 (6 oz.) can tomato paste
1 1/2 tsp. oregano
1 1/2 Tbsp. brown sugar
1/4 tsp. salt
2 cloves garlic, minced
1 c. cottage cheese, well
drained
1 c. shredded Mozzarella
cheese

Cook the spaghetti until just tender. Drain and stir butter, eggs and Parmesan cheese into spaghetti. Press the spaghetti mixture into a buttered 10 inch pie plate as a crust.

In a skillet, cook ground beef, onion and green pepper until meat is done. Drain off excess fat. Stir in the next 6 ingredients and simmer for 30 minutes. Spread cottage cheese over the spaghetti crust. Pour in meat-tomato mixture. Cover with foil and bake in a 350° oven for 45 minutes. Uncover and top with Mozzarella cheese. Bake 7 to 8 minutes more, until cheese has melted. Serves 8.

SPEEDY LASAGNA

Italian.

1 lb. ground beef
1 lb. (13 oz.) can tomatoes
1 (8 oz.) can tomato sauce
1 env. spaghetti sauce mix
1 clove garlic, chopped
8 oz. lasagne noodles
1 (6 oz.) pkg. Mozzarella,
**   sliced**
8 oz. lowfat cottage cheese
1/2 c. grated Parmesan
**   cheese**

In large skillet, brown ground beef and garlic. Spoon off excess fat. Add tomatoes, tomato sauce and spaghetti sauce. Bring mixture to boil and simmer 10 minutes or longer. Cook lasagne noodles in large amount of boiling salted water until tender. Drain and rinse in cold water.

Place 1/2 the noodles in lasagne pan or a deep 9x13 inch pan. Cover with 1/3 the sauce, 1/2 the cottage cheese and 1/2 the Mozzarella cheese. Repeat layers with rest of noodles, 1/3 of the sauce, rest of Mozzarella, and cottage cheese, ending with sauce. Top with Parmesan cheese. Bake 350° for 45 minutes. Let stand 10 minutes. Cut into squares. Serves 8.

Some lasagne can be used without boiling it first. Check label on package and bake according to the directions on package.

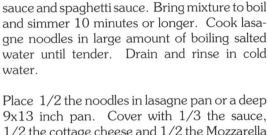

SUPER LASAGNE

This is one of those meals that is great to cut up into individual servings and freeze. Also good for company, because you can clean up the mess before they arrive.

1 lb. bulk Italian sausage
1/2 lb. ground round beef
1/2 c. chopped onion
2 cloves garlic, minced
1 Tbsp. sugar
1 tsp. salt
1 1/2 tsp. dried basil
1/2 tsp. fennel seeds
1/4 tsp. pepper
1/4 c. fresh parsley
1 (28 oz.) can Italian plum
  tomatoes
3 (6 oz.) cans tomato
  paste
1/2 c. water
2 c. Ricotta cheese
3 eggs, beaten
1/2 tsp. salt
12 lasagne noodles
3/4 c. freshly grated
  Parmesan cheese
3/4 lb. Mozzarella cheese,
  thinly sliced

Saute the sausage in a large skillet over medium heat for 3 or 4 minutes. Add the ground round, onion and garlic and saute, stirring until browned. Drain off the grease and discard. Add the sugar, salt, basil, fennel seeds, pepper, and half the parsley to the meat and stir well.

Squash the tomatoes. Combine the tomatoes, tomato paste and water. Add this to the meat mixture and simmer, covered, for 1 1/2 hours. In a bowl, combine the Ricotta cheese, eggs, salt, and the remaining parsley. Preheat oven to 350°. Cook the lasagne noodles according to package directions and drain.

Place a layer of noodles in a buttered 9x13 inch casserole dish. Cover with 1 1/2 cups of the sauce, 1/2 the Ricotta cheese mixture, 1/4 cup of the Parmesan cheese, and 1/2 the Mozzarella cheese. Repeat layering, ending with sauce sprinkled with the remaining 1 cup Parmesan cheese. Cover and bake for 25 minutes. Remove the cover and bake for 20 minutes longer. Let stand for 5 to 10 minutes before serving.

SICILIAN PIZZA

1 pkg. dry yeast
1 1/3 c. hi-altitude flour
1 Tbsp. sugar
1 1/2 tsp. salt
1 Tbsp. shortening
1 egg
2/3 c. hot milk

Pizza Sauce:
1 (8 oz.) can tomato sauce
1/2 tsp. oregano
1/2 tsp. marjoram
1/2 tsp. salt
1/2 tsp. sugar
1/2 tsp. parsley flakes

Place the first 7 ingredients in a small bowl in order listed. Beat at medium speed for 3 minutes. (Batter may climb beaters, just push down with rubber spatula.) Spread in greased 12 inch pizza pan. Spread sauce over dough to within 1/2 inch of edge. Add your choice of toppings (precook any raw meat). Sprinkle with 1 cup shredded Mozzarella cheese and 1/2 cup Parmesan. Let rise in warm place 20 minutes.

Pizza Sauce: Stir all ingredients together in small saucepan and simmer 5 minutes before putting on pizza. Bake 15 to 20 minutes in a 450° oven, until edges are lightly browned. Bake on bottom shelf. This will be a thick crust pizza.

Hint: If you like a lot of toppings on your pizza, let the pizza bake 10 minutes with only the sauce, then add the toppings. Finish baking.

Don't have time to make the crust? Make the sauce, and use French bread, cut in half, or pita bread for your crusts. The new pre-made crusts are also great.

MANICOTTI - HEALTHY

Italian pasta.

3/4 lb. ground beef or
  turkey
1/4 lb. Italian sausage
1 tsp. salt
1/2 tsp. pepper
3 Tbsp. chopped parsley
2 Tbsp. olive oil
2 tsp. Italian seasoning
4 tsp. sugar, divided
4 c. canned tomatoes,
  crushed
1 (6 oz.) can tomato paste
1 pkg. manicotti
1/2 lb. Mozzarella cheese,
  grated
1 egg, beaten
8 oz. lowfat cottage cheese
2 Tbsp. grated Parmesan
  cheese
1/2 green pepper,
  chopped
1 medium onion, chopped
1 cloves garlic, crushed

Saute meat; drain. Add salt and pepper. In another large skillet or pan, saute 2 tablespoons of the parsley, onion, garlic and green pepper in olive oil. Add Italian seasoning, 2 teaspoons of the sugar, tomatoes, tomato paste, and meat. Simmer 10 minutes. Boil manicotti in a large pot in lightly salted water for 2 minutes. Drain; rinse in cold water.

In a small bowl, combine egg, cottage cheese, 2 teaspoons of the sugar, Mozzarella and Parmesan cheese, and remaining parsley. Mix well and stuff into manicotti. Place in greased 9x13 inch pan. Pour meat sauce over all. Bake, uncovered, at 350° for 30 minutes. Serves 8.

SEAFOOD-TOMATO PASTA - HEALTHY/EZ

Italian.

2 (14 1/2 oz.) cans low
  sodium tomatoes
1 (6 oz.) can low sodium
  tomato paste
1/2 c. chopped onion
1 tsp. dried oregano
1 tsp. dried basil
Hot, cooked spaghetti
1/4 tsp. red pepper
1/2 tsp. garlic powder
1/4 tsp. dried thyme
1 lb. salad shrimp
1/2 c. chopped green
  peppers

Combine undrained tomatoes, tomato paste, onion, oregano, basil, red pepper, garlic powder, and thyme in a blender. Blend until well mixed. Put in saucepan and bring to a boil. Reduce heat and simmer, uncovered, for 10 minutes or until mixture thickens slightly, stirring occasionally. Add shrimp and green peppers and simmer 10 minutes more. Serve over cooked spaghetti. Serves 6.

CHICKEN ENCHILADAS SUPREME

Another great dish to cook, divide and freeze for a later day.

2 c. cooked, chopped
   chicken or turkey meat
1 (4 oz.) can chopped, mild
   green chiles
1 (7 oz.) can green chile
   salsa
1/2 tsp. salt
2 c. heavy cream
12 corn tortillas
1 1/2 c. grated Monterey
   Jack cheese

Combine chicken, green chiles and green chile salsa and mix well. Mix salt and heavy cream in a medium size bowl. Heat about 1/2 inch oil in a small skillet. Dip each tortilla into hot oil for about 5 seconds, just to soften. Drain on paper towels. Dip each fried tortilla into bowl containing cream and salt, coating each side. Fill each tortilla with chicken mixture. Roll and place in ungreased flat baking dish. Pour remaining cream over enchiladas and sprinkle with cheese. Bake, uncovered, at 350° for 20 to 25 minutes.

SOUR CREAM ENCHILADAS - EZ

Mexican.

12 large flour tortillas
1 1/4 c. ground beef or
   turkey
1/2 c. chopped onion
1 pt. sour cream
1 (4 oz.) can chopped
   green chili peppers
2 cans cream of chicken
   soup
1 c. shredded Cheddar
   cheese
Shredded lettuce
Diced tomatoes

Wrap tortillas in damp towel. Warm in microwave for 1 minute on REHEAT. Fry ground beef and onion in skillet; drain fat. Put in tortillas and roll tortillas. Put in a 9x13 inch pan. Mix sour cream, chili peppers and soup. Pour over tortillas. Top with cheese. Bake 300° for 15 to 20 minutes, until cheese melts. Serve with shredded lettuce and chopped tomatoes. Serves 6.

EASY MEXICAN CASSEROLE

1 medium size pkg. taco
  chips, crushed
1 pkg. taco mix
  seasonings
1 lb. hamburger
1 can tomato sauce plus
  1/2 c. water to rinse can
1/2 c. rice
Shredded lettuce
1 c. shredded cheese
Chopped tomatoes

Place taco chips in 9x13 inch pan. Cook rice according to directions on package. Brown hamburger in large skillet while rice is cooking. Add taco seasoning, tomato sauce and water to hamburger. Add rice and mix well. Pour mixture over crushed taco chips. Spread cheese on top. Bake in a 350° oven for about 10 minutes, or until cheese is melted. Serve with lettuce and tomatoes on top of each serving.

"Idea:" Guacamole and sour cream would also be great as toppings.

BEEF AND BEAN BURRITOS

Mexican.

1 (16 oz.) jar thick and
  chunky salsa
1 lb. ground beef
1 1/4 oz. taco seasoning
  mix
1 (16oz.) can refried beans
1 (4 oz.) can green
  chopped chiles
10 flour tortillas
3/4 c. shredded lettuce
3/4 c. shredded Cheddar

Drain salsa and reserve liquid. Brown ground beef; drain fat. Add seasoning, beans, chiles, and salsa liquid and simmer 5 minutes, uncovered. Spoon 1/3 c. mixture on each tortilla. Top with 1 tablespoon each of salsa, lettuce and cheese. Fold over and serve warm.

"Idea:" Make these ahead of time and freeze individually, but leave out the lettuce. When ready to eat later, pop them in the oven or microwave, then add lettuce. I like to smother mine with all or any of the following: salsa, sour cream, guacamole, tomatoes, or lettuce.

VEGETABLE PASTA TOSS - HEALTHY/EZ

1/2 (16 oz.) pkg. rotelle
   pasta
1/3 c. low calorie Italian
   salad dressing
1 tsp. Dijon mustard
1/2 (8oz.) pkg. lowfat
   Mozzarella cheese,
   cubed
1 (14 oz.) can artichoke
   hearts, drained and
   each cut in half
1/2 c. pickled sweet red
   pepper slices, cut in
   strips
1/2 c. frozen peas, thawed
1/4 tsp. salt

Prepare rotelle as label directs; drain. In a large bowl, combine and mix dressing and mustard. Add rotelle, cheese, artichokes, pepper strips, peas, and salt; toss until well mixed. Cover and refrigerate at least 1 hour to blend flavorings. To serve, toss lightly. Serves 4.

This is very good prepared the day before.

CHEESY NOODLE TOSS - HEALTHY/EZ

2 Tbsp. margarine or
   butter
1 small onion, minced
2 Tbsp. flour
1 tsp. salt
1/2 tsp. pepper
1 1/4 c. milk
8 oz. cottage cheese
1 c. frozen peas
1 (8 oz.) pkg. wide noodles
1/4 c. grated Parmesan
   cheese

In a 2 quart saucepan, on medium high, melt the margarine. Toss in the onion and cook until tender. Stir in flour, salt and pepper; cook 1 minute. Stir in milk; cook, stirring until thickened. Stir in cottage cheese and peas. Heat through.

In the meantime, cook noodles according to package directions; drain. Gently toss noodles with cottage cheese mixture and Parmesan cheese until heated. Serves 4.

"Idea:" Ham, turkey or tuna could be added or even salad shrimp, etc.

CREAM DRIED BEEF ON TOAST - EZ

**1 large or small pkg.
   smoked chipped dried
   beef
2 or 3 Tbsp. flour
2 Tbsp. margarine or
   butter
Salt and pepper (to taste)
White wine (optional)
Garlic powder
Milk (about 2 1/2 c.)**

In medium or large size skillet, melt margarine over medium high heat. Tear up beef into smaller size pieces and saute until lightly browned around the edges. Add enough flour to absorb the margarine until you have a slight pastelike substance. Add milk slowly, stirring constantly, until you have enough to give you a thin, gravylike texture. Continue stirring until mixture comes to a light boil. Turn down heat and add remaining seasonings and white wine until you like what you have. Gravy will thicken as it cooks. If it is too thin, combine about 1 tablespoon cornstarch with 1/4 cup cold water; stir until cornstarch is dissolved. Add to gravy. If too thick, add more wine, water or milk. Serve over toast or biscuits.

If you want to get fancier, try adding sauteed mushrooms or onions to gravy.

TURKEY OR CHICKEN STEW - HEALTHY/EZ

This is a great way to use the leftover carcass from the Thanksgiving turkey or a baked chicken. Reserve the broth from boiling the carcass to get the meat off the bones.

**Chicken or turkey, cooked
   and diced
Potatoes, cut in bite-size
Carrots, peeled and cut
   into 1/2 inch pieces
1/2 to 1 c. peeled and
   diced onions
Chicken bouillon or
   crystals
1 Tbsp. flour or more
1 Tbsp. cornstarch or more
1/4 c. cold water
Few drops of liquid smoke
   (optional)
1/2 tsp. Worcestershire
   sauce
1/2 tsp. garlic powder**

Place carrots and onions in large pot. Cover and cook over medium heat about 20 minutes. Mix flour, cornstarch with water and stir until dissolved; add to water. Make more of this mixture later, if necessary, to thicken liquid in stew. Add remainder of ingredients, except for the turkey or chicken, and cook, covered, until potatoes are just tender. Sample and add any additional spices you choose. Add the meat and the stew is ready to eat.

PERFECT FRENCH FRIES

These are perfect and saves a lot of time at last minute preparation. I remember these for our birthday dinners when we were kids.

Red potatoes or new Idaho Gold
Vegetable oil (enough for 2 inches in the bottom of deep-fryer or large pan)

Wash potatoes well; they are better if the skin is left on. At least 15 minutes or up to 5 hours before serving, using a French fry cutter, cut potatoes (may also be done by hand). Rinse potato strips under cold water, using a sieve. Drain on paper towels. Fill deep fat fryer or pan with 2 inches of vegetable oil.. Heat to 325°. If your fryer has a basket, immerse it in oil to preheat.

To pre-fry: Lift fryer basket from oil and place a generous handful of potatoes in basket. Fry 3 to 4 minutes. Remove potatoes and drain on paper towels. Repeat pre-frying with remaining potatoes. Cool for at least 15 minutes or leave at room temperature up to 5 hours. Turn off fryer. To second fry: Preheat oil to 375°. Fry potatoes as before until golden. Drain on paper towels. Serve, sprinkled with salt. By double frying, you will get crispier French fries.

EGG ROLLS

You can use shrimp or chicken and whatever vegetables you desire. The proportions are up to you.

Egg roll wrappers
Ground pork, cooked
Nappa cabbage, chopped
Onion, chopped
Bamboo shoots
Egg whites, beaten
Green onion, chopped
Bean sprouts
Celery, chopped
Dash of soy sauce
2 Tbsp. peanut or vegetable oil

Stir-fry all ingredients, except egg whites, in large wok, or use large skillet, in the vegetable or peanut oil until vegetables are lightly browned and tender (don't overcook). Fill egg roll wrappers and seal with egg whites. Place enough vegetable oil in deep frying pan to cover Egg Rolls (about 2 inches deep). Heat to almost boiling (350°). Drop Egg Rolls in, 2 at a time, and cook on one side until browned. Flip over and cook other side. Drain on paper towels and serve immediately while hot. Serve with sweet and sour sauce and Chinese mustard.

"Idea:" Cut the wrappers into smaller size; prepare the same way. Serve as appetizers. These also freeze well, cooked first, or freeze before deep-frying and cook them when ready.

HOMEMADE CHILE - EZ

Add a few of your own secret ingredients and enter one of the chile cookoffs. It's up to you! Do you like a lot of meat or would you rather have more beans? Do you like it very hot or mild, or do you want it heavy and thick, or light and thin? In any case, you'll beat anything you can buy in the stores. I've gotten great reviews on this recipe when I made it in my restaurant and was even noted on a talk show. This is also a great recipe for a single person. Make a large batch, pour into individual containers and freeze. Just take it out, let it thaw and heat up.

Canned tomatoes
Ground beef or turkey
Canned chile beans with
  sauce
Pepper
Seasoning salt
Garlic powder or salt to
  taste
Chili powder to taste
Green bell pepper, diced
Onion, diced
Cayenne pepper

Crush tomatoes with juice in large saucepan. Simmer over low heat, covered, for about 1 hour, stirring occasionally. Add chile beans with sauce. Cook an additional 15 minutes. Add seasonings to taste (never add seasonings more than a 1/2 teaspoon at a time).

Meanwhile, in a frying pan, cook ground beef or turkey until thoroughly cooked. Drain off grease. If using turkey, you will have to add 1 or 2 tablespoons vegetable oil to frying pan. Add meat to chile. In same pan, saute onion and green pepper in 1 tablespoon vegetable oil, until vegetables are tender. Add these to chile and it is ready to serve.

Try adding raw, diced onion and chunks of Cheddar cheese on the bottom of the serving dish before pouring in the chile. This is one meal that will warm your "innards" on a cold day.

Breads
Brunch

SESAME EGG BREAD

Braided bread with sesame seeds and a glaze. Beautiful for gift giving.

2 pkg. dry yeast
1 c. warm water
2 Tbsp. sugar
1/2 tsp. salt
1/2 c. bread or
  all-purpose flour
1 c. warm water
1/4 c. instant nonfat dry
  milk
2 Tbsp. sugar
2 eggs (reserve 1 egg
  white)
2 tsp. salt
2 c. bread or all-purpose
  flour
3 Tbsp. soft shortening

Combine first 5 ingredients in large mixing bowl. Beat until smooth. Cover; let stand in warm place 15 minutes. Add remaining ingredients; beat 2 minutes with mixer. Gradually stir in about 3 1/2 cups flour to make a very stiff dough. Form into smooth ball on well floured surface. Cover with bowl; let rest 10 minutes.

Roll out dough on floured surface to 1/2 inch thickness; fold in half. Roll and fold 4 more times. Divide dough in half. Mold into balls. Cover with bowl; let rest 10 minutes. Divide each ball of dough into 3 equal pieces. Shape each into 14 inch strips. Braid 3 strips together. Place on greased cookie sheet at least 5 inches apart. Combine the reserved egg white with 1 tablespoon water. Brush on loaves; sprinkle generously with sesame seed. Cover; let rise. Bake at 350° for 25 to 30 minutes.

OATMEAL MOLASSES BREAD - HEALTHY

2 pkg. dry yeast
1 c. warm water
1/4 c. dark molasses
1/2 tsp. salt
1/2 c. flour
1 1/4 c. warm water
1/4 c. instant nonfat dry
  milk
1/4 c. dark molasses
1 egg
2 tsp. salt
2 c. flour
2 Tbsp. shortening (soft)
1 c. quick cooking rolled
  oats

Combine first 4 ingredients in large mixing bowl; beat until smooth. Cover; let stand in warm place 15 minutes. Add remaining ingredients; beat 2 minutes with mixer. Gradually stir in about 3 1/2 cups flour to make a very stiff dough. Form into smooth ball on well floured surface. Cover with bowl; let rest 10 minutes.

Roll out dough on floured surface to 1/2 inch thickness; fold in half. Roll and fold 4 more times. Divide dough in half. Mold into balls. Cover with bowl; let rest 10 minutes. Shape each ball into a loaf. Place in well greased 9x5x3 inch bread pans. Cover; let rise in warm place 45 to 60 minutes, or until light and doubled in size. Bake at 375° for 35 to 40 minutes, or until deep golden brown. Remove from pans immediately.

HONEY YOGURT WHOLE WHEAT BREAD - HEALTHY

This is my favorite bread recipe for 2 reasons other than being healthy and tasting great. First of all, you can get the sourdough flavor by letting it set at the semi-liquid stage overnight, without the trouble of sourdough. Secondly, you can make it up in the morning, put it in the pans and it will rise by itself in the refrigerator in 3 to 8 hours. You can clean up the mess and when it comes time for dinner, just pop it in the oven.

1 tsp. dry yeast (1 pkg.)
2 c. warm water (120°)
1/3 c. vegetable oil
1 c. yogurt
1 Tbsp. salt
1/3 c. honey
6 c. whole wheat flour

Pour yeast into 1/2 cup warm water with a drop of honey. Set aside. In large bowl, mix honey, salt, oil, and 1 1/2 cups warm water. Add 3 cups of flour and yogurt. Beat until smooth. Stir in yeast mixture. (Cover with plastic wrap and let it set 5 to 8 hours or overnight if you desire a sourdough flavor.) Otherwise, add 3 more cups flour, 1/2 cup at a time, until mixed in. Pour out on well floured surface and knead until dough is stiff, but still a little sticky (a secret to baking with whole wheat flour), about 5 minutes. Cover with towel and let rest until doubled in size, about 45 minutes.

Divide dough into 2 greased 4x9 inch bread pans. (At this stage, if you'd like, place pans in plastic sacks, blow up with air and seal. Place the pans in the refrigerator at least 3 hours and up to 10 before baking. The bread will rise in the refrigerator, ready to go in the oven when ready.) Otherwise, let dough rise at room temperature about 40 minutes or until bread is nicely browned and a hollow thump is heard when you tap the crust.

WHOLE WHEAT BREAD - HEALTHY

Easy.

2 pkg. dry yeast
1/2 c. warm water (120°)
2 c. buttermilk
1/2 c. butter or margarine
4 Tbsp. sugar or 1/2 c.
  honey
1/4 tsp. baking soda
1/2 tsp. salt
3 eggs, lightly beaten
3 c. whole wheat flour
5 c. flour

Dissolve yeast in warm water. Heat butter and buttermilk in saucepan until butter melts. Don't worry if milk curdles. In large bowl, combine sugar or honey, baking soda, salt, and eggs. Add buttermilk mixture and yeast. Stir well. Slowly add whole wheat flour, mixing with fork. Add flour, a little at a time, until dough leaves sides of bowl. When dough becomes soft and satiny, turn out on floured surface and knead about 10 minutes. Place in greased bowl, turning dough to coat top. Cover with plastic wrap and towel. Set in a warm, draft free place. Allow to double in bulk (1 hour).

Punch down, knead lightly and return to warm place to rise again. After second rising, turn out dough onto lightly floured surface. Knead lightly; shape into 3 loaves. Place in well greased bread pans. (Dough should be just a little sticky, one of the secrets of making whole wheat bread so that it doesn't end up too heavy.) Cover with a towel and let rise until doubled (about 45 minutes). Bake at 375° about 30 minutes, or until bread has a hollow thump. Remove from pans and cool... that is, if you can stay away from warm bread out of the oven. *I can't!* Makes 3 loaves. *Freezes well.*

BRAN-SUNFLOWER NUT BREAD - HEALTHY

5 1/2 to 6 c. flour
1 1/2 c. shreds of bran
   cereal
2 Tbsp. sugar
2 tsp. salt
2 pkg. active dry yeast
1 1/2 c. water
1 c. milk
1/4 c. dark molasses
1/4 c. margarine or butter
1 c. sunflower nuts,
   toasted (unsalted)
Margarine or butter,
   softened

Mix 2 cups flour, cereal, sugar, salt, and yeast in large bowl. Heat water, milk, molasses and 1/4 cup margarine to 125° to 130° (margarine may not melt) in a small saucepan. Stir into flour mixture. Beat on low speed 1 minute. Stir in nuts and rest of the flour, one cup at a time, until dough is easy to handle and leaves the sides of the bowl. Turn onto lightly floured surface. Knead until elastic, about 5 minutes. Place in greased bowl; turn greased side up. cover and let rise in warm place until double, about 1 hour.

Punch down dough; divide into halves. Flatten each into oblong, pressing out air. Fold lengthwise into halves; flatten again. Lift at each end and pull, slapping on work surface several times, until the dough measures about 15x5 inches. Fold crosswise into thirds, overlapping; press down to seal. Roll dough tightly toward you, beginning at one open end. Pinch edge into roll to seal. Roll back and forth to tighten; press each end with side of hand to seal. Place seam side down in pans; brush with margarine. Let rise until double, 45 to 60 minutes. Heat oven to 375°. Place loaves on lowest rack. Pans should not touch each other or sides of oven. Bake until loaves sound hollow when tapped, 30 to 35 minutes. Remove from pans. Brush with margarine; cool on wire racks. Makes 2 loaves.

ITALIAN BREAD STICKS

These go great with cold salads in the summertime.

1 pkg. dry yeast
1 c. warm water
2 Tbsp. shortening
3 c. flour
2 Tbsp. sugar
1 1/4 tsp. salt
1 egg white

Soften yeast in water. Cut shortening into flour, sugar and salt. until very fine. Add softened yeast; mix until dough forms. Cover; let rise 20 minutes. Shape 1 1/2 inch pieces into sticks, 12 inches long. Place on greased cookie sheets. Brush with a mixture of 1 tablespoon each egg white and water. Sprinkle with sesame seeds. Let rise 30 minutes. Bake 12 to 15 minutes at 425°, until nicely browned.

NO KNEAD ROLL DOUGH

2 pkg. dry yeast
1 c. warm water
1/3 c. sugar
2 eggs
3 c. flour
1 Tbsp. salt
1/4 c. butter or other
   shortening (soft or
   melted)
1 c. warm milk

Place ingredients in mixing bowl in order listed. Beat at medium speed for 3 minutes. Stir in 3 to 3 1/2 cups flour to make a very stiff dough. Cover; let rest 15 minute. Toss on well floured surface until no longer sticky. Divide half of dough into 20 pieces. Shape each piece into a roll, 4 inches long. Brush sides with melted butter and place in 2 rows in greased 9x9 inch bread pan (small size). Cover; let rise in warm place until light and doubled in size, 45 to 60 minutes. Bake at 375° for 25 to 30 minutes or until golden brown.

You may shape the rolls any way you want to. If you are making separate rolls out of them on a cookie sheet, bake at 400° for 12 to 15 minutes.

WHOLESOME WHEAT AND OAT ROLLS - HEALTHY

1/2 c. rolled oats
1/3 c. unprocessed bran
1/3 c. wheat germ
1 c. water
1 c. plain yogurt
1/4 c. vegetable oil
5 to 5 1/2 c. flour
1/2 c. light brown sugar,
  packed
2 pkg. dry yeast
2 tsp. salt
2 eggs (room temperature)
Wheat germ or rolled oats
  for topping

In large bowl, combine rolled oats, bran and wheat germ; reserve. Heat water, yogurt and vegetable oil to boiling; pour over oat mixture. Cool to 125°, about 4 to 5 minutes.

Meanwhile, in small bowl, combine 1 cup flour, sugar, undissolved dry yeast, and salt. Add to grain mixture. Beat 2 minutes at medium speed of electric mixer, scraping bowl occasionally. Add 1 egg; beat at high speed 2 minutes. Stir in enough additional flour to make soft dough. Knead on lightly floured surface until smooth and elastic, about 5 minutes. Place in greased bowl, turning to grease top. Cover; let rise in warm, draft free place until double in size, about 45 minutes.

Punch down dough. Divide dough into 12 pieces. Roll each piece to 4 1/2 x3 inch oblong. Roll up tightly from wide end. Pinch seam to seal; taper ends. Place 2 inches apart on greased baking sheet. Cover; let rise in warm, draft free place until doubled in size, about 40 minutes. With sharp knife, make 3 diagonal slashes, 1/4 inch deep, on each roll. Lightly beat remaining egg; brush on rolls. Sprinkle with wheat germ or rolled oats, if desired. Bake at 375* for 25 to 30 minutes or until done. Remove from pans; cool on wire racks. Makes 12.

JUST PLAIN BUNS

2 c. warm water (120°)
1/3 c. sugar
2 pkg. dry yeast
3 c. flour plus more
2 eggs, beaten lightly
1/3 c. butter or margarine
1 1/2 tsp. salt

Combine water, sugar and dry yeast in a large bowl until yeast is dissolved and mixture becomes "bubbly". Add 3 cups flour and beat 2 minutes with electric mixer. Add eggs, melted butter and salt and beat 2 minutes or more. Add enough flour to make a soft dough. Let rise about 45 minutes in a warm place, until doubled in size.

Roll dough out on lightly floured board and cut with a big round cookie cutter or empty tin can. Place on lightly greased baking sheet, about 1 inch apart. Cover and let rise in warm place about 30 minutes or until doubled in size. Bake in preheated oven (400°) for 12 to 15 minutes, until lightly browned.

You may shape these rolls in any form you desire.

NO KNEAD REFRIGERATOR CRESCENT ROLLS

Start this one a day ahead of time!

3/4 c. milk
2 pkg. dry yeast
1/4 c. sugar
1/2 tsp. salt
1/2 c. butter
1/4 c. warm water (120°)
2 eggs, well beaten
4 c. flour

Heat milk and butter in saucepan over low heat until butter is melted. Cool to lukewarm. Sprinkle yeast in warm water and stir until dissolved. Add sugar, eggs and salt to milk mixture. Stir in dissolved yeast. Add flour gradually to make a soft dough. Cover and refrigerate for 24 hours.

Melt 1/2 cup butter and set aside. Divide dough in 4 parts. Roll each, one at a time, into circles about 3/8 inch thick on a lightly floured board. Cut each circle into 8 pie shaped wedges. Start with large side of each wedge and roll to the point. Dip in melted butter. Place on ungreased baking sheet, about 1 inch apart. Cover and let rise for about 1 hour, until doubled in size. Bake at 450° for about 10 minutes, until lightly browned.

BRAN BATTER ROLLS - HEALTHY

1 c. wheat bran cereal
2 1/2 to 3 c. flour
2 Tbsp. sugar
1 1/2 tsp. salt
1 pkg. dry yeast
1 c. milk
1/2 c. water
2 Tbsp. margarine
1 egg, slightly beaten
Poppy seed (optional)
Sesame seed (optional)

In large bowl of electric mixer, stir together cereal, 1 cup of the flour, sugar, salt, and yeast. Set aside. In small saucepan, heat milk, water and margarine until warm, about 120°. Add to cereal mixture. Reserve 1 tablespoon of egg. Add remaining egg to cereal mixture. Beat on low speed of electric mixer for 30 seconds, scraping bowl constantly. Beat on high speed for 3 minutes. By hand, stir in enough remaining flour to make a stiff batter. Cover lightly. Let rise in warm place until double in volume.

Stir down dough. Portion dough evenly into 16 greased muffin cups. Brush tops of rolls with reserved egg. Sprinkle with poppy or sesame seed if desired. Bake at 400 for 18 to 20 minutes, until golden brown. Serve warm.

OVERNIGHT CINNAMON OR PECAN ROLLS

These rolls do freeze nicely for unexpected company.

4 c. warm water (120°)
1 c. margarine
2 c. sugar
1 Tbsp. salt
1 pkg. dry yeast
3 eggs, lightly beaten
12 to 14 c. flour

At 2 P.M. the day before you are planning on baking the rolls, combine together the water and yeast, stirring until yeast has dissolved. Add margarine and stir until almost melted. Stir in sugar, salt and eggs; stir until well mixed. Add in flour, one cup at a time, until dough releases from edge of bowl. Pour out onto well floured surface and knead until dough becomes stiff, about 8 minutes. Place dough into large, greased bowl. Cover and place in warm area.

At 6 P.M., take dough out and once again slightly knead on well floured surface for a couple of minutes and return to bowl and cover again. At 9 P.M., form dough into desired cinnamon or caramel rolls. Place in greased pans. Cover until morning in a warm place. The next morning, roll will be ready to bake. Bake in preheated 350° oven about 25 minutes, until lightly browned.   Top with light frosting while warm if desired. Makes about six 9x13 inch cake pans.

Cinnamon Rolls:
1 c. butter, melted
2 c. sugar
2 Tbsp. cinnamon

Divide dough into 4 portions. Roll one portion out into rectangle, about 12x18 inches.   Stir sugar and cinnamon together. Brush butter over dough and sprinkle sugar mixture over top (enough topping for the entire batch). Tightly roll up dough lengthwise and cut into 1 1/2 inch circles. Place flat side down in lightly greased pans, about 2 inches apart. Follow directions.

Caramel Rolls:
1 c. butter
2 c. brown sugar
4 Tbsp. white corn syrup
Pecan halves

Melt butter, brown sugar and white corn syrup until well blended. Divide this on bottom of your pans. Spread pecan halves over this mixture and follow directions to make cinnamon rolls. (You may or may not want to use the cinnamon-sugar mixture.) Place rolls on top of caramel and nuts and bake as directed for cinnamon rolls.

CINNA-SWIRLS

3/4 c. milk
1/4 c. sugar
1 tsp. salt
1/4 c. vegetable oil
3 c. vegetable shortening
   (for deep-frying)
1/2 c. warm water
1 pkg. dry yeast
1 egg, beaten lightly
3 1/4 to 3 1/2 c. flour
3/4 c. sugar
1 tsp. cinnamon

Scald milk; stir in the 1/4 cup sugar, salt and vegetable oil. Cool to lukewarm.

Meanwhile, in a large bowl, dissolve the yeast in the warm water (120°). Stir in lukewarm milk mixture, egg and half of flour. Beat until smooth. Stir in remainder of flour, 1/2 cup at a time, until you have a soft dough and it doesn't stick to the sides of the bowl. Turn out onto lightly floured board; knead until smooth and elastic, about 8 to 10 minutes. Place in greased bowl, turning to grease top. Cover; let rise in warm place until dough is doubled in bulk, about 1 hour.

Combine remaining 3/4 cup sugar and cinnamon. Punch dough down. On lightly floured board, divide dough in half. Roll each half into 14x9 inch rectangle. Sprinkle with cinnamon and sugar mixture. Roll each roll tightly as a jelly roll and seal. Cut into 1 1/2 inch slices and place on greased baking sheets, cut sides up. Press down to flatten. Cover and let rise in warm place about 30 minutes. Heat shortening to 375° for deep-frying; a large skillet may be used. Fry rolls 2 to 3 minutes, until lightly browned. Turn once. Remove and drain on paper towels. While warm, dip in a powdered sugar glaze.

WHOLE WHEAT CINNAMON ROLLS

2 pkg. dry yeast
1/2 c. warm water (115°)
1/2 c. brown sugar
1/2 c. scaled lukewarm
  milk
1/2 c. butter or
  margarine, softened
2 eggs
1 tsp. salt
2 1/2 c. whole wheat flour
2 to 2 1/2 c. all-purpose
  flour

Filling:
4 Tbsp. butter or
  margarine, softened
1/2 c. sugar
4 tsp. cinnamon

Browned Butter Glaze:
1/2 c. butter or margarine
2 c. powdered sugar
1 tsp. vanilla
2 to 4 Tbsp. hot water

Dissolve yeast in warm water. Stir in brown sugar, milk, butter, eggs, salt, and whole wheat flour. Beat until smooth. Mix in enough of the all-purpose flour to make dough easy to handle. Turn dough onto lightly floured surface; knead until smooth and elastic, about 5 minutes. Place in greased bowl; turn greased side up. Cover; let rise in warm place until doubled, about 1 1/2 hours.

Punch down dough; divide dough into halves. Roll dough out, working with one half at a time, to a 15x9 inch rectangle. Mix sugar and cinnamon together. Spread half the butter over dough and sprinkle with half the sugar and cinnamon mixture. Roll up, beginning at wide side. Pinch edge of dough into roll to seal well; stretch to make even. Cut roll into 15 slices. Place slightly apart in greased oblong pan or in greased muffin cups, leaving about 2 inches between rolls. Repeat with other half of dough. Cover; let rise until doubled, 25 to 30 minutes. Heat oven to 375°. Bake 25 to 30 minutes. While warm, spread with glaze.

Browned Butter Glaze: Heat butter or margarine over low heat until golden brown. Remove from heat; blend in powdered sugar and vanilla. Stir in hot water until of spreading consistency. Makes 30.

SWEET DOUGH

Use for cinnamon rolls, bread rolls, Hungarian coffee cake or other sweet rolls.

1 1/2 c. milk
1/2 c. butter
2 tsp. salt
1/2 c. sugar
2 eggs
2 pkg. dry yeast
1/2 c. warm water (120°)
7 to 7 1/2 c. flour

Cinnamon Rolls:
1/2 c. butter, melted
3/4 c. sugar
2 tsp. cinnamon
1/2 c. raisins (optional)

Dissolve yeast in warm water. Scald milk; add butter to milk while scalding. Add salt and sugar. Beat eggs and add to cooled milk mixture. Add yeast mixture and stir well. Add 3 cups of flour and mix until smooth. Add rest of flour, 1/2 cup at a time, until dough forms and starts releasing from the side of the bowl. Put dough out on floured board and knead, adding flour as needed until smooth, about 7 to 10 minutes. Place into greased bowl and let rise until doubled in a warm place, about 45 minutes. Punch down and let rise a second time.

Cinnamon Rolls: Roll out Sweet Dough (1/2 recipe) into 16x20 inch rectangle to about 3/16 inch thickness. Brush with melted butter. Mix sugar and cinnamon together and sprinkle over dough. Add raisins if using. Roll dough, starting with the width and seal edges. Cut roll into 2 inch widths, placing flat side down into a 9x13 inch baking pan, leaving about 2 inches between each. Cover and let rise 45 minutes. Preheat oven to 375° and bake rolls until nicely browned, about 25 to 30 minutes. Remove and frost while warm if desired.

HUNGARIAN COFFEE CAKE

This has always been a special holiday morning treat in our family.

1/2 Sweet Dough recipe
1/2 c. butter
3/4 c. sugar
2 tsp. cinnamon
1 c. chopped walnuts

Prepare Sweet Dough as directed in recipe. Using 1/2 of the dough, break it up into walnut size pieces. Melt butter. Thoroughly grease one piece tube pan. Roll dough pieces into balls and dip each, first into butter, then cinnamon-sugar mix and finally into chopped walnuts. Place balls in layers in tube pan. Let rise 45 minutes.

Heat oven to 375° and bake 35 to 45 minutes, until lightly browned. Invert pan on clean towel or large plate so butter-sugar mixture runs down over cake. To serve, break apart with 2 forks, or just let everyone pull off pieces with their fingers.

PEANUT BUTTER-WHEAT GERM MUFFINS - HEALTHY/EZ

2/3 c. biscuit mix
1/3 c. wheat germ
1/4 c. sugar
1 egg, slightly beaten
1/3 c. water
2 Tbsp. peanut butter
1/2 tsp. vanilla

Preheat oven to 375°. Combine the biscuit mix, wheat germ and sugar in a small bowl. In another bowl, combine egg, water, peanut butter, and vanilla. Beat until smooth. Stir dry ingredients into mixture only until barely moistened. Spoon batter into greased muffin tins, filling cups 2/3 full. Bake 20 to 25 minutes. Makes 6 muffins.

FRENCH DOUGHNUTS

Make like a muffin, tastes like a doughnut!

5 Tbsp. butter, softened
1/2 c. sugar
1 egg, beaten
1 1/2 c. flour
2 1/4 tsp. baking powder
1/4 tsp. salt
1.4 tsp. nutmeg
1/2 c. milk

Cream together butter and sugar. Add egg and mix well. Sift dry ingredients and add alternately with milk. Pour into greased muffin tins. Bake at 350° for 25 to 30 minutes. Remove from pans and immediately roll in 1/3 cup melted butter and then in a mixture of 1/3 cup sugar and 1/2 teaspoon cinnamon. Makes 12.

"Idea:" Why not try adding some diced apples to this or how about chocolate or butterscotch chips? Maybe walnuts and maraschino cherries. The list goes on.

OAT BRAN MUFFINS - HEALTHY

2 1/2 c. oat bran or oat
** bran cereal**
1/3 c. brown sugar or
** honey**
2 tsp. baking powder
1 tsp. cinnamon
1 tsp. grated orange peel
1/2 tsp. nutmeg
1/2 c. raisins
1 c. nonfat milk or orange
** juice**
3 egg whites, lightly
** beaten**
1/4 c. safflower oil
2 tsp. vanilla
1/2 c. unsweetened
** applesauce or 2**
** bananas, mashed**

Combine dry ingredients, raisins and brown sugar or honey. Add milk, egg whites, oil, vanilla, and applesauce. Mix just until moist. Spoon batter into 12 lightly oiled muffin cups. Bake at 425° for 17 to 20 minutes. Makes 12 muffins.

APRICOT-ORANGE MUFFINS

11/3 c. flour
1/4 c. sugar
1 tsp. baking powder
1/2 tsp. salt
1 egg, slightly beaten
1/4 c. milk
1/4 c. oil
1/4 c. orange juice
  concentrate
1/4 c. apricot preserves

Topping:
2 Tbsp. flour
1 Tbsp. brown sugar
1/8 tsp. cinnamon
1 Tbsp. butter

Heat oven to 375°. Combine flour, sugar, baking powder, and salt in small bowl. In separate bowl, beat egg, milk, oil, orange juice, and preserves until smooth. Stir liquid mixture into dry and blend only until barely moistened. Spoon into 12 greased muffin tins to about 1/2 full.

Topping: Mix all ingredients for topping except butter. Cut in butter until mixture is crumbly. Sprinkle over batter and bake about 20 minutes, until nicely browned.

MORNING GLORY MUFFINS

1 1/4 c. sugar
1/2 c. vegetable oil
3 eggs
2 tsp. vanilla
2 c. flour
2 tsp.baking powder
1/4 tsp. salt
1 tsp. cinnamon
2 c. grated carrots
1/2 c. raisins
1/2 c. coconut
1/2 c. diced raw apple
Nuts (optional)

Combine sugar, oil, eggs, and vanilla in a large bowl; set aside. In another bowl, sift together flour, baking powder, salt, and cinnamon. Add to liquid ingredients and stir until just moistened. Gently fold in carrots, raisins, coconut, and apple. Spoon into greased muffin tins to about 2/3 full. Bake in a 350° oven for 20 to 25 minutes, until nicely browned. Makes about 18 muffins.

PINEAPPLE BRAN MUFFINS - HEALTHY/EZ

1 1/4 c. milk
1 1/2 c. Bran Buds
1 1/2 c. flour
1/3 c. sugar
1/2 tsp. salt
3 tsp. baking powder
1 egg, beaten
1/4 c. vegetable oil
3/4 c. crushed pineapple,
    drained

Preheat oven to 400°. Combine milk and cereal in large mixing bowl.

Meanwhile, grease muffin tins and sift together the flour, sugar, salt, and baking powder. Stir pineapple into dry ingredients. Add egg and oil to milk and cereal mixture, mixing well. Let stand 5 minutes. Add dry ingredients and mix only until moistened. Fill muffin tins 2/3 full and bake 20 to 25 minutes, until nicely browned. Makes 12 muffins.

PEANUT BUTTER BRAN MUFFINS

1 c. flour
1/3 c. light brown sugar,
    packed
2 tsp. baking powder
1/2 tsp. salt
1/4 tsp. baking soda
1 egg, beaten
1 c. milk
3 Tbsp. vegetable oil
1 c. 100% bran cereal
1/3 c. chunky peanut
    butter
2 Tbsp. honey

Preheat oven to 400°. Grease muffin tins. In medium size bowl, combine flour, brown sugar, baking powder, salt and baking soda. In separate small bowl, whip together the egg, milk, peanut butter, honey, and oil; stir in bran. Let stand about 5 minutes. Stir in flour mixture just until moistened. Fill muffin tins 2/3 full and bake 20 to 25 minutes, until nicely browned.

HIGH FIBER BRAN MUFFINS - HEALTHY/EZ

2 c. 100% bran cereal
1 1/4 c. milk
1/4 c. margarine, melted
1 egg
1 c. flour
1/3 c. brown sugar,
    packed
2 tsp. baking powder
1/2 tsp. baking soda

Preheat oven to 400°. Combine bran and milk; let stand 5 minutes.

Meanwhile, lightly grease 12 muffin pan cups. Beat egg and melted margarine into bran mixture until egg is well beaten. Stir in flour, brown sugar, baking soda, and baking powder only until barely moistened. Divide dough between muffin cups, filling about 3/4 full. Bake 18 to 20 minutes, until done.

HONEY WHEAT CAKES - HEALTHY

These are my favorite for entertaining at breakfast. Unlike pancakes, these are baked in a jelly roll pan so you don't have to stand, flipping pancakes, while your guests are eating. These beat pancakes in taste, nutrition, freezing ability, and versatility. They are especially good with fresh fruit and whipped cream or just plain butter and syrup. They are even great cold with peanut butter and jam. They are just as fresh the second and third day as the first (they must be kept refrigerated, however). They also freeze nicely, capable of going straight from the freezer to the microwave or even better, to a toaster oven.

1 c. Bran Buds
1/4 c. wheat germ
1/2 tsp. baking soda
1/2 c. hot water
1/4 c. vegetable oil
1/4 c. honey
1 c. flour
1 tsp. baking powder
1/2 tsp. salt
1 c. buttermilk
1 egg

Preheat oven to 425°. Grease 15x10 inch jelly roll pan. In large bowl, combine first 6 ingredients; stir to soften cereal. Let stand about 5 minutes. Beat in egg and buttermilk. Stir in remaining ingredients only until well blended. Pour onto cookie sheet. Bake 12 to 15 minutes, until firm to the touch. Cut into squares and serve.

"Idea:" Try adding a mashed banana, nuts or maple extract.

BEER PANCAKES

These pancakes bring back a lot of memories. While in high school, I worked at church doing odd jobs. One morning, while painting, Father Martin called me in, "Hey, Jerome, you want to try some Beer Pancakes?" They are great! The beer makes them light and they have a slight nutmeg flavor. The dough will keep in a covered jar in the refrigerator a couple of days. This does make a large batch.

1/3 c. olive or vegetable
  oil
2/3 c. beer
2 eggs, well beaten
1 3/4 c. milk
3 c. flour
4 tsp. baking powder
1 tsp. salt
2 Tbsp. brown sugar
1/4 tsp. nutmeg

Heat griddle to 375°. Combine oil, beer, eggs, and milk in large bowl and beat until frothy. Sift together flour, baking powder, salt, brown sugar, and nutmeg. Stir in dry ingredients, stirring only until smooth. A few small lumps are okay. Lightly grease griddle and cook pancakes, using a large spoon of dough for each. When edges start to brown and most of the bubbles have burst, flip pancakes and finish other side. Serve immediately.

SAVORY HOT CAKES - EZ

A favorite for Saturday mornings.

1 c. flour
1 tsp. baking soda
1/2 tsp. salt
1 egg, lightly beaten
1 tsp. sugar
1 Tbsp. vegetable oil
1 c. buttermilk

Mix all ingredients only until barely blended. If there are small chunks of flour, that's fine. Heat grill to about 375°. Lightly grease griddle and spoon batter on. When most of the bubbles pop and the edges are lightly browned, flip the cakes and cook about 1 more minute on the other side. It is important to flip them just once. Top with your favorite topping.

"Idea:" Add blueberries, apples or nuts. Add a dash of cinnamon with apples. Top with hot applesauce, walnuts and frozen yogurt. Make a glamorous breakfast, using you imagination and little work.

SOURDOUGH FRENCH TOAST - EZ

A family favorite for years and even better with sourdough bread. Use the following guide for 2 large slices. Double for 4, etc.

2 slices of extra sourdough
**   bread, sliced (large loaf)**
1/2 c. milk or evaporated
**   milk**
1 egg
1/2 tsp. cinnamon
1/2 tsp. nutmeg
1/2 tsp. vanilla

Beat all ingredients except bread together. Dip bread into mixture and grill on slightly greased, preheated (375°) griddle until lightly browned. Serve with warm syrup or fresh fruit, frozen yogurt and nuts.

STUFFED FRENCH TOAST

These will make your guests say, "WOW!".

1 (8 oz.) pkg. cream
  cheese, softened
1 1/2 tsp. vanilla
3/4 tsp. sugar
1/2 c. chopped pecans
1 (16 oz.) loaf soft French
  bread
4 eggs, beaten
1 c. milk
1/2 tsp. grated nutmeg
1 (12 oz.) jar apricot
  preserves
1/2 c. orange juice

Beat the cream cheese, 1 teaspoon of the vanilla and sugar in a small bowl until creamed. Stir in the pecans and set aside. Cut the bread into 10 to 12 slices, 1 1/2 inches thick. Cut a slit in each slice, creating a pocket. Fill each pocket with 1 1/2 tablespoons of the cheese mixture.

Beat the eggs, milk, the remaining 1/2 teaspoon vanilla, and the nutmeg together in a large shallow bowl. Dip the filled bread slices into the egg mixture on both sides, then cook in batches, on a lightly greased, hot griddle until both sides are golden brown. Remove to a platter and keep warm while cooking the remaining toast. Heat the preserves and orange juice in a small saucepan. Simmer for 3 to 4 minutes, or until slightly thickened. Drizzle the mixture over the French toast and serve immediately.

WHOLE WHEAT BISCUITS - HEALTHY

Nothing like warm biscuits out of the oven. Try them with creamed chicken or creamed dried beef over the top, then add jam to any leftover for a good dessert. You can't buy a canned biscuit that even starts to compare.

1 c. whole wheat flour
1 c. flour
1/2 tsp. salt
3 tsp. baking powder
1/3 c. butter flavored
  shortening
3/4 c. milk

Sift flours, baking powder and salt together in a bowl. Cut in shortening with fork until mixture resembles coarse corn meal. Add milk and stir with fork. Turn dough out onto lightly floured board and knead about 30 seconds. Roll out to about 1/2 inch depth and cut with biscuit cutter. Brush with melted butter or margarine and place on lightly greased cookie sheet. Bake in a 425° oven for 12 to 15 minutes, until golden brown. Bake in the middle of the oven and watch carefully not to burn the bottoms.

JERRY'S SUPERPOWER BREAKFAST DRINK - HEALTHY/EZ

A breakfast drink I created with no sugar. Tastes great, easy and fast, and stays with you for the morning. After telling a doctor about it, he said that it contained everything you needed and he highly recommended it.

1 1/2 c. milk
2 to 3 Tbsp. unflavored
   yogurt
3 Tbsp. unsweetened fruit
   juice concentrate,
   thawed
2 Tbsp. brewer's yeast
1 Tbsp. wheat germ
1 Tbsp. bran
Fresh fruit (your choice-
   bananas are great!)
Sunflower seeds or any
   other nuts (walnuts are
   great for a change)

Place all ingredients in a blender and blend well. Makes 2 glasses.

OVERNIGHT OMELET

Breakfast/brunch.

8 slices bread (try
   sourdough)
Butter (to butter bread)
8 eggs
3/4 tsp. salt
3/4 tsp. dry mustard
2 1/2 c. milk
1/2 lb. ham, diced
1/2 lb. grated Cheddar
   cheese

Butter both sides of bread and cover the bottom of a 9x13 inch baking pan. Beat together the eggs, salt, mustard, and milk. Pour over the bread. Sprinkle ham over the top and finish off with the cheese. Cover with foil and refrigerate overnight. Bake 1 1/2 hours at 325°, starting in cold oven.

"Idea:" As with any omelet, use whatever sounds good to you. Perhaps mushrooms, onions, green peppers, or why not small shrimp or crab. You may also vary the spices to match the ingredients, such as an Italian omelet with zucchini, tomatoes and Italian sausage, adding Italian seasonings like oregano, etc. *Be in control!*

MY FAVORITE OMELET

Breakfast/brunch.

3 eggs
2 Tbsp. water
3 Tbsp. butter
Dash of garlic powder
Salt and pepper to taste
1/3 c. salad shrimp,
    cooked
1/3 c. crabmeat or
    imitation
1/3 c. fresh mushrooms
1/4 c. diced Monterey Jack
    cheese
1/4 c. diced Cheddar
    cheese
2 Tbsp. evaporated milk
Avodaco slices
Alfalfa sprouts

In large frying pan or omelet pan, saute the mushrooms, crab and shrimp in 1 tablespoon of the butter until lightly browned. Remove and set aside on a plate.

Meanwhile, beat eggs, water, garlic powder, salt, and pepper together in a small bowl, using a wire whip, until eggs are well beaten. Melt remaining 2 tablespoonfuls of butter in omelet pan over medium low heat. Add eggs to pan and cook until edges are lightly browned and omelet becomes puffy. Turn omelet with large pancake turner and immediately add sauteed shrimp mixture. Fold over. While omelet is cooking, combine cheeses and evaporated milk in microwave and melt until cheese sauce is smooth. Remove omelet from pan onto serving plate. Slice avocados over the top and top this with the cheese sauce. Lightly toss a few alfalfa sprouts over the top and serve.

Besides tasting great, it's very impressive looking!

"Idea:" Omelets are great, because you can create anything that sounds good to you. Not only are they great for breakfast, but for lunch and dinner as well, and they are so versatile. Use anything you want, starting with the 3 eggs (or 2 for a smaller one), the water and seasonings. I've even used leftover Sloppy Joe mix and sour cream. You can even make dessert omelets, leaving out the seasonings, filling the omelet with fresh strawberries and cream cheese. Sprinkle the final product with powdered sugar.

"Note:" Don't want to try flipping the omelet? When the omelet is ready to flip, simply add the toppings over the top and place a lid over the top, with heat on very low until omelet is cooked, and you have a frittata.

Sweets

Cakes
Cookies
Pies
Desserts
Chocolate
Candy
Holidays

SWANS DOWN ANGEL FOOD (HIGH ALTITUDE)

**1 c. sifted cake flour plus
  1 Tbsp.
1 3/4 c. egg whites (room
  temperature - 10 to 12
  egg whites)
2 tsp. cream of tartar
1/4 tsp. salt
1/2 tsp. vanilla
1/2 tsp. almond extract
1 1/2 c. sugar (no lumps)**

Preheat oven to 400°. Sift together flour and 1 cup of the sugar 3 times. Set aside. In separate bowl, beat egg whites, cream of tartar and salt until fairly stiff, but not stiff peaks. Whites must be snowy, fluffy, slightly moist. Fold in 1/2 cup sugar slowly. Fold in vanilla and almond extracts. Fold the sifted flour and sugar mixture into egg white mixture, using a deep turning method. Folding should continue only until ingredients are blended.

Pour batter into ungreased angel food pan. Bake at 400° for about 30 minutes. Remove from oven. Invert pan over a bottle for 1 hour. To serve, cut gently with bread knife. Serve with fresh whipped cream, strawberries or raspberries.

This is an excellent cake to use with the Strawberry Angel Cake (page 177).

"Idea:" This cake does require careful attention in making. My mother likes the angel food cake mix and adds 2 extra egg whites. See our section on "What to do With What's Left," for some ideas as to what to do with the egg yolks.

"Idea:" Swirl in a package of dry gelatin into the batter. Also, you may add chopped walnuts and drained, chopped maraschino cherries. As a kid, a "Cherry-Nut Angel Food" was always my birthday cake.

ANGEL SPONGE CAKE

Whenever we went to Grandma's for dinner, this was often our dessert. No frosting is necessary, and it is great with ice cream, especially if it's homemade like ours often was. Mom says Grandma found the recipe in a farm journal several years ago.

**5 large eggs, separated
    (room temperature)
3/4 c. warm water
1 1/2 c. sugar
2 c. cake flour (must be
    cake flour)
1/2 tsp. salt
1 tsp. cream of tartar
1 tsp. vanilla
1/4 tsp. almond extract**

Beat egg yolks until thick and lemon colored. Add extracts to water. Beat in sugar and water mixture, alternately. Fold in flour. Beat egg whites and salt until frothy. Add cream of tartar and beat until stiff. Fold into egg yolk mixture. Pour into ungreased angel food cake pan. Bake in preheated 350° oven for about 50 minutes, until tested done. Cool upside down in pan about 1 hour before removing.

BEST EVER ORANGE CHIFFON CAKE

**6 egg whites (room
    temperature)
1 3/4 c. flour
1/2 tsp. salt
1 1/2 c. sugar
6 egg yolks
6 Tbsp. fresh orange juice
1 Tbsp. freshly grated
    orange peel
Powdered sugar for
    dusting**

Sift flour and *then* measure, then sift once more with salt added. Set aside. Place egg whites in large mixing bowl and beat at medium speed until they become foamy. Gradually beat in 1/2 cup of the sugar, beating after each addition. Continue beating until stiff peaks form when beater is slowly raised. Set aside. Preheat oven to 350°.

In small bowl, beat egg yolks at high speed until very thick and lemon colored, about 3 minutes. *Do not underbeat.* Gradually beat in remaining 1 cup sugar; continue beating until mixture is smooth. At low speed, blend flour mixture and orange juice alternately into egg yolk mixture, beginning and ending with flour and guiding batter into beaters with scraper. Add orange peel. With a whisk or rubber spatula, using under-and-over motion, fold yolk mixture gently into whites.

Pour batter into an ungreased 10 inch tube pan. Bake 35 to 40 minutes, until cake springs back when pressed with finger. Invert over bottle; cool completely (about 1 hour). Using and up-and-down motion, run spatula around edge of cake and tube. Invert cake and shake to release; Place on serving plate. Sift powdered sugar over top of cake. Serves 12.

BURNT SUGAR CAKE

This cake is a little more work than usual, but the results are impressive!

Filling:
1 (18 3/4 oz.) can
   apricots (heavy syrup)
1 Tbsp. brandy
2 Tbsp. corn starch
1/3 c. light brown sugar,
   packed
2 Tbsp. apricot preserves
1/8 tsp. cinnamon

Cake:
1 c. sugar
1/2 c. boiling water
2 1/2 c. flour
2 1/2 tsp. baking powder
1/4 tsp. salt
1/2 c. butter or
   margarine, softened
2 eggs
1 tsp. vanilla

Frosting:
1 1/2 c. whipping cream
2 Tbsp. sugar

Drain apricots; reserve 1/4 c. syrup. Chop and set aside. In small pan, combine syrup and brandy. Stir in corn starch until well dissolved. Add brown sugar, preserves and cinnamon and cook over low heat until thickened. Pour into small bowl; stir in chopped apricots. Cover and chill.

Meanwhile, in small skillet, stir 1/4 cup sugar over low heat until amber (burnt sugar). Add 1/2 cup boiling water. Stir over low heat until sugar is dissolved. Set aside.

Cake: Preheat oven to 350°. Combine flour, baking powder and salt. In separate bowl, beat butter and remaining 3/4 cup sugar until light and fluffy. Add eggs, one at a time, beating well after each and stir in vanilla. Blend in flour mixture alternately with burnt sugar mixture until well blended. Divide batter between two 8 inch, greased and floured cake pans. Bake 25 to 30 minutes or until tested done. Let cool in pans about 5 minutes. Remove and finish cooling on wire racks. Whip 1 1/2 cups whipping cream until stiff peaks form. Slowly add 2 tablespoons sugar and blend well.

To assemble: Cut each of the 2 cakes in half horizontally. Start with first layer and top with whipped cream. Add second and top with apricot mixture. Place on third layer and top with whipped cream. Finally, add the last layer and top with the apricot mixture. Put remaining whipped cream around the edge of the cake.

RASPBERRY WALNUT CAKE

Fancy.

2 3/4 c. flour
2 1/2 tsp. baking powder
1/2 tsp. salt
1/2 c. unsalted butter,
   softened
1 3/4 c. sugar
1 c. seedless raspberry
   preserves
1 tsp. vanilla
1/2 tsp. black walnut
   flavoring
2 eggs (room temperature)
1 1/4 c. millk
1 c. plus 2 Tbsp. ground
   walnuts

Cream Cheese Frosting:
6 oz. cream cheese,
   softened
6 oz. butter, softened
2 1/4 c. powdered sugar,
   sifted
3/4 tsp. vanilla

Preheat oven to 350°. Grease and flour two 9 inch round cake pans. Sift flour, baking powder and salt into a bowl. In a separate mixing bowl, cream butter and sugar until light and fluffy. Blend in vanilla and walnut flavoring. Beat in eggs, one at a time, blending well after each. Mix in dry ingredients and milk alternately in 3 additions. Fold in 1 cup of the nuts. Pour batter into pans and bake 30 to 35 minutes, until tested done. Leave in pans 10 minutes before removing to finish cooling on wire rack. Cool completely.

Cook jam over low heat until heated thoroughly. Spread jam between the 2 layers of cake and top with the Cream Cheese Frosting.

Cream Cheese Frosting: Cream butter, cream cheese and vanilla together until smooth. Add powdered sugar and mix well. Frost cake and use remaining walnuts to decorate the sides of the cake.

"Idea:" This is a great cake to use to decorate for a nice surprise for birthdays, weddings, etc.

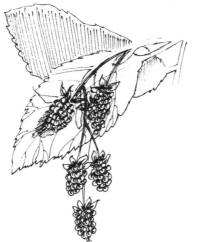

POPPY SEED TORTE

1/2 c. poppy seeds
2/3 c. milk
1/2 c. shortening
1 c. sugar
2 c. flour
2 tsp. baking powder
1/4 tsp. salt
3 egg whites, stiffly beaten

Filling:
1/2 c. sugar
1/2 c. sour cream
2 egg yolks, beaten
1 tsp. vanilla
1/2 c. chopped walnuts

Chocolate-Mocha
  Frosting:
6 Tbsp. butter, softened
3 Tbsp. cocoa
3 c. powdered sugar
Hot, strong coffee

Soak poppy seeds in milk for 2 hours. Cream shortening and sugar. Mix dry ingredients and add alternately with milk and poppy seeds. Fold in egg whites. Bake in 2 greased and floured 8 inch round cake pans at 350° about 20 minutes, until tested done. Cool 10 minutes; remove from pans to cool on wire racks.

Filling: Cook sugar, sour cream and egg yolks in top of double boiler, stirring constantly, until thickened, about 15 minutes. Remove from heat; add vanilla. Beat with a rotary beater until smooth; cool. Add nuts and spread between layers of cake. Frost with Chocolate-Mocha Frosting.

Chocolate-Mocha Frosting: Mix butter, cocoa and powdered sugar. Beat, moistening with hot coffee until spreading consistency. Frost cake.

POPPY SEED CAKE WITH CREAM CHEESE FROSTING

2/3 c. milk
1/3 c. poppy seed
2 1/4 c. sifted flour
1 Tbsp. baking powder
1/4 tsp. salt
1 1/4 c. sugar
1/2 c. butter, softened
2 tsp. vanilla
1/2 c. milk
3 large egg whites (room temperature)
1/4 c. sugar
2 Tbsp. poppy seed for decoration

Cream Cheese Frosting:
6 oz. cream cheese, softened
1/4 c. unsalted butter, softened
2 c. sifted powdered sugar
1 tsp. lemon juice

Preheat oven to 350°. Butter and flour two 8 inch round cake pans; line bottom of each with circle of waxed paper.

Bring the 2/3 c. milk to a boil; remove from heat. Stir in poppy seed; cool to room temperature.

Sift together flour, baking powder and salt; set aside. In large bowl, cream together the 1 1/4 cups sugar and butter; beat until light. Add vanilla. Combine poppy seed mixture and the 1/2 cup milk. Add this mixture alternately with flour to the creamed mixture, adding 1/3 of each mixture at a time. Beat egg whites until they hold soft peaks. Add the 1/4 cup sugar, a little at a time, and beat until whites hold stiff, glossy peaks (do not overbeat). Gently fold into batter. Divide batter evenly between the 2 cake pans. Bake 30 minutes or until tested done. Cool 10 minutes; turn out onto wire racks to finish cooling. Frost with Cream Cheese Frosting and decorate with poppy seed.

Cream Cheese Frosting: Cream together cream cheese and butter. Add powdered sugar and lemon juice; beat until creamy. If frosting is too runny, add more sugar. If it is too stiff, add a little milk.

A NEW KIND OF CARROT CAKE

2 c. sugar
1 1/3 c. vegetable oil
4 medium eggs
2 1/2 c. flour
2 1/2 tsp. baking soda
2 tsp. cinnamon
1 tsp. salt
1 1/2 Tbsp. vanilla
3 c. grated carrots
1 c. chopped pecans

Pineapple Cream Cheese
  Frosting:
8 oz. cream cheese,
  softened
1/2 c. butter, softened
1 lb. powdered sugar
  (about 4 c.)
1 (15 oz.) can crushed
  pineapple, well drained

Preheat oven to 350°. Combine sugar, oil and eggs in a large bowl and blend well. Thoroughly mix together the dry ingredients and add to the egg mixture. Stir in the carrots, nuts, and vanilla. Pour the batter into 3 greased and floured 9 inch or two 10 inch layer cake pans. Bake for 30 to 35 minutes, until cake tests done.   Let cool on racks for 10 minutes. Remove and finish cooling on wire racks. Frost with Pineapple Cream Cheese Frosting.

Pineapple Cream Cheese Frosting;   Cream together the cream cheese and butter. Beat in powdered sugar and vanilla. Stir in pecans and pineapple.   Frost cake. Garnish sides with additional chopped pecans if desired.

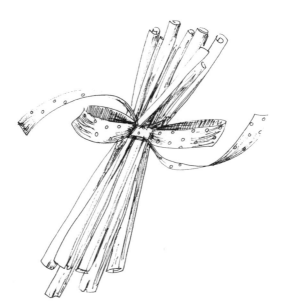

ORANGE CARROT CAKE - EZ

The best and easiest carrot cake you'll ever make or taste.

3 c. flour
2 c. sugar
1 c. shredded coconut
2 1/2 tsp. baking soda
2 1/2 tsp. cinnamon
1 tsp. salt
1 1/4 c. vegetable oil
2 tsp. vanilla
1 (11 oz) can mandarin
   oranges, undrained
3 eggs
2 c. carrots, shredded

Orange Cream Cheese
   Frosting:
1 (8 oz.) pkg. cream
   cheese, softened
1 tsp. orange extract
2 Tbsp. orange juice
   concentrate
2 c. powdered sugar
3 Tbsp. butter or
   margarine, softened

Blend 1 1/2 cups of the flour, sugar, coconut, vegetable oil, eggs, vanilla and mandarin oranges in large mixing bowl on high speed for 1/2 minute. Add remaining 1 1/2 cups flour, baking soda, cinnamon and salt. Blend on medium speed 45 seconds. Scrape bowl and stir in carrots. Pour into greased 9x13 inch cake pan or 2 greased and floured 10 inch round pans. Bake in preheated oven for 45 to 55 minutes (35 to 45 minutes for 10-inch pans) until tested done. Cool completely. For round pans, let cool 10 minutes before removing to wire racks to finish cooling. Frost with Orange Cream Cheese Frosting.

Orange Cream Cheese Frosting: Cream butter and cream cheese until smooth. Add the rest of the ingredients and blend until smooth. Frosting will not be as stiff as usual. I prefer it this way to get more cream cheese flavor. You may add more powdered sugar for a stiffer frosting. Frosting will harden with refrigeration. I like to garnish this cake with drained mandarin oranges.

RAVE REVIEW COCONUT CAKE

1 pkg. yellow or white cake
  mix
1 pkg. instant vanilla
  pudding mix
1 1/3 c. water
4 eggs
1/4 c. vegetable oil
2 c. flaked coconut
1 c. chopped nuts

Frosting:
2 Tbsp. margarine
2 c. flaked coconut
2 Tbsp. margarine,
  softened
1 (8 oz.) pkg. cream
  cheese, softened
2 tsp. milk
4 to 5 c. powdered sugar
1 tsp. vanilla

Blend cake mix, pudding mix, water, eggs, and oil in large bowl. Beat at medium speed for 4 minutes. Stir in coconut and nuts. Pour into 3 greased and floured 9 inch cake pans or one 9x13 inch cake pan. Bake at 350° for 35 to 45 minutes until tested done. Cool in pans for 15 minutes. Remove and cool completely on wire racks.

Frosting: Melt 2 tablespoons margarine in medium size skilled over medium heat. Stir in coconut and stir until light browned (toasted). Be careful not to let it burn. Spread on absorbent paper towel to cool.

Meanwhile, cream the other 2 tablespoons margarine, cream cheese and vanilla together until smooth. Add the milk and powdered sugar alternately, beating well. Add enough powdered sugar to get the spreading consistency you desire. Stir in 1 3/4 cups of the toasted coconut. Frost cake and sprinkle with remaining coconut on top.

High Altitude (over 6,000 feet): Increase water to 1 3/4 cups and add 1/4 cup flour.

PERFECT WHITE CAKE

This recipe was given to me by a very dear friend of Mom's, Pearl Paulicheck, many years ago.

1/2 c. shortening
1 c. sugar
1 1/4 c. milk, divided
2 1/2 c. flour
1 tsp. salt
1 tsp. vanilla
2 tsp. baking powder
2 egg whites (room
  temperature)
1/2 c. powdered sugar

Cream shortening and sugar until light and fluffy. Add 1 cup of milk and vanilla. Beat in flour and salt until well blended. Add baking powder to 1/4 cup remaining milk and dissolve. Add to cake mixture and beat well. In a separate bowl, beat egg whites until stiff. Slowly add powdered sugar until well dissolved. Fold egg whites gently into cake mixture. Pour into greased and floured 9x13 cake pan. Bake at 350° for about 25 to 30 minutes. At altitudes above 6,000 feet, bake at 375°.

YELLOW CAKE

This cake is a good cake for decorating and may also be used for any of the "jello" cakes instead of using a cake mix.

2 1/4 c. flour
1 1/2 c. sugar
3/4 c. shortening
3/4 c. milk
3 eggs
2 1/2 tsp. baking powder
1 tsp. salt
1 tsp. vanilla
1/2 tsp. almond extract

Preheat oven to 375°. Grease and flour two 9 inch round or one 9x13 inch cake pan. Into large bowl, measure all ingredients. Start mixing at slow speed; beat until well mixed, scraping bowl with spatula. Increase speed to medium and beat 5 minutes, stopping occasionally to scrape bowl. Pour batter into prepared pans and bake 25 minutes (30 for oblong pan) until tested done. Cool in pans on wire racks 10 minutes. Remove and cool completely. Frost with your choice of frosting.

PINEAPPLE UPSIDE-DOWN CAKE

This is another favorite childhood memory.

1/2 c. butter or margarine
2 c. packed brown sugar
1 (15 1/2 oz.) can
  pineapple chunks
Maraschino cherries,
  drained
Yellow Cake batter
  (preceding recipe)
Whipped cream or ice
  cream

Preheat oven to 375°. Before making cake batter, prepare topping. Place butter in 9x13 inch cake pan and place in oven until butter has melted. Remove from oven and sprinkle brown sugar over top of butter. Drain pineapple chunks and form "flowers" in sugar mixture. Use a cherry for the center of each flower.

Prepare cake batter and carefully spoon batter over design in the cake pan. Bake 35 to 40 minutes until tested done. Let cool 10 minutes, then invert onto serving dish. Any fruit that remains stuck in pan, gently remove with spatula and replace in design. Serve with whipped cream or ice cream.

Apples may also be substituted for pineapple. Use enough peeled and sliced apples to cover the bottom of the pan.

THE BEST GINGERBREAD

2 1/2 c. sifted flour
1 1/2 tsp. baking soda
1 tsp. ground ginger
1 tsp. cinnamon
1/2 tsp. salt
1/2 c. soft vegetable
  shortening
1/2 c. sugar
1 c. molasses
1 egg
1 c. hot water

Sift flour, baking soda, ginger, cinnamon, and salt onto wax paper. Cream shortening with sugar until fluffy in a large bowl; beat in molasses and egg. Stir in flour mixture, 1/2 at a time, just until blended. Beat in hot water until smooth. Pour into a well greased 9x13 inch baking pan. Bake in a 350° oven for 30 minutes until tested done. Serve warm or cold with your favorite topping, such as whipped cream or ice cream.

FRUIT COCKTAIL CAKE - EZ

This was always on the picnic menu; a fond memory of childhood days. Refrigerate if it lasts longer than a couple of days.

1 1/4 c. sugar
2 eggs
2 c. flour
2 tsp. baking soda
Pinch of salt
1 (17 oz.) can fruit
  cocktail, undrained
1/4 c. brown sugar,
  packed
1/2 c. chopped nuts

Topping:
3/4 c. sugar
1/2 c. margarine or butter
2/3 c. evaporated milk
1/2 c. coconut
1 tsp. vanilla

Blend sugar, eggs, flour, baking soda, and salt together in a large bowl until well mixed. Stir in fruit cocktail with liquid. Pour into an ungreased 9x13 inch cake pan. Mix together brown sugar and nuts and sprinkle over cake. Bake 45 minutes at 325° or until tested done. Frost while still partially warm.

Topping: Combine sugar, butter or margarine and evaporated milk in a small saucepan. Bring to a light boil and continue cooking 5 minutes, stirring constantly. Remove from heat and stir in coconut and vanilla. Pour hot topping over warm cake. Cool completely before serving. It may also be served with whipped cream; omit topping if you do.

GERMAN GOLD POUND CAKE

This is a great recipe to use when you have a lot of leftover egg yolks from making an angel food. Make the cake and freeze for later use.

2 c. sugar
1 c. butter, softened
3 1/2 c. flour
1 c. milk
1 1/2 tsp. baking
    powder
2 tsp. vanilla
1/8 tsp. salt
6 egg yolks

Preheat oven to 350°. Grease and flour 10 inch Bundt pan or two 9x5 inch loaf pans. In large bowl, beat sugar and butter at high speed until light and fluffy. Add rest of ingredients; at low speed, beat until well mixed, constantly scraping bowl with rubber spatula. Beat at high speed 4 minutes, occasionally scraping bowl. Pour batter into prepared pans and bake 1 hour for Bundt pan, 45 to 50 minutes for loaf pans or until tested done. Cool cake 10 minutes before removing. Cool completely on rack.

"Idea:" Use your imagination and leftovers for toppings. Mix cake with ice cream, fresh fruit, sauce or puddings. Or, try applesauce and walnuts with maple syrup over the top. Also a great cake to use for your own version of a Boston Creme Pie, using the custard filling and chocolate glaze from the eclair recipe.

PINEAPPLE CAKE - EZ

1 box yellow cake mix
1 large can crushed
    pineapple
Ingredients necessary for
    cake (see cake box)

Topping:
1 c. *cold milk*
1 large carton whipped
    topping
2 pkg. French vanilla
    instant pudding
Coconut

Bake cake as directed on the package, using 9x13 inch baking pan. Cool completely. Prick top with a fork and pour juice from the pineapple over the top. Spread pineapple over that.

Topping: Stir pudding and milk together until smooth. Fold in whipped topping and spread over the top of cake. Sprinkle with coconut.

DUMP CAKE - EZ

A recipe given me before I learned how to bake. No mixing, just "dump" the ingredients, one on top of each other. A great one for the kids to do!

1 (20 oz.) can crushed
  pineapple
1 large can cherry pie
  filling
1 box yellow cake mix
1 c. chopped pecans
1 stick margarine or
  butter

Spread the pineapple, juice included, in a 13x9 inch baking dish or pan. Next spoon the cherry pie filling on top and sprinkle the cake mix over them. Spread pecans over all and dot top with margarine or butter. Do not stir any of the ingredients. Bake in a 350° oven for 1 hour.

DOUBLE ORANGE REFRIGERATOR SHEET CAKE - EZ

1 pkg. orange cake mix
1 (3 oz.) pkg. orange jello
Ingredients necessary on
  the pkg. box

Topping:
1 env. instant whipped
  topping
1 small pkg. vanilla
  instant pudding
1 1/2 c. *cold* milk
1 tsp. orange extract

Preheat oven to 350°. Dissolve jello in 3/4 cup boiling water. Add 1/2 cup cold water; set aside at room temperature. Mix and bake cake as directed on package in a 9x13 inch cake pan. Cool cake for 25 minutes. Poke deep holes with a large serving fork about an inch apart. Slowly pour jello mixture over cake, filling the holes. Refrigerate cake while preparing topping.

Topping: In a chilled bowl, blend and whip topping mix, instant pudding, cold milk, and orange extract until slightly stiff, 5 to 8 minutes. Immediately frost cake. Cake must be stored in refrigerator.

"Idea:" Any flavor of jello, pudding or cake may be used. Some of the family favorites include lemon cake mix with lime jello and chocolate cake with cherry. Add nuts, coconut, any flavor chips, etc. How about some drained fruit mixed with the jello?

SUGARLESS CUPCAKES - HEALTHY

Mom makes these for the diabetics at local nursing home. They love them!

1 c. raisins
1 c. applesauce
   (unsweetened)
2 eggs
1 c. sugar substitute
3/4 c. vegetable oil
1 tsp. baking soda
2 c. flour
1 1/2 tsp. cinnamon
1/4 tsp. nutmeg
1 tsp. vanilla or rum
   extract
1/2 tsp. salt

Soak raisins in warm water about 1 hour before starting. Drain water off raisins. In large mixing bowl, combine applesauce, eggs, oil, and sugar and beat until well mixed. Add vanilla or rum extract. In a separate bowl, combine flour, baking soda, cinnamon, nutmeg and salt and add to liquid mixture. Beat until well mixed. Stir in raisins. Place cupcake liners in muffin tins. Fill each about 2/3 full of batter. Bake at 350° for 25 minutes or until tested done. Makes about 2 dozen.

PEANUT SQUARES

3 egg yoks, beaten
3/4 c. sugar
3 Tbsp. water
Pinch of salt
3/4 c. flour
1 tsp. baking powder
3 egg whites, beaten until
   stiff

Frosting:
2 c. powdered sugar
2 Tbsp. melted butter
1 lb. ground roasted
   peanuts
2 tsp. vanilla
Small amount of milk as
   needed

Beat yolks and sugar together until light and fluffy. Add all other ingredients except whites. Mix well. Fold in whites. Bake in greased and floured 9x13 inch cake pan in a 350° oven about 20 minutes until tested done. When cool, cut into 24 bars (4 lengthwise by 6 across).

Frosting: Blend together powdered sugar, vanilla, butter, and enough milk to make the frosting spreadable. Frost squares and roll them in the peanuts.

CHOCOLATE CHIP COOKIES - EZ

This is a great recipe, the best and it makes a lot! About 80 good size cookies and you will need them!

1 1/2 c. sugar
2 c. brown sugar
1 lb. butter or margarine,
  softened
3 eggs
2 Tbsp. vanilla
6 c. flour
1 1/2 tsp. salt
1 1/2 tsp. baking soda
3 c. chocolate chips
2 c. chopped nuts

Cream together the sugars and butter until light and fluffy in a *big* bowl. Add eggs and vanilla and blend well. Stir in flour, salt and baking soda until well mixed. Stir in chocolate chips and nuts until well mixed. Place by rounded teaspoonfuls onto lightly greased cookie sheets and bake in preheated 350° oven for 10 to 12 minutes, until lightly browned around edges. Remove and cool a few minutes before removing to wire racks to finish cooling.

OATMEAL-CHOCOLATE CHIP COOKIES - EZ

Mom's favorite chocolate chip recipe.

1/2 c. butter flavored
  shortening
1/2 c. sugar
1/2 c. packed brown
  sugar
1/2 tsp. vanilla
1 egg
1 Tbsp. water
1 c. flour
1/2 tsp. baking soda
1/2 tsp. salt
1 c. quick cooking oats
1 (6 oz.) pkg. (1 cup) semi-
  sweet chocolate chips
1/2 c. chopped walnuts

Preheat oven to 375°. Thoroughly cream shortening, sugars and vanilla. Beat in egg, then water and beat until light and fluffy. Sift together flour, baking soda and salt; add to creamed mixture, blending well. Stir in rolled oats, chocolate chips and walnuts. Drop by rounded teaspoonfuls onto lightly greased cookie sheet, about 2 inches apart. Bake 10 to 12 minutes, until browned around the edges. Remove and wait 3 minutes before removing cookies from sheet to finish cooling. Makes 3 1/2 to 4 dozen. Double the recipe, as these freeze well, if you have any left.

"Idea:" Substitute M&M's, butterscotch or peanut butter chips. Add cherry chips along with chocolate chips or maybe try maple flavoring with butterscotch chips, etc. Get the idea?

WHEAT AND RAISIN CHOCOLATE CHIP COOKIES - HEALTHY

Mom has a neighbor that always doubles this recipe. It is recommended to chill the dough about 30 minutes before baking.

1 1/2 c. softened
   margarine or butter
   flavored shortening
1 1/2 c. packed dark
   brown sugar
1 1/2 c. sugar
2 tsp. vanilla
4 eggs
2 1/2 c. whole wheat flour
1/2 tsp. salt
2 tsp. baking soda
2 Tbsp. hot water
1 c. chopped nuts
1 c. raisins
1 (12 oz.) pkg. semi-sweet
   chocolate chips

Preheat oven to 350°. Beat margarine or shortening in a very large bowl until soft and creamy. Gradually add sugars, beating until light and fluffy. Add vanilla. Add eggs, one at a time, beating after each addition. Blend flours and salt together and gradually add to the creamed mixture, beating at low speed until well mixed. Dissolve baking soda in hot water and add to mixture. Mix well. Stir in chocolate chips, nuts and raisins. Drop by generous tablespoonfuls (that's correct) of dough onto greased cookie sheet, flattening dough to about 2 1/2 inch circle. Bake 10 to 12 minutes, until browned around edges. Cool on cookie sheet a few minutes before removing to wire rack to finish cooling. Makes 45 large, delicious cookies.

SURPRISE MERINGUE COOKIES - EZ

These meringue cookies must be totally dry before tasting good.

2 egg whites (room
   temperature)
1/8 tsp. salt
1/8 tsp. cream of tartar
1 tsp. vanilla
3/4 c. sugar
6 oz. chocolate chips
1/2 c. chopped nuts

Beat egg whites with cream of tartar, salt and vanilla. When it is foamy, slowly add the sugar while beating. Beat until stiff. Fold in chocolate chips and nuts. Cover cookie sheet with brown paper. Drop by teaspoonfuls on paper. Bake at 300° for 25 minutes. Remove from oven and let cool thoroughly before removing from paper.

POPPY SEED SUGAR COOKIES

Another great recipe. I love poppy seed and these are different.

1 1/4 c. sugar
2/3 c. margarine or
   butter, softened
1 tsp. almond extract
1 tsp. vanilla
1 tsp. butter flavoring
1 Tbsp. orange juice
2 eggs
3 c. flour
2 Tbsp. poppy seeds
2 tsp. baking powder
1/2 to 1 1/2 tsp. salt

Glaze:
1/3 c. sugar
1/4 tsp. poppy seed
2 Tbsp. orange juice
1/4 tsp. almond extract
1/4 tsp. vanilla
1/4 tsp. butter flavoring

In large bowl, cream sugar, margarine or butter, almond extract, vanilla, and butter flavoring until light and fluffy. Add orange juice and eggs; blend well. Lightly spoon flour into measuring cup; level off. By hand, stir in flour, poppy seed, baking powder, and salt until well blended. (Soft dough can be refrigerated for easier handling or knead in small amount of flour until no longer sticky.)

Heat oven to 350°. On lightly floured surface, roll out dough, 1/3 at a time, to 3/16 of an inch thickness. Cut with 2 3/4 inch round cutter. Place 2 inches apart on ungreased cookie sheets. Bake 9 to 12 minutes or until lightly browned around the edges. While cookies are baking, combine all glaze ingredients; mix well. Immediately brush baked cookies with glaze, stirring glaze occasionally. Cool 1 minute; remove from cookie sheets. Cool on wire racks.

Cookie cutters of assorted shapes and sizes can be used. Makes 2 1/2 dozen.

Hint: Measure out all ingredients of glaze at the same time as you are preparing cookie dough, since they are all the same, to save time.

FROSTED CASHEW COOKIES

1 c. firmly packed brown
sugar
1/2 c. butter, softened
(must be butter)
1/2 tsp. vanilla
1 egg
2 c. flour
3/4 tsp. baking powder
3/4 tsp. baking soda
1/3 c. sour cream
3/4 c. coarsely chopped
salted cashew pieces

Frosting:
1/2 c. butter
2 c. powdered sugar
3 Tbsp. half & half or milk
1/2 tsp. vanilla

Heat oven to 375°. Lightly grease cookie sheets. In large bowl, beat brown sugar and 1/2 cup butter until light and fluffy. Add vanilla and egg; beat well. Lightly spoon flour into measuring cup; level off. Add flour, baking powder, baking soda, and sour cream; mix well. Stir in nuts. Drop by rounded teaspoonfuls, 2 inches apart, onto prepared cookie sheets. Slightly flatten with palms of hands. Bake 8 to 10 minutes only until edges are lightly browned. Immediately remove from cookie sheets. Cool completely.

In medium saucepan, lightly brown 1/2 cup butter; remove from heat. Stir in powdered sugar, half & half and vanilla; beat until smooth. Frost cooled cookies.

CREAM CHEESE SUGAR COOKIES

This is my favorite sugar cookie recipe. It's easy to handle. May I recommend the metal cookie cutters that have only the outline; they never stick.

1 c. sugar
1/2 tsp. salt
1 c. margarine or butter, softened
3 oz. cream cheese, softened
1/2 tsp. almond extract
1/2 tsp. vanilla
1 egg yolk (reserve white)
2 1/4 c. flour

In large bowl, combine sugar, salt, margarine, cream cheese, almond and vanilla extract, and egg yolk; blend well. Lightly spoon flour into measuring cup; level off. Stir in flour. Chill dough 30 minutes. Heat oven to 375°. On lightly floured surface, roll out dough, 1/3 at a time, to 1/8 inch thickness. Cut into desired shapes with lightly floured cutters; place 1 inch apart on ungreased cookie sheets. Sprinkle with sugar, or if desired, brush with slightly beaten egg white before sprinkling with colored sugar. Bake 7 to 10 minutes, until edges begin to brown. Remove from oven and let stand about 3 minutes until removing to wire rack to finish cooling.

Cherry Chip Pecan (Valentine's Day): Add cherry chips and pecan pieces (as many as you want) and cook the same way. When they are cool, partially dip in melted white chocolate (may be dyed red), using "paste" dye or melted chocolate, for a professional looking Valentine's Day cookie.

Snowflakes (Christmas): Using the same recipe, cut into star shaped cookies. Bake and cool as directed. Place 1/2 teaspoon seedless black raspberry jam on center of backside of a cookie. Adhere second cookie to first, back to back with jam, alternating points to form a 10 point "snowflake". Dust with powdered sugar.

DROPPED SUGAR COOKIES - EZ

2 3/4 c. flour
1 tsp. salt
1/2 tsp. baking soda
1/2 c. butter, softened
1 1/2 c. sugar
2 eggs
1 c. dairy sour cream
1 tsp. vanilla

Preheat oven to 375°. Sift salt, flour and baking soda together on a sheet of waxed paper; set aside. In large bowl, beat butter, sugar and eggs at high speed for 3 minutes. Stir in sour cream and vanilla. Add flour mixture in 3 parts, blending well after each addition to make a soft dough. Drop by rounded teaspoonfuls, about 2 inches apart, on ungreased cookie sheet; sprinkle with sugar. Bake about 12 minutes until lightly golden. Remove from cookie sheet and cool on wire rack.

OATMEAL PUDDING COOKIES - HEALTHY

1 1/4 c. flour
1 tsp. baking soda
1 c. butter, softened
1/4 c. sugar
3/4 c. packed brown sugar
1 pkg. instant vanilla
   pudding
3 eggs
3 1/2 c. quick oats
1 c. raisins (optional)

Preheat oven to 375°. Cream butter, sugars and pudding mix together until smooth and creamy. Beat in eggs, one at a time, mixing well after each addition. Add flour and baking soda to creamed mixture and blend well. Stir in oatmeal and raisins. Drop by rounded teaspoonfuls on ungreased cookie sheets and bake 10 to 12 minutes, until lightly browned. Let set on sheets for a couple of minutes before removing to wire racks to finish cooling..

THE $10,000 OATMEAL COOKIE

This is a cookie I created that was "supposed" to win me $10,000 in a recipe contest.

1 c. butter or margarine, softened
1 c. brown sugar
1 c. sugar
3 eggs
2 1/2 c. flour
1 tsp. salt
2 tsp. baking soda
2 c. quick oatmeal
2 (5 oz.) white chocolate candy bars with almonds, broken in small pieces
2 tsp. orange extract
1 tsp. cinnamon
1 tsp. vanilla
1/4 c. orange juice concentrate

Cream butter or margarine and sugars until light and fluffy in large mixing bowl. Add eggs, one at a time, beating well after each addition. Add orange and vanilla extracts and orange juice concentrate; mix well. Blend in flour, salt, baking soda, and cinnamon. Stir in oatmeal and candy bar pieces. Drop by rounded tablespoonfuls onto lightly greased cookie sheets, about 1 inch apart. Bake at 350° 10 to 12 minutes only, until lightly browned. Cool on cookie sheets about 5 minutes before removing to wire cooling racks to finish cooling. Store in an airtight container. Makes 5 to 6 dozen.

THE BEST OATMEAL COOKIES

The secret in these is soaking the raisins. I've learned to do this anytime I use raisins in baking, even if it's just soaking them in hot water a few minutes and draining them. Don't oversoak, though, as it will give your product an unstable texture.

3 eggs, well beaten
1 c. raisins
1 tsp. vanilla
1 c. butter or margarine, softened
1 c. packed brown sugar
1 c. sugar
2 1/2 c. flour
1 tsp. salt
1 tsp. cinnamon
2 tsp. baking soda
2 c. oatmeal
3/4 c. chopped pecans.

Combine eggs, raisins and vanilla and let stand for 1 hour, covered with plastic wrap. Cream together butter and sugars in a large bowl until light and fluffy. Add flour, salt, cinnamon, and baking soda to sugar mixture. Mix well. Blend in egg-raisin mixture, oatmeal and chopped nuts. Dough will be stiff. Drop by heaping teaspoonfuls onto ungreased cookie sheet or roll into small balls and flatten slightly on cookie sheet. Bake at 350° for 10 to 12 minutes, until just lightly browned around the edges. Cool a few minutes before removing from cookie sheet to finish cooling. Makes 5 to 6 dozen.

EASY DOES IT COOKIES

1 pkg. cake mix (any
flavor)
1 pkg. vanilla instant
pudding
1 c. sour cream
1 tsp. vanilla
2 eggs

Preheat oven to 350°. Mix all ingredients thoroughly. Drop by rounded teaspoonfuls on ungreased cookie sheet. Bake 10 to 12 minutes, until lightly browned. Cool a few minutes on cookie sheet before removing to wire rack to finish cooling. Makes about 8 dozen soft cookies.

GOLDIE COOKIES-RAISIN FILLED

Mom remembers how we four sons used to call these "little raisin pies" when we were kids. She sent them to us when we were away from home in the military.

1 c. sugar
1/2 c. vegetable
shortening
1/2 c. buttermilk
1 egg
2 1/2 c. flour
1 tsp. baking powder
1/4 tsp. salt
1/4 tsp. baking soda
1/4 tsp. vanilla

Filling:
1/2 c. sugar
2 Tbsp. flour
1/2 tsp. salt
1 c. raisins
1 tsp. vanilla
1/2 c. water

Cream sugar and shortening until light and fluffy, scraping sides of bowl as necessary. Add egg and blend well. Sift together 1/2 cup of the flour, baking soda, salt, and baking powder and add to creamed mixture. Mix well. Add buttermilk, vanilla and remainder of flour; stir until well mixed. Cover with plastic wrap and chill at least 2 hours. Meanwhile, prepare filling.

Filling: Combine all ingredients in small saucepan. Cook over medium heat until clear and slightly thickened. Cool.

Preheat oven to 400°. Roll out chilled dough to about 3/8 inch thick and cut out 3 inch circles with biscuit cutter. Place 1 circle on ungreased cookie sheet. Place 1 teaspoon filling in the center and top with a second cookie. Press edges together with a fork; bake 15 minutes.

"Idea:" Mom used to also use drained crushed pineapple instead of raisins.

PEANUT BUTTER SCOTCHIES

This is a favorite we almost had forgotten until Mom made them again after several years, just in time before this book went to print.

1 1/2 c. flour
2 tsp. baking powder
1/2 tsp. salt
1/3 c. butter or margarine
3/4 c. sugar
3/4 c. brown sugar,
  packed
1/2 c. evaporated milk
2 eggs
1 Tbsp. grated lemon rind

Melt butter in large saucepan. Remove from heat and add sugars and evaporated milk. Blend well. Add eggs and beat well. Sift flour, baking powder and salt together and stir into mixture. Add lemon rind and stir well. Pour into greased and floured 15x10 inch jelly roll pan. Bake in a 350° oven for 30 to 35 minutes, until lightly browned. Cool completely. Spread with topping. Let stand at room temperature until set. Cut into bars. Makes 24 bars.

Butterscotch Topping:
1 c. butterscotch chips
3/4 c. peanut butter
2 c. crushed corn flakes

Butterscotch Topping: Melt butterscotch chips in double boiler over low heat. Remove from heat and stir in peanut butter and corn flakes. Spread over cookies while topping is warm. Let set at room temperature until set.

HAZELNUT AND WALNUT COOKIES

A great cookie to take hiking or backpacking. These will last forever, if they last a day, if you know what I mean!

3 c. flour
1 c. brown sugar, firmly
  packed
1/2 c. sugar
2 tsp. cinnamon
1 tsp. baking powder
1/2 tsp. salt
2 3/4 c. walnuts, coarsely
  chopped
3/4 c. hazelnuts, toasted
  (do not husk) and
  coarsely chopped
3 eggs, beaten to blend
1/3 c. vegetable oil

Preheat oven to 375°. Grease 10 1/2 x 15 1/2 inch jelly roll pan. Sift first 6 ingredients into large bowl. Mix in all nuts. Reserve 2 tablespoons egg for glaze. Add remaining eggs and oil to flour and mix until crumbly dough forms. Pour into prepared pan. Brush with reserved eggs. Bake until beginning to color, about 15 minutes. Remove from oven; reduce temperature to 300°. Cut cookies into diamond, 1 1/2 inches long on each side. Place on baking sheets. Bake until beginning to dry, about 15 minutes. Transfer to racks and cool. Store airtight.

These cookies will be fairly hard like a "European cookie," but taste great and will literally keep for months.

TANGY ORANGE DROPS

1 1/2 c. flour
1 tsp. baking powder
1/2 tsp. salt
1/4 c. butter, softened
1/4 c. butter flavored
  shortening
3/4 c. sugar
1 egg
3 Tbsp. orange juice
3/4 c. coconut, shredded

Preheat oven to 350°. Sift together flour, baking powder and salt; set aside. Cream butter, shortening and sugar until light and fluffy. Add egg and beat well. Add sifted ingredients and mix thoroughly. Stir in orange juice and coconut until well blended. Drop by rounded teaspoonfuls onto greased cookie sheets. Bake 12 to 15 minutes, until lightly browned. Remove to wire racks and frost while warm.

Orange Frosting:
1 c. sifted powdered sugar
1 Tbsp. orange juice
1 Tbsp. water

Orange Frosting: Combine powdered sugar, orange juice and water; stir until smooth. Spread over cookies.

OATMEAL SCOTCHIES

1 c. flour
1 tsp. baking soda
1/2 tsp. salt
1/2 tsp. cinnamon
1 c. butter, softened
3/4 c. sugar
3/4 c. brown sugar
2 eggs
1 tsp. vanilla
2 c. quick oatmeal
2 c. (12 oz. pkg.)
  butterscotch chips

Preheat oven to 375°. In small bowl, combine flour, baking soda, salt, and cinnamon; set aside. In large bowl, combine butter, sugar, brown sugar, eggs, and vanilla; beat until creamy. Gradually add flour mixture. Stir in oats and butterscotch chips. Drop by level tablespoonfuls onto ungreased cookie sheets. Bake 7 to 8 minutes, until lightly browned around the edges. Cool 2 minutes before removing from sheets to complete cooling. Makes about 3 dozen.

BUTTERSCOTCH LEMON COOKIES

1 1/2 c. flour
2 tsp. baking powder
1/2 tsp. salt
3/4 c. sugar
1/2 c. butter, softened
1 egg
2 Tbsp. milk
1 Tbsp. lemon juice
1 tsp. grated lemon rind
1 1/2 c. butterscotch chips

Preheat oven to 375°. In small bowl, combine flour, baking powder and salt; set aside. In large bowl, combine sugar and butter; beat well. Add egg, milk, lemon juice, and lemon rind; beat well. Gradually beat in flour mixture. Stir in butterscotch chips. Drop by rounded table-spoonfuls onto greased cookie sheets. Bake 8 to 10 minutes. Until edges are lightly browned. Allow to stand 2 minutes before removing from sheets. Cool completely on wire racks. Makes about 1 1/2 dozen.

COCONUT-BUTTERSCOTCH DROPS

2 c. flour
1/2 tsp. baking soda
1/2 tsp. salt
1 (6 oz.) pkg. butterscotch
  chips
1/2 c. chopped nuts
1/2 c. butter or
  margarine, softened
1/2 c. brown sugar,
  packed
1/2 c. sugar
2 eggs
1 tsp. vanilla
1 tsp. coconut flavor

Cream butter and sugars together until light and fluffy. Add eggs, blending in well. Stir in flour, baking soda, salt, vanilla, and coconut flavoring until well mixed. Stir in nuts and butterscotch chips. Chill dough at least 2 hours. Drop dough by teaspoonfuls into 1 1/2 cups shredded coconut; roll to coat. Place on greased cookie sheet. Bake at 375° for 10 to 12 minutes, until lightly browned. Let cool on cookie sheets 5 minutes before removing.

MEXICAN WEDDING COOKIES

Great idea to go with the Christmas package.

1 c. butter, softened
1 c. powdered sugar
1 tsp. vanilla
1 tsp. almond extract
2 c. flour
1/2 tsp. salt
1 c. finely chopped pecans
Powdered sugar

Cream butter, sugar, vanilla and almond extracts together. Blend flour, salt and pecans into butter and sugar mixture. Mix dough until it holds together. Form into 1 inch balls. Place balls on ungreased baking sheet, about 1 inch apart. Bake at 400° for 10 to 12 minutes or until lightly browned (watch closely). Cool cookies for a few minutes and roll in powdered sugar several times until well coated. Makes 4 dozen.

PURE FRUIT COOKIES - HEALTHY/EZ

"O" cholesterol

3 medium size ripe
  bananas
1/3 c. peanut or safflower
  oil
1 tsp. vanilla
1 1/2 c. rolled oats
1/8 tsp. salt
1/2 c. uncooked fine
  grained oat bran creamy
  style hot cereal
1 1/2 c. coarsely chopped
  mixed dried fruit
1 c. chopped nuts

Preheat oven to 350°. Mash bananas in large bowl until smooth. Stir in oil, vanilla and salt. Add oats, oat bran, mixed fruit, and nuts; stir well to combine. Drop by rounded measuring tablespoonfuls onto lightly greased cookie sheets, about 1 inch apart. Flatten out slightly with back of spoon. Bake 20 to 25 minutes or until bottom and edges of cookies are lightly browned. Let set about 3 minutes after removing from oven, before removing cookies from pan to cooling racks.

HI-PROTEIN ENERGY BARS - HEALTHY

This is a very favorite of mine to take on hikes or ski trips. It's a hit with everyone. Kids will like them too. You may substitute carob chips for peanut butter for an even healthier treat.

1/2 c. butter or
  margarine, softened
1 1/3 c. packed brown
  sugar
2 eggs
1 tsp. vanilla
1/3 c. cocoa
1/4 c. milk
1/4 c. dry milk
1/4 c. wheat germ
1 c. whole wheat flour
1/2 tsp. baking powder
1/4 tsp. baking soda
1 (12 oz.) pkg. peanut
  butter chips
1/2 c. raisins

Cream butter, sugar, eggs, and vanilla until light and fluffy. Blend in cocoa and milk. Add dry milk, wheat germ, flour, baking powder, and baking soda. Fold in peanut butter chips and raisins. Spread mixture evenly in greased 13x9 inch cake pan. Bake at 350° for 30 to 35 minutes. Cut into bars. Wrap each bar separately if desired.

BLOND GRANOLA BROWNIE BARS - HEALTHY

1/2 c. margarine
1 3/4 c. firmly packed
  brown sugar
2 extra large eggs, lightly
  beaten
1 tsp. vanilla
3/4 c. flour
3/4 c. whole wheat flour
1 1/2 tsp. baking powder
3/4 tsp. salt
1 1/2 c. granola style
  cereal
1/2 c. chopped nuts

Melt butter. Remove from heat and add sugar, mixing well. Stir in eggs and vanilla. In mixing bowl, stir together white and whole wheat flours, baking powder and salt. Add sugar mixture, mixing until well combined. Stir in granola, then nuts. Spread batter in greased 9x13 inch baking pan. Bake in preheated 350° oven for 25 minutes or until wooden pick inserted in center comes out clean. (*Do not overbake* or brownies will become dry.) Let cool in pan on rack . Cut into desired size bars. Store in airtight container. Makes about 2 dozen.

CARAMEL BROWNIES

1 c. flour plus 1/8 c.
2 Tbsp. baking powder
1 tsp. salt
1/2 c. butter
2 c. packed brown sugar
2 eggs
2 Tbsp. vanilla
1 c. chocolate chips

Melt butter; add eggs, sugar and vanilla, beating until light and fluffy. Combine dry ingredients and stir into egg mixture until well mixed. Stir in chocolate chips. Spread mixture in 10x15 inch, lightly greased jelly roll pan. Bake in a 350° oven for about 30 minutes, until top springs back when lightly touched. Cool and cut into squares. You may frost if you wish.

DELICIOUS DATE DROPS

1 c. finely chopped, pitted
  dates
1/2 c. water
1 egg
1/2 c. brown sugar,
  packed
1/2 c. butter, softened
1/4 c. milk
1 1/2 c. flour
1/2 tsp. salt
1/2 tsp. baking powder
1/4 tsp. baking soda
1/2 c. chopped nuts

Date Frosting:
3 Tbsp. butter, softened
1 1/2 c. sifted powdered
  sugar
1/2 tsp. vanilla
2 Tbsp. reserved date
  mixture

Preheat oven to 375°. Combine dates and water; bring to a boil. Reduce heat and simmer 5 minutes. Cool. Set aside 2 tablespoons date mixture for frosting. Beat in egg, sugar, butter and milk into the rest of the date mixture. Beat well. Stir together flour, salt, baking powder, and baking soda. Add to egg mixture; mix well. Stir in nuts. Drop by teaspoonfuls on ungreased cookie sheet. Bake 10 to 12 minutes, until lightly browned. Remove to wire rack. Cool and frost.

Date Frosting: Beat together all ingredients until smooth. Add just enough milk to make the frosting spreadable. Makes 3 dozen.

POTATO CHIP COOKIES

These taste like shortbread.

1 lb. butter or margarine,
  softened
1 c. sugar
1 tsp. vanilla
3 1/2 c. flour
2 c. crushed potato chips
1/2 c. chopped pecans

Cream butter and sugar. Add vanilla and stir in flour. Add potato chips and nuts. Drop by teaspoon onto greased cookie sheet. You can place these fairly close together, as they do not spread. Bake at 350° for about 15 minutes.

DOUBLE PEANUT BUTTER COOKIE

As a peanut butter "freak", this is my favorite peanut butter cookie.

1 1/2 c. sifted flour
1/2 c. sugar
1/2 tsp. baking soda
1/4 tsp. salt
1/2 c. butter flavored
shortening
1/2 c. creamy peanut
butter
1/4 c. light corn syrup
1 Tbsp. milk

Combine flour, sugar, baking soda, and salt. Cut in shortening and peanut butter until mixture resembles coarse meal. Blend in corn syrup and milk. Shape in roll, 2 inches in diameter; chill. Slice 1/8 to 1/4 inch thick. Place half the slices on ungreased cookie sheet; spread each with 1/2 teaspoon peanut butter. Cover with remaining slices; seal with edge of a fork. Bake at 350° for 12 minutes. Makes about 2 dozen.

PEANUT BUTTER REFRIGERATOR COOKIES

1 c. butter, softened
1 c. sugar
1 c. packed brown sugar
1 c. crunchy peanut butter
2 eggs
2 1/2 c. flour
2 tsp. baking soda
1/4 tsp. salt

In large bowl, beat butter, sugars, peanut butter, and eggs until light and fluffy. Sift flour with baking soda and salt and add to creamed mixture; blend well. Shape dough into long rolls about 2 inches in diameter, and chill thoroughly. When chilled, slice rolls into 3/8 inch thick circles. Place on ungreased cookie sheets, about 2 inches apart. Bake at 400° for 8 to 10 minutes, until lightly browned. Makes 5 to 6 dozen.

PEANUT BUTTER BURST COOKIES

2 c. flour
1 tsp. baking powder
1/4 tsp. salt
1 c. butter or margarine,
softened
3/4 c. packed brown sugar
1/2 c. sugar
1/2 tsp. vanilla
1 egg
2 c. (12 oz. pkg.) peanut
butter chips

Preheat oven to 375°. In large bowl, cream butter and sugars until light and fluffy. Add vanilla and egg; beat well. Stir in flour, baking powder and salt. Blend well and stir in peanut butter chips. Drop by rounded teaspoonfuls onto ungreased cookie sheets. Bake 7 to 9 minutes. Cool on cookie sheets 2 minutes. Remove and cool completely. Cookies will be a light golden color with a light brown edge. Makes about 4 dozen.

GINGERSNAPS, POP'S FAVORITE - HEALTHY

These are Dad's favorite kind of his favorite cookies!

2 1/2 c. whole wheat flour
1 1/2 tsp. baking soda
1 tsp. ground ginger
1/2 tsp. cinnamon
1/2 tsp. ground cloves
1/2 tsp. salt
3/4 c. butter, softened
1 c. packed brown sugar
1 egg
1/2 c. molasses
Sugar (to roll dough in)

Preheat oven to 375°. Mix flour, baking soda, ginger, cinnamon, cloves, and salt in small bowl. Set aside. In large bowl, beat butter, brown sugar and egg until light and fluffy. Add molasses, blending thoroughly. Stir in flour mixture. Drop rounded tablespoonfuls of dough into palm and form into balls. Roll in sugar and place 2 inches apart on lightly greased cookie sheet. Bake about 8 minutes, until lightly browned. Remove and leave on cookie sheets about 5 minutes before removing to finish cooling.

NO BAKE COOKIES - EZ

2 c. sugar
1/4 c. milk
1/4 c. cocoa
1/2 c. butter
1/2 c. peanut butter
2 tsp. vanilla
3 c. quick oatmeal

Melt sugar, milk, cocoa, and butter together in mid-size saucepan until mixture comes to a boil for 1 minute. Remove from heat and stir in remainder of ingredients. Drop by rounded teaspoonfuls onto waxed paper and let stand until cool and firm.

SWEDISH ROSETTES

This recipe is worth the investment in a rosette iron, which you will need. Because of the design, this is an excellent Christmas cookie.

2 eggs
2 tsp. sugar
1 c. milk
1 c. flour
1/2 tsp. salt
1 Tbsp. lemon extract

Beat eggs slightly. Add sugar and then milk until smooth and well blended. Sift flour and salt into egg mixture and stir until smooth (should be the consistency of heavy cream). Add lemon extract. Add about 2 1/2 quarts vegetable oil to a 5 quart deep fryer (or heavy skillet) to fill it about 2/3 full and heat to 400°. Dip rosette irons in hot oil to heat them; drain excess oil on paper towels. Dip heated forms into the batter to not more than 3/4 of their depth. Plunge batter coated form into hot oil and cook until active bubbling ceased. Remove. With a fork, ease rosettes off forms and onto paper towels to drain. While still warm, dip in powdered sugar. Makes 6 dozen.

FAVORITE REFRIGERATOR COOKIES

Mother's advice: "I always double this recipe and usually bake half at a time. My children and grandchildren used to love the dough raw. They thought I spoiled it when I baked the cookies!

1 1/2 c. flour
1/2 tsp. baking soda
3/4 tsp. salt
2 tsp. vanilla
1/2 c. butter or
  margarine, softened
1 c. sugar
1 egg

Mix flour, baking soda and salt in flour sifter; set aside. In large bowl, cream butter until light and fluffy. Add sugar and vanilla; beat until well mixed. Add egg and continue beating until light and fluffy. Stir in flour mixture until smooth and well mixed. Turn dough (it will be quite soft) out on large pieces of waxed paper and shape into a roll, about 2 inches in diameter. Tightly wrap in wax paper and refrigerate a few hours, overnight or even a few days (cook them fresh as you need them).

When ready to bake, preheat oven to 375°. Cut dough in slices, about 1/4 inch thick; place them about 1 inch apart on greased cookie sheets. Bake about 10 minutes, until lightly browned. Remove at once and cool on wire rack.

"Idea:" Add pecans, chocolate chips, maybe cherry or lemon, or try macadamias. Use your imaginations!

PARTY BUTTER COOKIES

2 c. flour
3/4 c. butter, softened
1 egg yolk, beaten
1/2 c. sugar
1/2 tsp. vanilla

Sift flour. Cream butter and add sugar gradually. Cream until light and fluffy. Add egg yolk and beat well. Add flour, a small amount at a time, mixing thoroughly after each addition. Add vanilla and blend. Divide dough into 2 parts; shape in rolls, 1 1/2 inches in diameter, rolling each in waxed paper. Chill 3 hours or overnight. Cut in 1/8 inch slices. Bake on ungreased baking sheet in a 400° oven for 4 to 5 minutes, watching carefully so as not to burn. Makes about 6 dozen cookies.

This is a great recipe to serve with ice cream or at a tea party. The dough keeps well in the refrigerator up to 3 weeks or freezes well up to 5 months.

NEVER FAIL PIE CRUST

4 c. flour
1 Tbsp. sugar
2 tsp. salt
1 3/4 c. butter flavored
   shortening
1 egg, lightly beaten
1 Tbsp. vinegar
1/2 c. *ice cold water*

Mix flour, sugar and salt in large bowl. Cut in shortening until mixture resembles coarse oatmeal. Stir in remaining ingredients until dough is cohesive. Chill dough about 30 minutes before using. Dough can be refrigerated for 2 weeks or frozen for longer periods.

Hint: When rolling out pie dough, chill rolling pin and board if possible. Also handle as little as possible for a flaky crust. This is a great recipe if you have trouble with crusts. Makes enough for two 9 inch double crusts. (It is possible, and for me, preferable to use half whole wheat flour. It holds the crust together better.) The dough will hold in the refrigerator up to 3 weeks. It also freezes well, if tightly wrapped in plastic wrap, then foil. Let thaw in refrigerator a few hours before using.

VANILLA PUDDING PECAN PIE - EZ

1 (3 1/4 oz.) vanilla
   pudding (not instant)
1 c. dark corn syrup
1/4 c. evaporated milk
1 egg, slightly beaten
1 c. chopped pecans
1 unbaked 8 inch pie shell

Blend pie filling mix with corn syrup. Gradually stir in evaporated milk and egg, then add pecans. Pour into pie shell. Bake at 375° until top is firm and just begins to crack, about 40 minutes. Cool at least 3 hours before serving.

GLAMOUR RASPBERRY PIE-LATTICE TOP

2 (10 oz.) pkg. frozen
   rasberries, thawed
   (undrained)
10 large marshmallows,
   finely cut
1 c. sugar
3 Tbsp. quick tapioca
1 Tbsp. lemon juice
2 Tbsp. butter or
   margarine, melted
1 (9 inch) unbaked pie shell
Pastry for lattice top

Black or red raspberries can be used.

Combine berries, marshmallows, sugar, tapioca, and lemon juice with butter; mix lightly. Pour into unbaked pie shell. Put on lattice top. Bake at 425° for 10 minutes. Lower heat to 325° and bake 25 minutes longer.

TOASTED COCONUT PECAN PIE - EZ

3 eggs, beaten
1 1/2 c. sugar
1/2 c. butter or
    margarine, melted
2 tsp. lemon juice
1 tsp. vanilla
1 1/3 c. flaked coconut
1/2 c. coarsely broken
    pecans
1 unbaked 9 inch pie crust

Preheat oven to 350°. Thoroughly combine eggs, sugar, butter, lemon juice, and vanilla. Stir in coconut and pecans. Pour into pie shell and bake 45 to 50 minutes or until filling is set. Cool. Garnish with whipped cream and pecans. Makes 6 large size servings.

STRAWBERRY BANANA PIE

Another one of my grandmother's recipes. If in a hurry, use a pre-made crust from your grocer.

1 large banana
1 baked 8 inch pastry shell
1 (No. 2) can strawberry
    pie filling
2 tsp. grated lemon rind,
    divided
2 egg whites (room
    temperature)
1/4 tsp. cream of tartar
1/4 c. sugar

Slice banana into cooked pastry shell. Combine strawberry pie filling and 1 teaspoon lemon rind. Pour over banana. Beat egg whites and cream of tartar until foamy. Gradually add sugar, beating until stiff peaks form. Add remaining 1 teaspoon lemon rind. Spread meringue over pie filling, sealing it to crust all around. Bake in preheated oven (350°) for 12 to 15 minutes, until meringue is golden brown.

"Idea:" How about melting a chocolate bar on bottom of crust instead of using banana? Eliminate the lemon rind.

AMARETTO BREAD PUDDING - EZ

1 loaf French bread
1 qt. half & half
2 Tbsp. unslted butter,
    softened
3 eggs
1 1/2 c. sugar
2 Tbsp. almond extract
3/4 c. golden raisins
3/4 c. sliced almonds

Amaretto Sauce:
8 Tbsp. unsalted butter,
    softened
1 c. powdered sugar
1 egg, well beaten
4 Tbsp. Amaretto liquor

Break up bread into small pieces; place in a bowl. Cover with the half & half. Cover the bowl and let stand for an hour. Preheat oven to 325°. Grease a 9x13 inch baking dish or cake pan with butter. In a small bowl, beat together eggs, sugar and almond extract. Stir into bread mixture. Gently fold in raisins and almonds. Spread mixture evenly into baking dish. Bake 50 minutes until golden. Remove and let cool.

Amaretto Sauce: In top of double boiler, over simmering water, stir together butter and sugar. Stir constantly until sugar and butter are dissolved and mixture is very hot. Remove from heat. Whisk the egg well into the butter and sugar mixture until sauce has come to room temperature. Add the Amaretto.

To serve: Preheat broiler. Cut pudding into 8 to 10 squares and place on ovenproof serving dish. Spoon Amaretto Sauce over pudding and place under broiler until sauce bubbles. Serves 8 to 10.

CARAMEL-PECAN CHEESECAKE

1 c. graham cracker
    crumbs
2 Tbsp. sugar
1/4 c. margarine, melted
3 (8 oz.) pkg. softened
    cream cheese
3/4 c. sugar
2 Tbsp. flour
1 tsp. vanilla
3 eggs (room
    temperature)
1/2 c. caramel topping
1/2 c. chopped pecans
1 Tbsp. brown sugar
1 1/2 tsp. margarine
1 1/2 tsp. water
1/2 c. pecan halves
2 Tbsp. caramel topping

Combine graham cracker crumbs, 2 tablespoons sugar and 1/4 cup melted margarine. Press into bottom of 9 inch springform pan. Bake at 325° for 10 minutes.

Combine cream cheese, 3/4 cup sugar, flour, and vanilla; beat until smooth. Add eggs, one at a time, mixing well after each addition. Reserve 1 cup cream cheese batter and add 1/2 cup of the caramel topping to it. Spoon half of plain batter over crust; cover with caramel batter. Sprinkle chopped pecans over caramel layer; spread remaining plain batter over pecans. Bake at 450° for 7 minutes. Reduce oven temperature to 250°; continue baking for 30 minutes. Loosen cake from rim of pan; cool before removing pan. Chill.

Melt brown sugar and 1 1/2 teaspoons margarine. Add water; bring to boil. Add pecan halves; cook 2 minutes, stirring constantly. Spread on waxed paper; cool. Arrange pecan halves on top of cheesecake. Brush top of cheesecake with topping before serving. Serves 12.

CHEESECAKE SUPREME

This is the New York style cheesecake. Great with strawberries or other topping. This also freezes very well, so you don't have to consume all of those calories in one day!

Crust:
1 c. sifted flour
1/4 c. sugar
1 tsp. grated lemon zest
1/2 c. butter
1 egg yolk
1/4 tsp. vanilla

Filling:
5 (8 oz.) pkg. cream cheese, softened
1/2 tsp. vanilla
Grated zest of 1 lemon
3 Tbsp. lemon juice
1 3/4 c. sugar
3 Tbsp. flour
1/4 tsp. salt
1 c. eggs (4 or 5)
2 egg yolks
1/4 c. cream

Crust: Preheat oven to 400°. Combine flour, sugar and lemon zest in small bowl. Cut in butter until crumbly. Add the egg yolk and vanilla. Blend thoroughly. Pat 1/3 of the dough on bottom of 9 inch springform pan with sides removed. Bake about 8 minutes until lightly browned. Cool. Attach sides, then pat remaining dough on sides to 1 3/4 inches high. Increase temperature to 450°.

Filling: Beat cream cheese until light and fluffy. Add vanilla, zest and lemon juice. Add sugar, salt and flour. Add eggs and egg yolks, one at a time, mixing well after each. Gently stir in cream. Pour into pan. Bake 12 minutes. Reduce to 300° and continue baking for 55 minutes until done. (To test for doneness, lightly insert point of sharp knife; it should come out clean). Chill at least 4 hours before serving.

ECLAIRS

I think this has to be my favorite dessert. It's a little bit of work, but worth it!

Choux Paste (pg. 178)

Vanilla Pastry Cream:
3/4 c. sugar
1/4 c. flour
1/4 tsp. salt
1 1/2 c. milk
6 egg yolks, slightly beaten
1 1/2 tsp. vanilla
1 1/2 c. heavy or whipping cream

Semi-sweet Chocolate Glaze:
2 sq. semi-sweet chocolate
2 Tbsp. butter
1 c. powdered sugar
3 Tbsp. milk

Preheat oven to 375°. Make Choux Paste as for strawberry cream puffs.. Drop by 1/4 cupfuls onto cookie sheet, 2 inches apart, and in rows 6 inches apart to make 10. Spread each mound into rectangle, rounding edges, or pipe out of a pastry bag. Bake 40 minutes or until lightly browned. Cut slit in side of each shell and bake 10 minutes longer. Turn off oven; dry shells in oven 10 minutes. Cool on rack.

Meanwhile, prepare Vanilla Pastry Cream and Semi-sweet Chocolate Glaze. Slice about 1/3 from top of each shell and fill bottom of shells with cream filling. Replace tops and spread with glaze. Refrigerate until serving time.

Vanilla Pastry Cream: In 2 quart saucepan, combine the sugar, flour and salt; stir in milk. Over medium heat, cook, stirring until mixture thickens and boils, about 10 minutes; boil 1 minute. Beat small amount of hot milk mixture into yolks; slowly pour egg mixture back into milk mixture, stirring rapidly. Cook over medium low heat, stirring constantly, until mixture thickens and coats spoon well, about 8 minutes. *Do not boil.* (To check thickness, lift metal spoon from mixture and hold up 15 seconds; spoon should not show through mixture.) Remove from heat; stir in vanilla. Cover surface with plastic wrap and chill at least 2 hours. In small bowl with mixer at medium speed, beat whipping cream until stiff peaks form. Fold into custard mixture.

Semi-sweet Chocolate Glaze: In 1 quart pan over low heat, melt chocolate and butter, stirring constantly until melted. Stir in powdered sugar and milk until smooth.

The pastry cream recipe makes enough for a double batch of eclairs. You may want to cut the recipe in half or use the remainder in creative ways with fresh fruit or your own version of a Boston Cream Pie. The chocolate glaze is great for the Boston Cream Pie.

CHERRY PRETZEL SALAD OR DESSERT

2 c. crushed pretzels
3/4 c. melted butter or
  margarine
3 Tbsp. sugar
1 (8 oz.) pkg. cream
  cheese, softened
3/4 c. sugar
1 (8 oz.) ctn. frozen
  whipped topping,
  thawed
1 (16 oz.) can sweet
  cherries, drained
  (reserve juice)
1 (6 oz.) pkg. cherry jello

Place pretzels in ungreased 9x13 inch pan. Pour butter over pretzels and sprinkle the 3 tablespoons of sugar over mixture. Bake in a 325° oven for 20 minutes, until lightly browned. Cool.

Meanwhile, beat cream cheese with the 3/4 cup sugar. Fold in whipped cream and spread over pretzel mixture. In a separate bowl, prepare jello according to directions, using the juice as part of the hot water. Let cool until slightly thickened. Add drained cherries and pour over cream cheese mixture. Refrigerate until set or overnight.

Cherries may be chopped, if you want, before adding to jello. Everyone will guess you have lots of pecans in the first layer. This can be used as a salad, but I prefer to call it dessert.

"Idea:" Can you think of any other flavors of fruit and jello?

PISTACHIO DESSERT

1/2 c. butter or
  margarine, melted
1 c. flour
1 c. chopped pecans
1 (8 oz.) pkg. cream
  cheese, softened
1 c. powdered sugar
2 c. instant whipped
  topping, prepared
  according to directions
  on package
2 boxes instant pistachio
  pudding mix
3 c. milk

Mix the melted butter, flour and pecans together and press into the bottom of a 9x11 inch oblong Pyrex or cake pan. Firmly press the mixture until it is well lined and the bottom is covered. Bake at 350° for 20 minutes. Cool.

Meanwhile, beat cream cheese and sugar together until smooth, then fold in prepared whipped topping. Spread 1/2 of this mixture over the cooled crumb mixture. This completes the second layer. Spread the remaining 1/2 of the cream cheese/whipped topping mixture over the pudding. Sprinkle top with nuts and chill at least 2 hours.

"Idea:" Why not butterscotch or chocolate? For a great Christmas dessert or party time, add a little red food coloring to cream cheese layer.

QUICK STRAWBERRY DESSERT

1 small loaf angel food or
   pound cake
1 (3 oz.) pkg. instant
   vanilla pudding
1 c. cold milk
1 pt. vanilla ice cream
1 c. boiling water
1 (3 oz.) pkg. strawberry
   jello
1 (12 oz.) pkg. frozen
   strawberries

Break cake into small pieces and place in 9x13 inch cake pan.   In separate bowl, dissolve pudding in cold milk. Add ice cream and beat until smooth. Pour over cake. Dissolve jello in boiling water.   Add strawberries.   Stir and refrigerate until it thickens slightly. Pour over pudding and cake. Chill at least 2 hours before serving.

ORANGE OR APRICOT SPARKLE

1 (3 oz.) pkg. orange or
   apricot jello
1 c. boiling water
1 c. ice cubes
1 large banana, sliced
1 (10 oz.) can crushed
   pineapple, drained
   (reserve juice)
1/2 c. miniature
   marshmallows

Topping:
1/4 c. pineapple juice
   (reserved)
1/2 c. sugar
1 Tbsp. flour
1 Tbsp. butter
2 Tbsp. cream cheese,
   softened
1/2 pkg. instant whipped
   topping, whipped
   according to directions
   on pkg.
1 egg, slightly beaten

Prepare jello as directed on package, but add ice cubes instead of cold water. Stir until ice cubes have melted. Stir in pineapple, marshmallows and banana. Chill in dessert or parfait glasses until set.

Topping: In medium size saucepan, combine pineapple juice, sugar, slightly beaten egg, flour, and butter.   Stir until sugar is dissolved and mixture has thickened, stirring constantly. Add cream cheese, blending well. Cool. Fold in instant whipped topping and chill.

When ready to serve, top jello servings with topping.

RICE CUSTARD PUDDING

This is one I remember well from my childhood days. Great hot or cold with a little milk.

2 eggs
1/2 c. sugar
1/4 tsp. salt
1/2 tsp. vanilla
2 1/2 c. milk
1 c. boiled rice
1/2 c. raisins
Nutmeg

Beat eggs; add sugar, salt and vanilla. Stir well. Add milk, rice and raisins, stirring once more. Pour into a buttered 2 1/2 quart casserole dish and sprinkle lightly with nutmeg. Set casserole in larger pan filled with hot water and bake at 350° for about 30 minutes or until center is set. Cool some before serving. Serve with light cream or whipped cream.

GLORIFIED RICE - EZ

1 c. cold rice
1/2 c. sugar
1 1/2 c. crushed
   pineapple, drained
1/2 tsp. vanilla
1 c. whipping cream,
   whipped
8 large marshmallows,
   cut up
1/4 c. chopped
   maraschino cherries

Mix all ingredients and chill thoroughly. Makes 6 to 8 servings.

"Idea:" Here's one you can go wild with . Use any flavor yogurt and fruit, fresh or canned, nuts, honey, cinnamon, peanut butter, etc. Use whatever sounds good to you; see how easy it is to be creative. A great way to use up rice from the night before.   One we've always liked is simply adding raisins to leftover rice, warming it up and serving with sugar and milk the next morning for breakfast. It's still one of my favorites!

CARAMEL CUSTARD CUPS - EZ

This is another childhood memory Mom used to make. We served it in the restaurant I used to own. One customer commented, "This is just like my mom used to make." I replied, "Where do you think I got the recipe?"

4 Tbsp. brown sugar
2 eggs
1 c. evaporated milk
2/3 c. water
1/2 c. sugar
1 1/2 tsp. vanilla
Few grains of salt

Preheat oven to 350°. Press 1 tablespoon each of the brown sugar into 4 custard cups. In small bowl, lightly whip eggs and stir in evaporated milk, water, sugar, vanilla, and salt.   Pour mixture carefully over brown sugar in cups. Set cups in pan with 1 inch of water in pan. Bake 50 minutes or until custard is set.   Cool and refrigerate, covering with plastic wrap if kept more than a day.

RITZ CRACKER TORTE - EZ

3 egg whites (room
  temperature)
1/2 c. chopped nuts
1 c. sugar
30 Ritz crackers, crushed

Beat egg whites until stiff.   Gradually beat in sugar. Fold in crackers and nuts. Bake in lightly buttered 8 inch pie plate for 20 minutes at 350°. Remove from oven and cool completely. Add topping just before serving.

Topping:
1/2 c. whipping cream
Maraschino cherries
2 Tbsp. powdered sugar
1 c. crushed pineapple,
  drained, or 1 c. fruit
  cocktail, drained

Topping: Whip cream until peaks start to form. Slowly add powdered sugar and continue beating until well whipped; fold in pineapple. Spread on top of torte. Cut and top each piece with a maraschino cherry. Serve immediately. If not eating soon, don't put on fruit and whipped cream until ready to serve. *Easy! Looks and tastes great!*

"Idea:" Try any kind of fruit you'd like on it. Fresh fruit is very good to use, like strawberries. Also you might want to try chocolate chips over the top or chocolate syrup.

BASIC CREPES

Good for dessert or dinner.

2/3 c. all-purpose flour
2 eggs
3 Tbsp. butter, melted
1/8 tsp. salt
1 c. milk
2 tsp. sugar

Blend all ingredients until smooth. Refrigerate at least 2 hours or overnight. Heat a 7 or 8 inch skillet or crepe pan. Brush with *butter*. Pour a scant 1/4 cup batter into the pan. Tilt pan to coat bottom evenly. Cook over medium heat until golden. Turn crepe and cook other side. Turn crepe out on plate; keep warm. Repeat with remaining mixture. Makes about 8 crepes.

Crepes can be stored, layered between waxed paper and covered, in refrigerator 2 or 3 days. To reheat, place in single layer on baking sheet. Heat in a 350° oven until warm, about 5 minutes, or use microwave for about 5 seconds. Proceed with recipe.

"Note:" This is a great recipe. Good for dessert or dinner, and like omelets or quiches, anything goes. Following are just a few ideas, but one of my favorite is simply to fill with ice cream and top with a sundae topping, or make your own topping as follow in the Orange Crush Crepes.

ORANGE CRUSH CREPES

Crepes (from basic recipe)
1/4 c. crushed pineapple,
   drained
2 Tbsp. butter
1 Tbsp. brown sugar
2 scoops vanilla ice cream
1/4 c. peeled and
   sectioned orange, cut up

Scoop ice cream into crepe and fold over. Saute remaining ingredients and pour over top.

This recipe is for individual servings. Multiply ingredients accordingly.

GRAPE CREPES

4 oz. cream cheese,
   whipped
Crepes (from basic recipe)
1/3 c. chopped pecans
4 tsp. cornstarch
1 (6 oz.) can frozen grape
   juice concentrate
1 tsp. grated lemon peel
2 Tbsp. sugar

Spread cream cheese over unbrowned side of crepe, leaving 1/4 inch rim around edge. Sprinkle with nuts. Roll up as for jelly roll. Repeat with remaining crepes. In chafing dish or skillet, stir grape juice into cornstarch; add 1/2 cup water. Cook and stir until sauce is thickened and bubbly. Stir in sugar and lemon peel. Add crepes; heat through, spooning sauce over crepes. Serves 6.

"Idea:" Here, once more, try any flavor of juice concentrate available such as orange, pineapple, etc. Some of the thicker ones, you may need to add a little water to get the right consistency.

DOUBLE COCOA CAKE

1/2 c. butter or margarine
1/2 c. vegetable oil
1 c. boiling water
2 c. flour
2 c. sugar
4 Tbsp. cocoa
1 tsp. baking soda
1/2 tsp. salt
2 eggs
1 tsp. vanilla
1/2 c. buttermilk

Frosting:
1/2 c. butter or margarine
4 Tbsp. canned milk
4 Tbsp. cocoa
1 lb. powdered sugar
   (2 1/2 c.)
1 c. chopped walnuts
1/2 tsp. vanilla

Preheat oven to 350°. Combine butter or margarine, vegetable oil and the boiling water in a small saucepan over low heat until butter has melted.

Meanwhile, in large bowl. Combine the flour, sugar, cocoa, baking soda, and salt. Stir in saucepan mixture until well blended and add the eggs, vanilla and buttermilk. Beat until well blended (mixture will be runny). Pour into a greased and floured "deep" jelly roll pan and bake 15 to 20 minutes at 350°.

Frosting: Melt butter or margarine, canned milk and cocoa in a small saucepan over low heat. Bring to a boil and add remaining ingredients. Add more milk, if necessary, to achieve a drizzle mixture. Drizzle over cooled cake.

DEVIL'S FOOD

An excellent cake for chocolate lovers and the frosting is "satiny". You will notice a difference with no powdered sugar that is in most other frostings.

4 sq. unsweetened
  chocolate
1 1/2 c. sugar
1 1/2 c. milk
1 tsp. white vinegar
2 c. sifted cake flour
3 tsp. baking powder
1/2 tsp. baking soda
1/2 tsp. salt
2 eggs, separated
1/2 c. butter or
  margarine, softened
1 tsp. vanilla

Frosting:
1 1/2 c. sugar
6 Tbsp. cornstarch
1/4 tsp. salt
1 1/2 c. boiling water
3 sq. unsweetened
  chocolate
1/4 c. butter or margarine
1 tsp. vanilla

Grease and flour two 9 inch round cake pans. Combine chocolate, 1/2 cup of the sugar and 1 cup of the milk in a small heavy saucepan. Cook, stirring constantly, until mixture thickens and turns a deep chocolate color. Cool slightly. Stir vinegar into the remaining 1/2 cup milk in a cup to sour; reserve. Sift flour, baking powder, baking soda, and salt onto wax paper; reserve.

Meanwhile, cream butter, remaining cup of sugar and egg yolks in a large bowl at high speed 3 minutes. Beat in cooled chocolate mixture until light and fluffy at medium speed on mixer. Stir in flour mixture alternately with soured milk and vanilla, beating after each addition until batter is smooth. Beat egg whites until stiff, but not dry, in small bowl; fold into batter. Pour batter into prepared pans. Bake in 350° oven for 30 minutes or until tested done. Cool layers in pan on wire racks 10 minutes; loosen around edges with a knife. Turn out onto wire racks; cool completely. Put layers together with Chocolate Velvet Frosting. Frost side and top with remaining frosting.

Chocolate Velvet Frosting: Combine sugar, cornstarch and salt in a medium size saucepan; stir in boiling water until well blended. Cook stirring constantly, until mixture thickens. Add chocolate squares and butter. Continue cooking and stirring until chocolate and butter melt; remove from heat. Stir in vanilla. Pour into a medium size bowl and place over a larger bowl with ice. Stir frosting several times until thick enough to spread.

SOUR CREAM CHOCOLATE CAKE

This recipe has been a family favorite for at least 50 years.

4 Tbsp. cocoa
1 3/4 c. flour
1 1/4 c. sugar
1/4 tsp. salt
2 Tbsp. margarine or
   butter, melted
1 1/2 c. sour cream
2 eggs
2 tsp. soda
4 Tbsp. boiling water

Fudge Frosting:
2 oz. unsweetened
   chocolate
3 Tbsp. butter or
   margarine
5 Tbsp. evaporated milk
Dash of salt
1 tsp. vanilla
2 c. powdered sugar or
   more

Combine cocoa, flour, sugar, and salt in large mixing bowl. Add margarine, sour cream and eggs. Beat well on medium speed on mixer. Dissolve soda in boiling water and add to cake mixture. Pour into greased 9x13 inch cake pan and bake at 350° for about 25 to 30 minutes or until inserted toothpick comes out clean. Cool completely and frost with Fudge Frosting.

Fudge Frosting: Combine chocolate, butter and milk in top of double boiler. On low heat, melt ingredients until mixture is smooth. Add salt and vanilla. Remove from heat. Stir in enough powdered sugar for spreading consistency. Spread quickly over cooled cake. This is also a good frosting for brownies.

COCA-COLA CAKE

One of the best chocolate cakes you'll ever eat.

2 c. flour
2 c. sugr
1 c. butter or margarine
1 c. Coca-Cola
2 Tbsp. cocoa
1/2 c. buttermilk
2 eggs
2 tsp. vanilla
1 tsp. baking soda
1/4 tsp. salt
1 1/2 c. mini
   marshmallows

Icing:
1/2 c. butter or margarine
6 Tbsp. Coca-Cola
2 Tbsp. cocoa
1 c. chopped pecans
3 3/4 c. powdered sugar
1 tsp. vanilla

Preheat oven to 350°. Butter 9x13 inch cake pan. Sift flour and sugar into large bowl. Melt butter in heavy saucepan. Add Coca-Cola and cocoa and bring just to a boil. Stir into flour mixture. Blend in buttermilk, eggs, vanilla, baking soda, and salt. Fold in marshmallows. Pour into prepared pan. Bake about 35 minutes, until tested done

Meanwhile, prepare icing. Melt butter in heavy saucepan. Add Coca-Cola and cocoa and bring just to a boil. Remove from heat. Stir in powdered sugar and vanilla. Add pecans. Spread over hot cake.

CHOCOLATEY CREAM FROSTING

This is my favorite chocolate frosting and is great on the Black Forest Cake or the Black Raspberry Cream Cheese Filled Chocolate Cake.

3 1/2 c. powdered sugar
1/2 c. butter, softened
3 (1 oz.) sq. unsweetened
**   chocolate**
1 tsp. vanilla
1/8 tsp. salt
2 Tbsp. egg substitute
1/4 c. milk

In large bowl, combine 1 cup of the powdered sugar, butter, melted chocolate, vanilla, and salt; beat until creamy. Beat in egg substitute. Alternately blend in remaining sugar and milk. Continue beating until thick enough to spread. Spread frosting over cake and chill. Any frosting left may be refrigerated or put between graham crackers.

ORANGE-FROSTED COCOA BUNDT CAKE

3/4 c. butter or
**   margarine, softened**
1 2/3 c. sugar
2 eggs
1 tsp. vanilla
3/4 c. sour cream
2 c. flour
2/3 c. unsweetened cocoa
1/2 tsp. salt
2 tsp. baking soda
1 c. buttermilk or sour
**   milk**

Orange Frosting:
1 c. powdered sugar
2 Tbsp. butter or
**   margarine, melted**
1 1/2 Tbsp. orange juice
1/2 tsp. vanilla
1/4 tsp. grated orange peel

Cream butter or margarine, sugar, eggs, and vanilla in large bowl; blend in sour cream. In a separate bowl, combine flour, cocoa and salt. Stir baking soda into buttermilk; add alternately with dry ingredients to creamed mixture. Beat 2 minutes at medium speed. Pour batter into greased and floured 9 or 12 cup Bundt pan. Bake at 350° for 45 to 50 minutes, until cake tester comes out clean. Cool 10 minutes; remove from pan. Cool completely on a wire rack. Frost with orange or vanilla frosting.

Orange Frosting: Combine all ingredients in small bowl; beat until smooth. Drizzle over cake.

GERMAN CHOCOLATE CAKE

This is the best and original German Chocolate Cake; 3 layers of delicious sin.

1 (4 oz.) bar German chocolate
1/2 c. boiling water
2 c. flour
1 tsp. baking soda
1/2 tsp. salt
1 c. butter or margarine, softened
2 c. sugar
4 eggs, separated
1 tsp. vanilla
1 c. buttermilk

Coconut-Pecan Filling and Frosting:
1 c. evaporated milk or cream
1 c. sugar
3 egg yolks, slightly beaten
1/2 c. butter or margarine
1 tsp. vanilla
1 1/3 c. coconut
1 c. chopped pecans

Melt chocolate in boiling water; cool. Mix flour, baking soda and salt. Cream butter and sugar until light and fluffy. Add egg yolks, one at a time, beating thoroughly after each. Blend in vanilla and chocolate. Alternately add flour mixture and buttermilk, beating after each addition until smooth. Beat egg whites until stiff peaks form. Fold into batter.

Preheat oven to 350°. Line three 9 inch round cake pans with waxed paper on the bottoms. Pour batter into the pans. Bake 30 to 35 minutes, until tested done. Immediately run spatula around pans between cakes and sides. Cool in pans 15 minutes. Remove from pans; remove paper. Finish cooling on racks. Spread filling and frosting between layers and over top.

Coconut-Pecan Filling and Frosting: Combine evaporated milk or cream, sugar, egg yolks, and butter in saucepan. Cook and stir over medium heat until mixture thickens, about 12 minutes. Remove heat and stir in vanilla, coconut and pecans. Cool until of spreading consistency, beating occasionally.

TOLL HOUSE CAKE

A combination between the famous chocolate chip cookie and a torte.

1 c. butter or margarine,
  softened
1 c. brown sugar, packed
2/3 c. sugar
4 eggs
2 tsp. vanilla
1/2 tsp. salt
2 c. flour
2 c. (12 oz. pkg.) semi-
  sweet mini chocolate
  chips, divided

Frosting:
1 c. chocolate chips,
  reserved from cake
3/4 c. butter, softened
1 1/2 c. sifted powdered
  sugar
2 tsp. vanilla

Preheat oven to 350°. Grease bottom of 15 1/2x10 1/2x1 inch jelly roll pan. Line with waxed paper; set aside. In large bowl, combine butter, brown sugar and sugar; beat until creamy. Add eggs, one at a time, beating well after each addition. Add vanilla extract and salt; mix well. Gradually add flour. Stir in 1 cup chocolate chips. Spread batter into prepared pan. Bake 20 to 25 minutes. Cool completely.

Frosting: Melt chocolate chips over hot (not boiling) water; stir until smooth.. Set aside. In small bowl, combine butter and powdered sugar; beat until creamy. Add melted chocolate and vanilla extract; blend until smooth.

To assemble: Loosen sides of cake. Invert onto lightly floured cloth. Peel off waxed paper. Trim edges of cake; cut cake crosswise into four 3 3/4x10 inch sections. Spread 3 slightly rounded tablespoonfuls frosting on one cake layer. Top with second cake layer. Repeat layers of frosting and cake. Frost entire cake with remaining frosting.

BLACK RASPBERRY CREAM CHEESE FILLED CHOCOLATE CAKE**

This is a very popular cake for decorating, because of its firmness. This is also the cake recipe to use for the Black Forest Cake.

4 (1 oz.) sq. unsweetened chocolate
1 c. butter or margarine, softened
2 1/4 c. sugar
1 1/2 c. buttermilk
3 c. flour
1 tsp. baking soda
1/4 tsp. baking powder
1/2 tsp. salt
5 eggs, separated (room temperature)
1 tsp. vanilla

Black Raspberry Cream Cheese Filling:
3 oz. cream cheese, soft ened
1/4 c. seedless black raspberry jam
1 c. powdered sugar

Preheat oven to 350°. Grease and flour two 10 inch or three 9 inch round cake pans. Melt chocolate in small saucepan on low heat. Set aside to cool slightly. In small bowl, combine flour, baking soda, baking powder, and salt. Set aside. In large bowl, cream butter and sugar until light and fluffy. Beat egg yolks and add, mixing well. Stir in melted chocolate. Add buttermilk and flour mixture alternately until well blended. Whip egg whites and fold into cake mixture until well blended. Stir in vanilla. Divide batter between pans and bake 30 to 35 minutes, until tested done. Remove from oven and cool 10 minutes before removing cakes from pans. Continue cooling on wire racks.

Black Raspberry Cream Cheese Filling: Blend ingredients until smooth. Spread filling between layers and refrigerate, covered, 45 minutes before frosting with Chocolatey Creamy Frosting (see page 133).

BLACK BOTTOM CUPCAKES

A very impressive gift for a chocoholic!

8 oz. cream cheese, softened
1 egg
1/3 c. sugar
1/8 tsp. salt
1 c. semi-sweet chocolate chips
1 1/2 c. flour
1 c. sugar
1/4 c. cocoa
1 tsp. baking soda
1/2 tsp salt
1 c. water
1/3 c. vegetable oil
1 Tbsp. white vinegar
1 tsp. vanilla

Preheat oven to 375°. Line muffin tins with cupcake papers. Using wooden spoon, blend cream cheese, egg, the 1/3 cup sugar, and 1/8 teaspoon salt in mixing bowl. Carefully fold in chocolate chips. Set aside.

Combine dry ingredients in another bowl and mix well. Add remaining ingredients and blend thoroughly. Fill cupcake papers about 3/4 full with batter. Drop 1 heaping tablespoonful cream cheese mixture into center of each. Bake until done, 25 to 30 minutes. Cool completely and top with your favorite chocolate frosting for an even richer taste or eat plain. Makes 18.

HURRY-STIR BROWNIES - EZ

2/3 c. margarine
1 1/2 c. packed brown
    sugar
1/2 c. cocoa
2 eggs, beaten
1 1/3 c. flour
3/4 c. chopped nuts

Melt margarine in large skillet. Remove skillet from heat. Stir in sugar and cocoa. Mix well. Add eggs, flour and nuts. Mix well. Spread dough in greased 8 inch square pan. Bake at 350° for about 40 minutes. Put on your favorite chocolate frosting.

PERFECT FUDGE BROWNIES

1 c. butter or margarine
4 (1 oz.) sq. unsweetened
    chocolate
1 1/2 c. plus 2 Tbsp. flour
1/2 tsp. baking powder
1 tsp. salt
4 eggs, slightly beaten
2 c. sugar
1 tsp. vanilla
3/4 c. chopped nuts
Fudge frosting

Place margarine and chocolate in a heavy pan. Cover and place over very low heat until margarine and chocolate melt, stirring mixture occasionally; cool. Sift together flour, baking powder and salt. Place eggs in large bowl of mixer. Gradually add sugar, beating on medium speed until mixture is creamy. Add vanilla and cooled chocolate mixture. Thoroughly blend in dry ingredients, then nuts. Spoon batter into greased 9x13 inch pan. Bake in preheated oven at 375° for 30 minutes or until tested done.   Cool thoroughly. Spread with fudge frosting if desired. Makes about 3 dozen.

MOCHA CHIP MUFFINS

These can be used as a dessert as well as a muffin. I made one batch and forgot the baking powder; gave them almost a brownie-like texture. Tasted great!

2 1/4 c. flour
3/4 c. cocoa
1/2 c. sugar
1 Tbsp. baking powder
2 tsp. instant coffee
    powder
2 large eggs
1 1/2 c. milk
1/2 c. margarine, melted
1 tsp. vanilla
1 1/2 c. chocolate chips

In large bowl, combine flour, cocoa, sugar, baking powder, and instant coffee powder. In medium bowl, whisk eggs, milk, margarine, and vanilla until blended.   Pour liquid ingredients into dry ingredients; add chocolate chips, stirring just until mixed.   Spoon batter into 18 greased muffin cups. Bake in a preheated 400° oven 20 minutes or until lightly browned.

"Idea:" Try these with white chocolate instead of chocolate chips.

DOUBLE CHOCOLATE OATMEAL COOKIES

This is a very popular cookie with a brownie type texture. Great for chocolate lovers!

1 1/2 c. sugar
1 c. margarine, softened
1 egg
1/4 c. water
1 tsp. vanilla
1 1/4 c. flour
1/3 c. cocoa
1/2 tsp. baking soda
1/2 tsp. salt
3 c. quick cooking oats
1 (6 oz.) pkg. chocolate
  chips (semi-sweet)

Preheat oven to 350°. Beat sugar, margarine, egg, water, and vanilla together until light and fluffy. Stir in remaining ingredients. Drop by rounded teaspoonfuls on ungreased cookie sheet. Bake 10 to 12 minutes.

FUDGY FRUITCAKE DROPS

1/4 c. butter or
  margarine, softened
1/2 c. sugar
1 egg
1/2 c. grape jelly
1 tsp. vanilla
1 c. flour
1/4 c. unsweetened cocoa
2 tsp. baking powder
2 c. chopped walnuts
1 1/2 c. raisins
1 c. chocolate chips
Powdered sugar (optional)

In large mixer bowl, beat butter for 30 seconds; add sugar. Beat until fluffy. Add egg, jelly and vanilla; beat until well combined. Stir together flour, cocoa powder and baking powder. Stir flour mixture into beaten mixture. Stir in nuts, raisins and chocolate chips. Drop by rounded teaspoonfuls onto greased and floured cookie sheets. Bake in a 350° oven about 10 minutes or until just set. Cool 1 minute. Remove to wire rack; cool. If desired, sift powdered sugar over cooled cookies. Makes about 3 dozen.

THE REESE'S FUDGE COOKIE

1 1/4 c. butter or
  margarine, softened
2 c. sugar
2 eggs
2 tsp. vanilla
2 c. flour
3/4 c. cocoa powder
1 tsp. baking soda
1/2 tsp. salt
2 c. (12 oz. pkg.) peanut
  butter chips

Cream butter or margarine and sugar in large mixing bowl. Add eggs and vanilla; blend well. Combine flour, cocoa, baking soda, and salt; blend into creamed mixture.   Stir in peanut butter chips. Drop by teaspoonfuls onto ungreased cookie sheet. Bake at 350° for 8 to 9 minutes. (Do not overbake; cookies will be soft.) Cool on cookie sheet until set, about 1 minute. Remove to wire rack to cool completely. Makes 3 1/2 dozen.

SNAPPY TURTLE COOKIES

A cookie similar to the turtle candies.

1/2 c. packed brown sugar
1/2 c. margarine or
   butter, softened
1/4 tsp. vanilla
1/8 tsp. maple flavoring
2 eggs (reserve 1 white)
1 1/2 c. flour
1/4 tsp. salt
1/4 baking soda
1 1/2 to 2 c. split pecan
   halves

Frosting:
1/3 c. semi-sweet
   chocolate chips
3 Tbsp. milk
1 Tbsp. margarine or
   butter
1 c. powdered sugar

In medium bowl, blend brown sugar and margarine. Add vanilla and maple flavoring, egg and egg yolk; beat well. By hand, stir in flour, salt and baking soda; mix thoroughly. Chill dough for 30 minutes. Heat oven to 350°. Lightly grease cookie sheets. Arrange pecan pieces in groups of 3 or 5 on prepared cookie sheets to resemble head and legs of turtle. Beat reserved egg white. Shape rounded teaspoonfuls of dough into balls; dip bottoms into egg white. Press lightly onto nuts. Tips of nuts should show after baking. Bake 10 to 12 minutes, until light golden brown around edges. Cool, then frost.

Frosting: In small saucepan, melt chocolate chips, milk and margarine over low heat. Stir until smooth. Remove from heat; stir in powdered sugar. If too thin, add powdered sugar until you reach the desired consistency. Generously frost cooled cookies. Makes 3 dozen.

BAKED FUDGE PIE

1 oz. sq. baking chocolate
1/2 c. butter
1 c. sugar
2 eggs, beaten
1 scant c. flour
1 tsp. vanilla

Melt chocolate with butter in medium size saucepan over low heat. Add sugar, eggs, flour, and vanilla. Pour into greased 8 inch pie pan (this recipe needs no crust). Bake at 350° for 25 minutes; chill. Top with whipped cream or ice cream. Serves 8.

FROZEN STRAWBERRY FUDGE PIE

2 (10 oz.) pkg. frozen
  strawberries, thawed
  and drained
1/4 c. corn syrup
1 (12 oz.) tub non-dairy
  whipped topping
1 (9 inch) prepared
  chocolate crumb crust
1 c. semi-sweet chocolate
  chips

Place drained strawberries in blender or food processor. Process until pureed. Transfer to large bowl. Add corn syrup; mix well. Fold in 2 cups of the whipped topping. Spoon into crust. Freeze until firm (about 1 1/2 hours).

Combine over hot (not boiling water), 1 cup of the whipped topping and chocolate chips. Stir until morsels are melted and mixture is smooth. Spread evenly over strawberry layer. Freeze until firm (about 1 1/2 hours). Garnish with remaining whipped topping and chocolate dipped strawberries (fresh) if desired.

ROCKY ROAD CANDY - EZ

1 (12 oz.) pkg. semi-
  sweet chocolate chips
1 (14 oz.) can
  sweetened condensed
  milk
1 (10 1/2 oz.) pkg.
  miniature
  marshmallows
2 Tbsp. butter
2 c. dry roasted nuts

In heavy saucepan, over low heat, melt the chocolate chips with sweetened condensed milk and butter. Remove from heat. In large bowl, combine nuts and marshmallows. Stir in chocolate mixture. Spread on wax paper-lined cookie sheet. Chill 2 hours until firm. Remove from pan; peel off wax paper. Cut into squares. Store, loosely covered, at room temperature.

CHOCOLATE CLUSTERS

2 bars German chocolate
2 Tbsp. vegetable
  shortening
3/4 c. raisins
1/2 c. coconut
1 tsp. vanilla
2 c. dry roasted peanuts

In top of double boiler, melt chocolate and shortening over low heat. Stir until smooth. Remove from heat and put cold water in bottom of double boiler. Return top part of boiler and add vanilla, raisins, coconut, and peanuts to chocolate mixture. Stir until well mixed. Drop by teaspoonfuls on waxed paper. Chill.

COCONUT CREMES

1 1/2 lb. powdered sugar
1 cube butter, softened
3 c. flaked coconut
2 tsp. vanilla
1 can sweetened
    condensed milk
1 c. chopped nuts
1 lb. almond bark or milk
    chocolate

Mix all ingredients except milk chocolate or almond bark. Roll in balls and chill (may use powdered sugar to roll). Melt almond bark or milk chocolate and dip balls in this and place on waxed paper.. Let cool.

COCONUT CANDY DROPS

This recipe is from a dear friend of Mom's, Barbara.

1/2 c. butter or
    margarine, softened
1 can sweetened
    condensed milk
2 (9 oz.) pkg. flaked
    coconut
1 1/2 c. chopped nuts
5 1/2 c. powdered sugar
1 c. maraschino cherries,
    drained and chopped
1 lb. almond or chocolate
    bark

Mix butter, coconut, nuts, powdered sugar, and maraschino cherries in a large bowl. Add condensed milk and stir until well mixed. Put in refrigerator and chill overnight. Make into balls. Chill for 1 hour. Dip in melted chocolate or almond bark. Place on wax paper. Let cool.

CRISPY CHOCOLATE PEANUT BUTTER BALLS

3 3/4 c. powdered sugar
1/2 c. margarine,
    softened
2 c. crunchy peanut butter
2 c. crispy rice cereal

Chocolate Coating:
6 oz. German's sweet
    chocolate
6 oz. semi-sweet
    chocolate chips
2 oz. paraffin wax

Combine first 4 ingredients in large bowl and mix well. Roll dough into 1 inch balls. Chill.

Chocolate Coating: In top of double boiler over boiling water, melt German's sweet chocolate and chocolate chips with paraffin wax, stirring constantly, until smooth. Using a wooden pick inserted in balls, dip balls into chocolate mixture, one at a time. Set on waxed paper to harden. Store in airtight container in refrigerator.

ORANGE FUDGE

2 c. sugar
1 (5 1/3 oz.) can
  evaporated milk
  (2/3 cup)
10 large marshmallows (or
  100 miniature)
1 (6 oz.) pkg. semi-sweet
  chocolate chips
1 c. chopped walnuts
1/2 c. butter or
  margarine, cut into
  small pieces
Grated peel of 2 oranges

In saucepan, combine sugar, evaporated milk and marshmallows. Bring to boil over medium heat, stirring to dissolve the sugar. Boil for 6 minutes, stirring constantly. Remove from heat and add remaining ingredients. Beat well until fudge thickens, about 5 minutes. Pour into a buttered 8 inch square baking pan. Chill until firm and cut into squares.

CHOCOLATE RASPBERRY TRUFFLES

12 oz. milk chocolate
1/3 c. heavy whipping
  cream
Powdered sugar
1/4 c. raspberry flavored
  liquor or raspberry
  Schnapps

Break chocolate into very small pieces. Place in mixing bowl. In small saucepan, combine cream and liquor. Heat just to boiling. Immediately pour over chocolate pieces. Beat until smoothly blended. Chill 1 to 2 hours until firm.

Roll between palms of hands into 1 inch ball. Chill at least 30 minutes. Roll truffles in powdered sugar; chill. Makes about 2 dozen truffles.

AMARETTO TRUFFLES

8 oz. semi-sweet
  chocolate, melted
1/4 c. Amaretto liqueur
2 Tbsp. strong coffee
1/2 c. unsalted butter,
  softened
1 Tbsp. pure vanilla
3/4 c. vanilla wafer crumbs
1/2 c. powdered sugar
1/2 c. unsweetened cocoa
  powder

In small bowl, mix melted chocolate, Amaretto and coffee until smooth. Add butter, vanilla and cookie crumbs. Mix well. Set bowl in ice water and beat until firm. Form into balls and chill. Mix powdered sugar and cocoa. Roll truffles in sugar mixture and store in airtight container. Refrigerate until serving. Makes 1 pound.

"Idea:" Use any flavor liqueur you prefer, and for a different change, try coating chilled balls in melted almond bark for a white chocolate truffle.

CHOCOLATE TRUFFLES

2/3 c. whipping cream
3 Tbsp. unsalted butter
1 Tbsp. sugar
6 (1 oz.) pieces semi-sweet
  chocolate, chopped
2 Tbsp. desired liquor
  (brandy, Amaretto,
  Kahlua, rum, etc.)
Cornstarch
1 lb. dipping chocolate,
  chopped

In a 1 quart saucepan, combine whipping cream, butter and sugar. Cook and stir until butter is melted and mixture is very hot. Remove from heat. Stir in semi-sweet chocolate until it is melted. Add liquor; stir. Transfer mixture into a chilled bowl. Cover and chill 1 hour or until mixture is completely cold, stirring often. Drop mixture by teaspoonful into cornstarch, rolling each until coated. Transfer to wax paper-lined cookie sheet. Chill 30 minutes or until firm.

To dip candies: Place water in the bottom of a double boiler. Bring water to hard boil. Remove from heat. Place half of dipping chocolate in top of double boiler; set over hot water until chocolate begins to melt. Add remaining chocolate, 1/2 at a time, stirring constantly after each addition, until smooth. Refill bottom of double boiler with cool water. Stir until chocolate reaches 96°. Dip candies, one at a time, into the melted chocolate. Turn to coat. Remove. Let excess chocolate drip off. Place on wax paper. Let candies stand until chocolate is set. Store in cool, dry place.

HOT FUDGE SAUCE - EZ

1/2 c. evaporated milk
1/2 c. sugar
Dash of salt
1 c. semi-sweet chocolate
  chips

In small saucepan, combine evaporated milk, sugar and salt. Bring *just* to a boil; remove from heat. Add chocolate morsels and stir until morsels melt and mixture is smooth. Serve warm over ice cream or cake. Makes 1 1/4 cups.

"Idea:" Substitute butterscotch morsels for the chocolate for a great butterscotch sauce.

GERMAN CHOCOLATE CHEESECAKE SQUARES

This is probably my favorite of any desserts.

1 pkg. dry yeast
1/2 c. warm water (110°)
2 to 2 1/2 c. flour
1/4 c. sugar
1/2 tsp. salt
1 egg
1/2 c. margarine, softened
2 (8 oz.) pkg. plus 1 (3 oz.)
  pkg. cream cheese,
  softened
1 c. sugar
1/3 c. cocoa
3 eggs
2 tsp. vanilla

Coconut-Pecan Topping:
1/2 c. sugar
1 egg
1/2 c. evaporated milk
1/4 c. margarine or butter
2/3 c. flaked coconut
1/2 c. chopped pecans
1 tsp. vanilla

Dissolve yeast in warm water in large bowl. Stir in 1 cup flour, 1/4 cup sugar, salt, 1 egg, and margarine vigorously until smooth. Add enough flour to make dough easy to handle. Turn onto lightly floured surface. Knead until smooth and elastic, 3 to 5 minutes. Cover; let rest 20 minutes. Heat oven to 350°. Grease jelly roll pan (15 1/2x10 1/2 inches). Press dough in bottom and up sides of pan.

Beat cream cheese in large bowl on medium speed. Gradually add 1 cup sugar and the cocoa until fluffy. Beat in 3 eggs, one at a time. Add vanilla, scraping bowl occasionally. Pour into crust. Bake until crust is golden brown and center is set, about 25 minutes; cool. Spread with Coconut-Pecan Topping. Refrigerate at least 1 hour. Cut into about 2 inch squares. Refrigerate any remaining squares. Makes 3 dozen.

Coconut-Pecan Topping: Heat sugar, egg, milk and margarine in 1 quart saucepan over medium low heat, stirring constantly, until thick, about 12 minutes. Remove from heat; stir in remaining ingredients. Spread over cake.

CHOCOLATE CHEESECAKE SQUARES

1/2 c. butter or margarine
1 1/2 c. chocolate wafer
  crumbs
3/4 c. finely chopped nuts,
  divided
6 oz. cream cheese,
  softened
1/2 c. sugar
1/3 c. cocoa
1 egg
1 tsp. vanilla

Melt butter in 9 inch square baking pan in oven during preheating to 350°. Stir in crumbs and 1/2 cup nuts until well blended. Pat evenly to cover bottom. In small bowl, beat cream cheese, sugar, cocoa, egg, and vanilla until smooth and well blended. Pour over crust. Sprinkle with remaining 1/4 cup nuts. Bake 20 minutes. Cool in pan on rack . Cut into 1 1/2 inch squares. Keep chilled. Makes 36.

HOT FUDGE PUDDING (MUD PUDDING) - EZ

Mom found this recipe one day when company was coming and she didn't have any eggs. It became a family favorite.

1 c. flour
2 tsp. baking powder
1/4 tsp. salt
3/4 c. sugar
2 Tbsp. cocoa
1/2 c. milk
2 Tbsp. butter or
    margarine, melted
1 c. chopped nuts
1 c. brown sugar
1/4 c. cocoa
1 3/4 c. hot water

Heat oven to 350°. Combine flour, baking powder, salt, sugar, and the 2 tablespoons cocoa in a bowl. Stir in milk and margarine; blend in nuts. Spread in ungreased 9 inch square baking pan. Mix together the brown sugar and 1/4 cup cocoa and sprinkle over mixture. Pour hot water over all. Bake 45 minutes.

The cake rises to the top while baking and sauce will be on the bottom. Serve warm with ice cream or whipped cream if desired.

INDIVIDUAL CHOCOLATE SOUFFLES

Great idea for a Christmas dinner!

1/4 c. sugar plus 1/2 c.
    sugar
1 1/4 c. milk
3 sq. unsweetened
    chocolate
5 eggs, separated (room
    temperature)
1/4 c. flour
1/4 tsp. salt
2 tsp. vanilla
1/2 c. whipping cream,
    whipped
1/2 c. chocolate syrup (if
    desired)

Butter six 10 ounce souffle dishes, then lightly sprinkle them with sugar. In large saucepan, combine flour and 1/4 cup sugar; gradually add milk, stirring constantly, until mixture is smooth. Cook mixture over medium heat, stirring constantly, until mixture is thickened. Remove from heat. Stir in chocolate until melted. Rapidly beat in egg yolks all at once until well mixed. Set aside and cool to lukewarm.

Preheat oven to 375°. In large bowl, beat egg whites, salt and vanilla at high speed and gradually add 1/2 cup sugar, 2 tablespoons at a time. Whites should stand in stiff peaks. With rubber spatula, gently fold chocolate mixture into beaten egg whites until blended; spoon into the prepared souffle dishes. Place filled cups in jelly roll pan for easier handling. Bake 30 to 35 minutes, until puffy and brown. Serve immediately. Pass whipped cream and syrup to pour over each.

CHOCOLATE MOUSSE

6 (1 oz.) sq. semi-sweet
  chocolate
2 Tbsp. water
2 Tbsp. butter or
  margarine
5 egg yolks
5 egg whites (room
  temperature)
2 to 3 Tbsp. rum
1 tsp. vanilla

Melt chocolate, butter and water together in large saucepan over low heat, only until barely melted. Remove from heat and beat in egg yolks, one at a time, until thoroughly mixed. In a separate bowl, beat egg whites until stiff. Fold into chocolate mixture. Stir in rum and vanilla. Divide into parfait glasses or brandy snifters and chill at least 2 hours before serving. Top with whipped cream before serving. Serves 6.

ALMOND ROCA

1 3/4 c. sugar
1/2 c. water
2 Tbsp. corn syrup
1 lb. butter
1 lb. blanched split
  almonds (2 c.)
1 (12 oz.) pkg. semi-sweet
  chocolate chips
Extra chopped nuts for
  topping

Combine sugar, water, corn syrup, butter, and almonds in large skillet and cook to hard crack stage or until almonds are golden brown, stirring constantly (at least 35 to 40 minutes). Pour onto a large cookie sheet. Melt chocolate chips and spread on candy. Sprinkle with crushed almonds or other nuts. When cool, break into pieces. *This freezes very well.*

MACADAMIA BRITTLE - EZ

1 c. unsalted (if possible)
  macadamia nuts,
  coarsely chopped
1/2 c. butter (room
  temperature
1/2 c. sugar
1 Tbsp. light corn syrup
3/4 c. semi-sweet
  chocolate chips

Line bottom and sides of 8 inch square cake pan with foil. Butter foil generously. Cook nuts, butter, sugar, and corn syrup in heavy large skillet over low heat, stirring until butter melts and sugar dissolves. Increase heat and boil until mixture turns golden brown and begins to mass together, stirring constantly, about 5 minutes. Pour into prepared pan, spreading evenly. Sprinkle with chocolate chips; let melt. Spread evenly over top. Cool 15 minutes. Remove candy from pan. Peal off foil. Cool completely. Break into pieces and store, airtight, at a cool room temperature. Makes 1 pound or 36 pieces. (Also works well with cashew nuts.)

"Idea:" There's no reason any other kind of nuts couldn't be used or other flavor chips. How abour pistachios and white chocolate?

CHOCOLATE MARSHMALLOW TREATS

The traditional Rice Krispie Marshmallow Treat with a twist.

1/4 c. margarine or butter
1 (10 oz.) pkg. regular
marshmallows or 4 c.
miniature
marshmallows
6 c. crispy rice cereal
2 c. milk chocolate chips
optional)
Maraschino cherries,
drained and chopped
(optional)
2 Tbsp. shortening
(optional)

Melt margarine in large saucepan over low heat. Add marshmallows and stir until completely melted. Remove from heat. Add cereal and cherries stir until well coated. Using buttered spatula or waxed paper, press mixture evenly into buttered 15 1/2 x 10 1/2 x 1 inch pan. Set aside to cool. If you wish to omit chocolate, you are finished. *Enjoy!*

For chocolate filling, combine milk chocolate chips with shortening in small saucepan or in top section of double boiler. Stir over very low heat, or over hot (not boiling) water, until chips melt and mixture is smooth. Remove from heat. Cut cooled cereal mixture in half crosswise, reserving about 1/3 cup of the melted chocolate mixture. Spread remaining over one half. Top with other half, gently pressing halves together. Drizzle reserved chocolate mixture over top. Chill just until chocolate is firm. Cut into 2 1/2 inch squares. Store, tightly covered, at room temperature in cool, dry place. Makes 35 squares.

ALMOND BARK KRISPIES - EZ

1 lb. almond bark
1/2 c. peanut butter
2 c. crispy rice cereal
2 c. miniature
marshmallows
2 c. dry roasted salted
peanuts

Melt almond bark and peanut butter in top part of a double boiler. Add rest of ingredients. Mix well. Drop by teaspoonfuls on waxed paper. Let cool.

POPCORN BALLS - EZ

Great for making popcorn "snowmen" for Christmas parties!

2 gal. popped corn
1 (10 oz.) bag
  marshmallows
1/2 c. butter or margarine
1 tsp. vanilla
Extra butter for hands
Food coloring (if desired)
Peanuts (if desired)

Melt butter in large heavy saucepan. Add marshmallows and melt until smooth. Remove from heat and stir in vanilla. Pour over popped corn and stir until well mixed. Butter hands and form into balls. Place on waxed paper. If using food coloring and peanuts, add to marshmallow mixture after removing from heat.

CARAMEL CORN

5 qt. popped popcorn
2 c. packed brown sugar
1 3/4 c. margarine or
  butter
1/2 c. white corn syrup
1 tsp. vanilla
1 tsp. salt
1/4 tsp. baking soda
1 c. peanuts or other nuts
  (optional)

Remove as many of the "old maids" from the popcorn as possible. In medium size saucepan, melt the brown sugar, margarine and corn syrup. Bring to a low boil and boil for 5 minutes, stirring constantly. Remove from heat and stir in vanilla, salt and baking soda. Mix well. Add nuts and pour over corn, tossing well. Spread mixture on well buttered or greased cookie sheets. Place in a 250° oven and bake for 40 minutes. Toss every 10 minutes. Remove from oven and spread out on wax paper. When cool break up the larger pieces. Allow about 2 hours to dry, then store in airtight container.

DATE NUT CRISPS

1 tsp. vanillla
1/2 c. chopped nuts
2 1/2 c. crispy rice cereal
1/4 lb. butter
1 c. sugar
2 eggs, lightly beaten
8 oz. pitted, chopped dates
Shredded coconut or
   chopped nuts to roll
   candy in

Melt butter in skillet over low heat. Add sugar, eggs and dates. Cook over medium heat, stirring constantly, until smooth and fairly thick, about 10 minutes. Remove from heat; add vanilla, chopped nuts and cereal. Mix thoroughly. Remove by teaspoonfuls and roll each in either shredded coconut or chopped nuts. Put them on waxed paper. Refrigerate to set quickly.

CHOCOLATE TORTE WITH RASPBERRY SAUCE

An easy, very impressive dessert; great for Christmas dinner. The raspberry sauce can be used for other things, such as ice cream topping or on cakes, etc.

6 oz. semi-sweet
   chocolate chips
1 c. unsalted butter,
   softened
1 c. sugar
8 large egg yolks
8 large egg whites (room
   temperature)
Sweetened whipped cream

Raspberry Sauce:
2 (10 oz.) pkg. frozen
   raspberries in syrup,
   thawed
1/4 c. sugar
2 to 3 Tbsp. Grand Marnier
   or Triple Sec

In top of double boiler over boiling water, melt chocolate. In large bowl, combine melted chocolate, butter and sugar. Cool. Add egg yolks, 2 at a time, beating well after each addition. In separate bowl, beat egg whites until stiff. Gently fold egg whites into chocolate mixture. Pour 2/3 of the batter into buttered and floured 9 inch springform pan. Bake at 325° for 35 to 40 minutes or until wooden pick inserted in center comes out clean. Cool to room temperature (center will fall) and spread remaining batter on top. Refrigerate for at least 8 hours or overnight. Use a hot knife to cut into wedges. Serve with sweetened whipped cream and Raspberry Sauce.

Raspberry Sauce: Drain 1 package raspberries and discard juice. Retain juice from other package. Puree fruit, sugar and liqueur in food processor or blender; strain puree to remove seeds. Chill until ready to use.

CHOCOLATE PIXIES

A brownie textured cookie. Great for a Christmas plate, because of its "frosty" look.

1/4 c. butter or margarine
4 oz. unsweetened
  chocolate
2 c. flour
2 c. sugar
1/2 c. chopped walnuts
2 tsp. baking powder
1/2 tsp. salt
3 eggs
Powdered sugar

In large saucepan, melt margarine and chocolate over low heat, stirring constantly. Remove from heat; cool slightly. Lightly spoon flour into measuring cup; level off. Stir in remaining ingredients except powdered sugar; blend well. Chill dough 30 minutes.

Heat oven to 300°. Shape dough into 1 inch balls; roll in powdered sugar (coat heavily). Place 2 inches apart on ungreased cookie sheets. Bake 15 to 18 minutes or until edges are set. Remove from cookie sheets immediately. Makes about 3 dozen.

BLACK FOREST CAKE

This is the real thing, complete with kirsch liquor. A cake with a little bit of work involved, but well worth the work. *Impressive!*

1 1/2 c. frozen,
   unsweetened black
   cherries, thawed and
   drained (reserve liquid)
3 Tbsp. cornstarch
2/3 c. liquid (drained
   cherry juice plus water)
3 Tbsp. sugar
1 1/2 c. whipping cream
1 c. powdered sugar
2 tsp. vanilla

Cake: Follow directions for the cake in the Black Raspberry Cream Cheese Filled Chocolate Cake (page 136). Use two 10 inch round pans.

Stir sugar, cornstarch and liquid together in saucepan. Over medium heat, stir mixture constantly until thickened, about 5 minutes. Stir in cherries. Chill 30 to 45 minutes.

Meanwhile, prepare Chocolatey Cream Frosting (page 133). Cut each cake in half horizontally, so that you have 4 pieces. Place first cake, cut side up, on serving plate. Sprinkle about 2 tablespoons kirsch liquor or cherry brandy so that it soaks into the cake. Spread about 3/4 cup frosting and place second half of cake on top. Spread cherry filling over top. Add third layer and again sprinkle with another 2 tablespoons of kirsch and another 3/4 cup frosting over that. Add top layer and chill, covered, at least 30 minutes.

Top with whipped cream. Whip cream until stiff. Add powdered sugar and vanilla until well blended and whipped cream is stiff. Apply whipped cream over entire cake. Garnish with chocolate shavings and maraschino cherries, cut in halves and drained, or whole cherries, with stems, drained.

BLACK FOREST CHEESECAKE

A masterpiece for the Christmas holidays!

1 1/2 c. chocolate
   sandwich cookies,
   crushed
1/4 c. butter, melted
1 Tbsp. sugar
Dash of cinnamon
3 (8 oz.) pkg. cream
   cheese, softened
1 1/2 c. sugar
4 eggs (room
   temperature)
1/3 c. cherry flavored
   liquor
4 sq. semi-sweet
   chocolate
1 tsp. shortening
Whipped cream, flavored
   with a little cherry
   flavored liquor or
   maraschino cherry juice
Maraschino cherries with
   stems

Combine crushed cookies, butter, cinnamon, and 1 tablespoon sugar. Mix well and press into the bottom and about 1 inch up sides of a 9 inch springform pan. Beat cream cheese until light and fluffy; gradually add 1 1/2 cups sugar, mixing well. Add eggs, one at a time, beating well after each. Stir in liquor and mix until blended. Pour into prepared pan. Bake at 350° for 1 hour. Let cake cool in oven for 30 minutes. *Do not open oven door.* Cool to room temperature.

Place chocolate in double boiler. Bring water to boil. Reduce heat to low. Cook until chocolate melts. Cool slightly. Stir in shortening until it melts. Drizzle in crisscross pattern on top of cheesecake. Garnish with dollops of whipped cream with green and red cherries with stems on top.

NUTMEG COOKIE LOGS

A butter type cookie made to look like miniature logs for the Christmas season.

3/4 c. sugar
1 c. butter, softened
2 tsp. vanilla
2 tsp. rum extract
1 egg
3 c. flour
1 tsp. nutmeg

Frosting:
2 c. powdered sugar
3 Tbsp. butter or
   margarine, softened
2 Tbsp. half & half or milk
3/4 tsp. rum extract
1/4 tsp. vanilla

In large bowl, combine sugar, butter, vanilla, rum extract, and egg. Beat on medium speed until light and fluffy. Stir in flour and nutmeg; mix well. Chill dough 30 to 45 minutes. Heat oven to 350°. Divide dough into 6 pieces. On lightly floured surface, shape each piece of dough into long ropes, 1/2 inch in diameter. Cut into 3 inch lengths; place on ungreased cookie sheets. Bake for 12 to 15 minutes or until light golden brown. Cool.

Frosting: In small bowl, combine all ingredients; mix well. Spread on top and sides of cookies. If desired, mark frosting with tines of fork to resemble bark. Sprinkle lightly with nutmeg. Store in tightly covered container. Makes about 2 1/2 dozen.

CHERRY WINKS

Everyone's favorite! Great for Christmas or Valentine's Day.

1 c. sugar
3/4 c. butter flavored
  shortening
2 eggs
2 Tbsp. milk
1 tsp. vanilla
2 1/4 c. flour
1 tsp. baking powder
1/2 tsp. salt
1/2 tsp. baking soda
1 c. chopped pecans
1 c. chopped dates
1/2 c. chopped and
  drained maraschino
  cherries
2 1/2 c. crushed corn
  flakes
15 maraschino cherries,
  quartered

Preheat oven to 375°. In large bowl, combine sugar, shortening, eggs, milk, and vanilla; blend well. Stir in flour, baking powder, salt, baking soda, pecans, dates, and the 1/2 cup cherries; blend well. If desired, chill dough for easier handling. Drop by rounded teaspoonfuls into crushed cereal; coat thoroughly. Form into 1 inch balls; place 2 inches apart on greased cookie sheets. Top each with 1/4 of a maraschino cherry. Bake 10 to 15 minutes or until light golden brown. Makes 4 to 5 dozen.

CHRISTMAS ROCK COOKIES

1 c. butter, softened
1 1/2 c. brown sugar
3 eggs
2 1/2 c. flour
1/2 c. flour (for fruit)
1/2 tsp. salt
1 tsp. vanilla
1 tsp. baking soda
1 tsp. cinnamon
1 lb. dates, diced
1/2 lb. glazed cherries
4 rings candied pineapple,
  diced
2 c. walnuts
1 c. almonds
1 c. Brazil nuts
1 c. pecans

In small bowl, combine the 1/2 cup of flour with the candied fruit, tossing well, so that the fruit is well coated. In large mixing bowl, cream together the butter, brown sugar and eggs until light and fluffy. Stir in 2 1/2 cups flour, baking soda, salt, cinnamon, and vanilla until well mixed. Stir in fruit mixture and nuts (all nuts are whole). Spoon out in rounded teaspoonfuls onto lightly greased cookie sheets. Bake in a 350° oven for 12 to 15 minutes. Let cool on cookie sheets about 5 minutes before removing to wire racks to finish cooling. Store in an airtight container.

CRUNCHY BANANA BREAD

An excellent fruit bread. It is a combination of banana bread and a light fruit cake. Great to give as a gift!

1 1/4 c. flour
3/4 c. whole wheat flour
1/3 c. wheat germ
1 Tbsp. baking powder
1 tsp. salt
1/2 tsp. nutmeg
2 eggs
1 1/2 c. sugar
1 c. mayonnaise
1/2 c. milk
3 very ripe bananas, mashed
1 1/4 c. flaked coconut, divided
1 c. dried pineapple and papaya pieces, diced small

Grease two 8x4 inch loaf pans. Heat oven to 325°. Combine flours, wheat germ, baking powder, salt, and nutmeg. In large mixer bowl with electric mixer on medium, beat eggs with sugar until light and thick. Beat in mayonnaise. Alternately beat milk and bananas with flour mixture into egg mixture just until moistened. Fold in 3/4 cup of the coconut and fruit bits. Pour into loaf pans. Sprinkle each with 1/4 cup of remaining coconut.. Bake 1 1/4 hours or until cake tester inserted in center comes out clean. Cool in pan 10 minutes. Remove from pan to wire rack and cool completely.

Tip: Dust dried fruit in flour before folding into batter. It keeps them from sinking.

ALICE'S CRANBERRY SALAD

This recipe was from a dear friend of Mom's, Alice Martin. Even people who don't care for cranberries love this. Great with turkey or chicken, especially for Thanksgiving or Christmas.

1 lb. raw cranberries
1 whole orange (seedless)
1 1/3 c. sugar
1 small can crushed pineapple, drained
2 c. boiling water
2 (3 oz.) pkg. jello (lemon, raspberry or orange)
3 peeled and diced sweet apples
1/2 c. chopped nuts

Grind the cranberries and orange, skin included, together. Add sugar and pineapple. Stir and set aside. Dissolve jello in water and partially chill just until mixture starts to thicken. Add fruit mixture to jello and then add the apples and nuts. Mix well and place in 9x13 inch pan. Refrigerate for at least 3 hours.

TANGERINE SNOWBALLS - EZ

**1 (10 oz.) pkg. shortbread
cookies, crushed
1 c. flaked coconut
2/3 c. sifted powdered
sugar (for cookies)
1/2 c. thawed frozen
concentrate (tangerine
or orange juice)
Sifted powdered sugar (to
coat cookies)**

Mix cookie crumbs, coconut and the 2/3 cup powdered sugar in a medium size bowl. Stir in tangerine juice until well blended. Roll mixture, a teaspoonful at a time, into balls between palms of hands. Roll each in powdered sugar in a pie plate to coat generously.

MYSTY'S TREATS (DOG BISCUITS)

Yes, even a gift for the dogs!

**1 c. rolled oats
1/3 c. margarine
1 c. boiling water
3/4 c. corn meal
1 Tbsp. sugar
1 to 2 tsp. chicken or beef
flavored instant bouillon
1/2 c. milk
4 oz. (1 c.) shredded
Cheddar cheese
1 egg, beaten
2 to 3 c. whole wheat flour**

Heat oven to 325°. Grease cookie sheet. In large bowl, combine rolled oats, margarine and boiling water; let stand 10 minutes. Stir in corn meal, sugar, bouillon, milk, cheese, and egg; mix well. Lightly spoon flour into measuring cup; level off. Add flour, one cup at a time, mixing well after each addition to form a stiff dough. On floured surface, knead in remaining flour until dough is smooth and no longer sticky, 3 to 4 minutes. Roll or pat out dough to 1/2 inch thickness; cut with bone shaped cookie cutter. Place 1 inch apart on prepared cookie sheets. Bake at 325° for 35 to 45 minutes or until golden brown. Cool completely. Makes 3 1/2 dozen large dog biscuits or 8 dozen small dog biscuits.

Fresh Fruits

**DANISH APPLE BARS

These are a great substitute for apple strudel. Much easier, tastes great and looks professional.

2 1/2 c. flour
1/2 tsp. baking powder
1 Tbsp. sugar
1 c. butter or margarine
1 egg yolk plus milk to
   equal 2/3 c. (reserve egg
   white)
1/2 tsp. vanilla
1 c. crushed corn flakes
5 to 6 medium size apples,
   peeled and freshly sliced
1 c. sugar
1 tsp. cinnamon
2 egg whites

Icing:
2 Tbsp. butter or
   margarine, softened
2 c. powdered sugar
1 tsp. vanilla or almond
   extract
5 to 7 Tbsp. milk

Mix flour, baking powder and 1 tablespoon sugar together in a bowl. Cut in butter or margarine with a pastry cutter or large fork until mixture is crumbly. Stir in egg yolk plus milk and vanilla until you have a dough ball. Divide dough in half. Reserve half and roll out half to fit 12x15 inch jelly roll pan. Place in pan. Sprinkle corn flakes over dough. Layer apples over top of corn flakes. Stir cinnamon into 1 cup sugar and sprinkle over all. Roll out remaining dough and put on top. Moisten edges and press to seal. Make vents in top crust as for a pie. Beat egg whites slightly and brush on top. Bake at 400° for 10 minutes; reduce heat to 350°. Bake 30 to 40 minutes longer. While hot, drizzle with icing. Cool slightly and cut into bars.

APPLE SLICE CAKE WITH CREAM CHEESE ICING

3 eggs
1 c. vegetable oil
2 c. sugar
2 c. flour
1 tsp. baking soda
2 tsp. cinnamon
1/4 tsp. salt
1 tsp. vanilla
4 c. yellow apples, peeled
    and sliced
1/2 c. chopped nuts

Frosting:
1 (8 oz.) pkg. cream
    cheese, softened
3 Tbsp. melted butter or
    margarine
1 tsp. vanilla
1 1/4 c. powdered sugar

Beat eggs and oil in a large mixing bowl until foamy. Stir in sugar, flour, baking soda, cinnamon, salt, and vanilla. Add apples and nuts; mix well. Pour batter into a greased and floured 9x13 inch cake pan. Bake at 350° for 1 hour or until tested done. Cool completely and frost.

Frosting: Cream melted butter, vanilla and cream cheese. Add powdered sugar; mix well. Spread evenly over cake.

APPLE RAISIN CAKE

3 c. flour
2 c. sugar
1 c. mayonnaise
1/3 c. milk
2 eggs
2 tsp. baking soda
1 1/2 tsp. cinnamon
1/2 tsp. nutmeg
1/2 tsp. salt
1/4 tsp. cloves
3 c. peeled and diced
    apples
1 c. raisins
1/2 c. walnuts, chopped

Rum Cream Cheese
    Frosting:
1 oz. cream cheese,
    softened
2 Tbsp. butter, softened
1 tsp. rum flavoring
2 1/2 to 3 c. powdered
    sugar

Beat all ingredients except apples, nuts and raisins together until well mixed. Stir in remainder. Preheat oven to 350°. Grease and flour two 8 inch round pans or one 9x13 inch cake pan. Pour batter into pan and bake 35 to 40 minutes (45 to 50 minutes for sheet pan), until tested done. If baking in round pans, let cakes set for 10 minutes before removing from pans. Finish cooling on wire racks.

Rum Cream Cheese Frosting: Blend all ingredients until smooth.

This is also a great frosting for a fresh banana cake.

"Idea:" Using this basic cream cheese recipe for different cakes, vary it by using the new fruit juice concentrates, such as pineapple, banana, guava.

CHOCOLATE APPLE SPICE CAKE

1/4 c. butter, softened
1 1/2 c. sugar
2 eggs
2 1/2 c. flour
1/4 tsp. cinnamon
1/2 tsp. nutmeg
1/4 tsp. cloves
1 tsp. vanilla
4 tsp. cocoa in hot water
  to make 1 1/2 c.
1 tsp. soda in hot water to
  make 1/2 c.
3 c. peeled and chopped
  apples
1/2 c. nuts, chopped
Powdered sugar or
  whipped cream (for
  topping)

Grease 13x9 inch cake pan. Preheat oven to 375°. In bowl, combine flour, cinnamon, nutmeg, and cloves; set aside. In large bowl, cream butter, sugar and eggs. Alternately add cocoa and soda mixtures with spiced flour mixture into creamed mixture. Add chopped apples and nuts. Pour batter into greased pan and bake in a 375° oven until inserted toothpick comes out clean, about 30 minutes. Cool completely and dust with powdered sugar.

APPLE CAKE WITH HOT CARAMEL SAUCE

1/4 c. butter, softened
1 c. sugar
1 egg
1 c. flour
1/2 c. chopped walnuts
1 tsp. cinnamon
1 tsp. nutmeg
1 tsp. baking soda
1/4 tsp. salt
3 medium apples, peeled
  and grated

Hot Caramel Sauce:
1/4 c. butter
1/2 c. brown sugar
1/2 c. sugar
1/2 c. whipping cream
1 tsp. vanilla
Pinch of salt

Cream butter and sugar until smooth. Beat in egg. Add flour, cinnamon, nutmeg, walnuts, baking soda, and salt; mix well. Stir in apples. Spoon into lightly greased 8 inch square pan. Bake in a 350° oven for 35 to 40 minutes. Cool completely. Cut into squares and serve with Hot Caramel Sauce.

Hot Caramel Sauce: In a small saucepan, over medium heat, melt butter. Add remaining ingredients and bring to a light boil, stirring constantly. Stir until thickened. Serve warm over cake.

APPLE COBBLER CAKE - EZ

6 medium size tart apples,
   pared, quartered and
   sliced
2 Tbsp. sugar
1 tsp. cinnamon
1 pkg. yellow cake mix
1/2 c. butter or
   margarine, melted
Light or table cream
1/2 c. chopped walnuts

Combine apples, sugar and cinnamon in a large bowl. Sprinkle 1/4 cup of the dry cake mix over top; toss until apple are evenly coated. Spoon into a buttered baking pan (9x13 inches). Cover and bake in a 350° oven for30 minutes; remove from oven.

Mix remaining cake mix and walnuts in a medium size bowl; drizzle melted butter over top. Toss until mixture forms large crumbs. Sprinkle evenly over partly cooked apple mixture. Bake 20 minutes longer, or until topping is puffed and golden. Cool slightly. Serve warm with cream. Serves 8.

CARROT-APPLESAUCE CAKE - HEALTHY

2 c. whole wheat flour
1 Tbsp. baking soda
2 tsp. cinnamon
1 tsp. ground cloves
1 tsp. ground nutmeg
1 (15 oz.) jar unsweetened
   applesauce
3 c. carrots, coarsely
   shredded (1 lb.)
1/2 c. bran
4 eggs
1/3 c. oil
1 1/2 tsp. vanilla

Sift the flour, baking soda and dry spices into a large bowl. Stir in the 1/2 cup of bran. Beat the eggs lightly in a medium bowl. Add all the remaining ingredients to the eggs and stir. Pour all this into the flour mixture and stir just to moisten thoroughly. Pour the batter into a lightly oiled 9 inch tube pan and bake at 350° for about 60 to 65 minutes. Cool the cake in pan for about 10 to 15 minutes, then turn it onto a rack to cool completely. Dust with powdered sugar, if desired, and wrap tightly to store. Refrigerate if keeping more than 3 days.

WHOLE WHEAT APPLESAUCE COFFEE CAKE - HEALTHY

1/3 c. butter or
  margarine, melted
1 1/2 c. applesauce
1 egg
3/4 c. brown sugar, firmly
  packed
1 1/2 c. whole wheat flour
3/4 tsp. baking soda
1 1/2 tsp. cinnamon
1/2 tsp. allspice
1/2 tsp. salt
1/2 c. raisins

Topping:
1/4 c. firmly packed brown
  sugar
2 Tbsp. whole wheat flour
1/8 tsp. cinnamon
1/8 tsp. nutmeg
1 Tbsp. margarine or
  butter, softened
1/4 c. chopped nuts

Melt butter or margarine in saucepan. Remove from heat. Add applesauce, egg and brown sugar; mix well. Sift or stir whole wheat flour, baking soda, spices, and salt together in a large bowl. Add liquid mixture. Mix well. Stir in raisins. Pour into 9 inch square cake pan that has been greased on the bottom. Sprinkle topping over batter. Bake in oven, preheated to 375°, for 45 minutes or until top springs back when touched lightly in center.

Topping: Combine all ingredients. Follow preceding directions.

APPLE NUT BREAD

This bread is great and freezes well. Ideal for gifts.

1 c. vegetable oil
2 c. sugar
4 eggs
3 c. flour
1 tsp. cinnamon
1/2 tsp. salt
1 tsp. baking soda
1 tsp. vanilla
3 c. Delicious apples,
  peeled and diced
1 c. pecan pieces

Beat together oil, sugar and eggs in large mixing bowl. In separate bowl, mix flour, cinnamon, salt, and baking soda. Add to sugar mixture and beat well. Stir in vanilla, apples and pecans. Pour mixture into 2 greased and floured 9x5x3 inch loaf pans. Bake at 325° for 1 1/2 hours or until tested done with toothpick.

APPLE OATMEAL MUFFINS - HEALTHY

1 1/3 c. flour
1 c. quick oats
1/3 c. brown sugar
1 Tbsp. baking powder
1 tsp. cinnamon
1/2 tsp. nutmeg
Dash of salt
2/3 c. skim milk
1/3 c. apple juice
1/4 c. vegetable oil
1 egg, beaten
1 medium apple, peeled
  and diced

Heat oven to 400°. Grease, spray with vegetable spray or use 12 paper baking cups. Combine dry ingredients. Add everything else, except the apples, and mix just until moistened. Gently fold in apples. Fill prepared muffin cups 2/3 full. Bake 20 to 22 minutes, until lightly browned.

EDNA'S APPLE MUFFINS

Given to Mom by a neighbor; has always been a family favorite from the time we were kids. My brother loves these!

2 1/4 c. flour
3 1/2 tsp. baking powder
1/4 tsp. cinnamon
1/2 tsp. nutmeg
4 Tbsp. vegetable oil
1/2 c. sugar
2 eggs
1 c. milk
1 c. chopped apples

Topping:
2 Tbsp. sugar
1/4 tsp. nutmeg
1/4 tsp. cinnamon

Preheat oven to 400°. Grease, spray with vegetable spray or use 18 paper baking cups. Mix together all dry ingredients, including sugar, in a large bowl. Add eggs, salad oil and milk. Beat at low speed just until moistened. Fold in apples and spoon into tins. Sprinkle topping on muffins and bake for about 20 minutes, until lightly browned.

Topping: Stir together sugar, nutmeg and cinnamon.

APPLESAUCE OATMEAL MUFFINS - HEALTHY

1 1/2 c. oats (quick or
  regular)
1 1/4 c. flour
3/4 tsp. cinnamon
1 tsp. baking powder
3/4 tsp. baking soda
1 c. unsweetened
  applesauce
1/2 c. skim milk
1/2 c. packed brown sugar
3 Tbsp. vegetable oil
1 egg white

Topping:
1/4 c. oats (quick or
  regular)
1 Tbsp. brown sugar,
  packed
1/8 tsp. cinnamon
1 Tbsp. margarine, melted

Heat oven to 400°. Line 12 medium size muffin cups with paper baking cups, or grease and flour muffin tin. Combine oats, flour, cinnamon, baking powder, and baking soda. Add applesauce, milk, brown sugar, oil, and egg white; mix just until dry ingredients are moistened. Fill muffin cups almost full. Combine remaining ingredients; sprinkle evenly over batter. Bake 20 to 22 minutes or until deep golden brown. Serve warm.

APPLESAUCE NUGGET COOKIES

2 c. flour
1/2 tsp. cinnamon
1/2 tsp. nutmeg
1/2 tsp. allspice
1/4 tsp. cloves
1/2 c. margarine,
  softened
1 c. brown sugar, packed
1 c. applesauce
1 tsp. baking soda
1 egg, well beaten
1 (6 oz.) pkg. butterscotch
  chips
1 c. chopped walnuts

Cream together the margarine and brown sugar until light and fluffy. Add egg and applesauce and beat until well mixed. Stir in all dry ingredients except butterscotch chips and walnuts. Blend in well. Fold in butterscotch chips and nuts.

Preheat oven to 350°. Scoop dough out by teaspoonfuls onto lightly greased cookie sheets. Bake 10 to 12 minutes, until lightly browned around edges. Let cool on cookie sheets 5 minutes before removing to wire racks to finish cooling. Frost with a burnt sugar frosting or buttercream frosting if desired.

CANDY APPLE CREPES

6 medium size tart apples,
  peeled and sliced
1/2 c. sugar
1/2 tsp. cinnamon
1/2 tsp. mace
2 Tbsp. butter
1 tsp. lemon juice
Crepes (pg. 128)
1 c. whipping cream
2 Tbsp. powdered sugar
1 tsp. vanilla

Caramel Pecan Topping:
4 Tbsp. butter or
  margarine
1/2 c. brown sugar
2 Tbsp. light cream
1/2 c. chopped pecans

Place first 6 ingredients in large, heavy saucepan and cook over low heat just until apples start to soften (about 20 minutes). *Don't let them get mushy.* Warm up crepes and place 2 tablespoons filling in each. Fold over. Top with Caramel Pecan Topping. Whip cream until stiff; add powdered sugar and vanilla. Place whipped cream on top of crepe.

Caramel Pecan Topping: Stir butter and brown sugar together in small saucepan and place over medium heat until butter is melted and sugar is dissolved. Add cream and stir constantly, just until mixture comes to a boil. Remove from heat and stir in pecans.

CANDY APPLE PIE

This is my brother's favorite! I have to make him one on his birthday every year.

Pastry for double pie crust
6 c. thinly sliced, pared
  tart apples
3/4 c. sugar
4 Tbsp. flour
1/2 tsp. ground mace
1/4 tsp. salt
6 Tbsp. butter or
  margarine
2 Tbsp. lemon juice
1/2 c. brown sugar
2 Tbsp. cream
1/2 c. chopped pecans

Roll out half of the pastry and line a 9 inch pie plate. Trim overhang to 1/2 inch. Combine sliced apples with sugar, flour, mace, and salt in a large bowl; toss lightly to mix. Spoon into prepared pastry shell. Dot with 2 tablespoons of the butter and sprinkle with lemon juice. (Set remaining butter aside for topping.)

Roll out remaining pastry and cover top of pie. Trim overhang to 1/2 inch; turn edges under, flush with rim. Flute to make a stand-up edge. Cut several slits in center to let steam escape. Bake in a 400° oven for 50 minutes, or until pastry is golden and juices bubble up. Remove from oven.

Melt remaining 4 tablespoons butter in a small saucepan; stir in brown sugar and cream. Heat slowly to boiling; remove from heat. Stir in pecans. Spread over top of pie; return to oven. Bake 5 minutes longer, until topping bubbles and crust is richly glazed. Cool on a wire rack at least an hour before cutting.

BLUE RIBBON APPLE PIE

This is my Dad's favorite pie and has won Mom several blue ribbons at the county fair.

Pastry for 2 crust pie
6 c. apples, peeled and sliced (mixture of Golden Delicious and Jonathan recommended)
3/4 c. sugar
1 Tbsp. flour
3 Tbsp. margarine or butter
1/4 tsp. mace
1/4 tsp. nutmeg
1/2 tsp. cinnamon
1 tsp. lemon juice
Dash of salt

Orange Glaze:
1 c. powdered sugar
1 tsp. grated orange peel
3 Tbsp. fresh orange juice

Toss apples with flour, lemon juice and spices. Turn into pastry lined 9 inch pie plate. Dot with butter. Cover with top crust; seal and flute edge. Cut slits for steam to escape. Bake at 425° for about 40 minutes. It is recommended to put a narrow piece of foil around edge of pie to prevent crust from burning. Remove as soon as pie is baked. Top pie with Orange Glaze while warm.

Orange Glaze: Mix together all ingredients and spread over pie.

SUGARLESS APPLE PIE - HEALTHY

6 medium Red or Golden Delicious apples, peeled and sliced (or more)
1 (6 oz.) can frozen sugarless apple juice, thawed
1 1/2 Tbsp. cornstarch
1 tsp. cinnamon
3 Tbsp. margarine
Whole wheat crust (see Never Fail Pie Crust recipe, pg. 119)

Place apples and undiluted apple juice in large pan. Bring to boil. Reduce heat and simmer, covered, about 5 minutes. Dissolve cornstarch in small amount of water. Gently stir into apples; bring to boil. Reduce heat and simmer, covered, 10 to 15 minutes or until apples begin to soften and mixture is thickened. Gently stir in cinnamon.

Fill pastry shell with apples. Use a 10 inch pie plate. Dot margarine over top. Cover with top crust and seal edges. Cut slits in top crust to allow steam to escape. Bake in preheated 350° oven about 45 minutes, or until crust is golden brown and filling is bubbly.

APPLE-MAPLE COTTAGE PUDDING - HEALTHY

An excellent lighter dessert; quite different.

**6 c. (about 2 lb.) peeled,
  cored and cubed apples
3/4 c. maple syrup
4 1/2 tsp. cornstarch
1 Tbsp. water
1/4 c. softened butter
3/4 c. sugar
1 egg
1 1/2 c. flour
1 Tbsp. baking powder
1 tsp. cinnamon
3/4 c. evaporated milk
Vanilla ice cream**

Combine apples and syrup in large, heavy saucepan. Cook, covered, over moderate heat until apples are tender. Combine cornstarch and water; add to apple mixture. Cook over moderately high heat, stirring constantly, until mixture is clear and comes to a boil. Pour into a greased, shallow 2 quart baking dish.

Cream together butter and sugar; add egg. Beat until light and fluffy. Combine flour, baking powder and cinnamon. Add dry ingredients to creamed mixture alternately with evaporated milk. Spread batter evenly over apple mixture. Bake in preheated 350° oven about 40 minutes, or until golden brown all over top and bubbly around edges. Cut in squares and serve warm, upside-down with vanilla ice cream on top. Serves 9 to 10.

CARAMEL-APPLE CHARLOTTE

**2 env. unflavored gelatin
10 Tbsp. brown sugar
3 eggs, separated
3 c. milk
2 apples, peeled and
  chopped
2 Tbsp. butter
1 1/2 tsp. vanilla
1 1/2 c. whipping or heavy
  cream, whipped
1/2 c. chopped pecans**

In medium saucepan, mix gelatin with 8 tablespoons brown sugar. Blend in egg yolks, beaten with milk. Let stand 1 minute. Stir over low heat until gelatin is dissolved, about 5 minutes. Add apples, butter and vanilla. Continue cooking, stirring constantly, until apples are tender, about 5 minutes. Pour into large bowl and chill, stirring occasionally, until mixture mounds slightly when dropped from spoon.

Beat egg whites into soft peaks. Gradually add remaining sugar and beat until stiff. Fold egg whites, then whipped cream and pecans, into gelatin mixture. Turn into 9 inch springform pan and chill until firm. Serves 10 to 12.

APPLE BANANA SALAD

This has always been a special part of our family Thanksgiving dinner and one of my favorite salads. Here, once more, the ingredients are not exact, it just depends on your tastes.

1 large Red Delicious apple
1 medium to large banana
1/2 c. chopped walnuts
3/4 c. miniature
**   marshmallows**
1 c. whipped cream or
**   substitute**
1 tsp. mayonnaise

Peel and dice apple into bowl. Peel banana. Dice and add to apple. Add other ingredients and stir well. Serves 2 to 3.

"Idea:" Add maraschino cherries, drained pineapple, kiwi, or star fruit. Use your favorite yogurt instead of mayonnaise and whipped cream.

APPLE-RICE PUDDING WITH MERINGUE

4 c. cooked rice
3 c. peeled and chopped
**   apples**
1/2 c. raisins
1 Tbsp. grated lemon rind
4 eggs, separated
3 c. half & half
1 tsp. vanilla
3/4 tsp. salt
1 c. sugar, divided

Combine rice, apples, raisins, and lemon rind in 2 1/2 quart casserole dish. In a separate bowl, slightly beat egg yolks and add half & half, vanilla, salt, and 3/4 cup of the sugar; mix well. Pour over the rice mixture. Set casserole in large pan and fill halfway with very hot water. Bake in a 350° oven for 2 hours, or until a knife inserted in center comes out clean. Carefully remove casserole from pan in oven.

In small bowl, with mixer at high speed, beat egg whites until soft peaks form. Gradually sprinkle in the remaining 1/4 cup sugar, beating well after each addition. Spread egg whites over rice mixture, making sure whites touch the edge of the casserole dish. Pull up points of egg whites to make a decorative top. Place casserole in same pan of water; return to oven. Bake an additional 10 minutes or until top is golden. Serve warm or cold. Refrigerate leftovers. Serves 10.

BANANA NUT BREAD - EZ

1 1/2 c. sugar
3/4 c. butter, softened
3 eggs, well beaten
6 Tbsp. milk
3 extra ripe bananas,
  mashed
3/4 c. chopped nuts
3 c. flour
3/4 tsp. baking soda
1 1/2 tsp. baking powder
1 1/2 tsp. vanilla
Pinch of salt

Cream sugar and butter; add well beaten eggs. Add bananas and milk; mix well. Add flour, baking soda, baking powder, and salt. Stir in vanilla and nuts. Pour batter into 2 greased 9x5x3 inch loaf pans. Bake at 350° for 45 to 50 minutes, until tested done.

OAT BRAN BANANA BREAD - HEALTHY

2 ripe bananas
3/4 c. oat bran, soaked in
  3/4 c. apple juice for 10
  minutes
1 c. brown sugar
1 c. white flour
1 c. whole wheat flour
1 1/2 tsp. baking soda
4 egg whites
1 tsp. cinnamon
1/2 tsp. nutmeg
1/4 tsp. salt

Soak bran. Mash bananas with brown sugar; beat in egg whites. Mix in oat bran. Mix dry ingredients together; stir into banana mixture. Bake in greased loaf pan at 350° for 40 minutes.

WHOLE WHEAT CARROT-BANANA BREAD - HEALTHY

1/2 c. butter or
  margarine, softened
1 c. packed brown sugar
2 eggs
1 c. flour
1 c. whole wheat flour
1 tsp. baking soda
1/2 tsp. baking powder
1/2 tsp. ground
  cinnamon
1 c. ripe, mashed bananas
1 c. finely shredded
  carrots
1/2 c. chopped walnuts
1/2 tsp. salt

Cream butter for 30 seconds in a mixing bowl. Add sugar; beat until fluffy. Beat in eggs.

In a separate bowl, stir together flour, whole wheat flour, baking soda, baking powder, cinnamon, and 1/2 teaspoon salt. Add dry ingredients and banana alternately to beaten mixture, beating after each addition. Fold in carrots and nuts. Pour into 2 greased 7 1/2x3 3/4 x2 inch loaf pans (the smaller size). Bake in a 350° oven for 40 to 50 minutes. Makes 2 loaves.

OAT BRAN BANANA MUFFINS - HEALTHY

Contain 0 cholesterol, 150 calories per muffin.

1 1/4 c. oat bran cereal *
1 c. flour
2 1/2 tsp. baking powder
1/2 tsp. baking soda
1/2 tsp. cinnamon
2 egg whites, slightly
   beaten
3/4 c. skim milk
3/4 c. mashed bananas
1/2 c. brown sugar
1/4 c. vegetable oil
1/2 tsp. vanilla
1/2 c. chopped nuts

Preheat oven to 400°. In large bowl, mix oat bran, flour, baking powder, baking soda, and cinnamon. In another bowl, mix together the egg whites, skim milk, mashed bananas, brown sugar, oil, and vanilla. Add to dry ingredients, stirring only until moistened. Fold in nuts. Grease or spray 12 muffin cups with vegetable spray. Divide batter between cups, filling almost full. Bake 20 to 25 minutes, until browned.

*Use a fine grain oat bran cereal or grind up cereal in a food processor or blender.

BANANA MOCHA CAKE - EZ

2 extra-ripe large
   bananas, peeled
1 tsp. dry instant coffee
1 1/4 c. flour
2/3 c. sugar
1/4 c. cornstarch
3 Tbs. cocoa
1 tsp. baking soda
1/2 tsp. salt
1 egg, lightly beaten
1/3 c. vegetable oil
1 Tbsp. vinegar
1 tsp. vanilla

Silky Mocha Frosting:
3 Tbsp. butter, softened
1 1/2 c. sifted powdered
   sugar
2 Tbsp. cocoa
1 tsp. dry instant coffee
2 Tbsp. milk
1/2 tsp. vanilla

Smash or puree bananas until smooth. Stir coffee into pureed bananas. In a 9 inch square pan, combine flour, sugar, cornstarch, cocoa, baking soda, and salt. Blend well. Make a well in center of dry ingredients. Add banana mixture, egg, oil, vinegar, and vanilla. Stir in dry mixture with a fork until well blended. Bake 20 minutes in a 350° oven. Cool completely. Spread with frosting. Serves 12.

Silky Mocha Frosting: Combine butter, sugar, cocoa, and coffee until mixed. Add milk and vanilla; beat until smooth.

FRESH BANANA NUT CAKE

2 1/2 c. flour
1 2/3 c. sugar
1 1/4 tsp. baking powder
1 1/4 tsp. baking soda
1 tsp. salt
2/3 c. butter flavored
    shortening
2/3 c. buttermilk
1 1/4 c. mashed bananas
3 eggs
2/3 c. chopped nuts

Blend flour, sugar, baking powder, baking soda, and salt. Add shortening, half of buttermilk and mashed bananas. Beat 2 minutes on medium speed. Add eggs and remainder of buttermilk; beat 2 more minutes. Fold in nuts. Bake in greased 9x13 inch pan 40 minutes at 350°, until tested done. Cool.

Top with your favorite frosting. My favorite is Rum-Cream Cheese Frosting (pg. 160).

SPECIAL BANANA CREAM PIE

This is my very favorite pie!

Pastry for 1 (9inch) pie
    crust
2/3 c. sugar
2 Tbsp. cornstarch
2 c. milk
2 large egg yolks
1 Tbsp. butter
2 large bananas, sliced
1 c. heavy cream
1/2 tsp. vanilla
About 4 Tbsp. powdered
    sugar

Roll out pie crust to fill a 9 inch pie plate. Prick bottom and sides. Have high fluted edge. Bake at 450° until light brown, 5 to 10 minutes. Remove from oven and cool.

In 2 quart saucepan, stir sugar and cornstarch together. Gradually stir in milk, keeping smooth. With a wire whisk, beat in egg yolks until well blended. Cook over medium heat, stirring constantly, until mixture comes to a light boil. Boil for 1 minute, until mixture is thick like heavy cream. Remove from heat and stir in butter and vanilla until well blended. Put in bowl and cover with plastic wrap. Refrigerate until cool, about 1 hour.

Arrange sliced bananas in baked pie shell; pour filling over bananas. Cover pie plate with plastic wrap and refrigerate overnight (or at least 5 hours). At serving time, whip cream. Add powdered sugar and vanilla. Spread over top of pie.

COUPE WITH BANANAS FLAMBE

This is a very impressive ending to a very romantic dinner.

**2 medium size bananas
(firm and ripe)
2 Tbsp. honey
1/4 c. pineapple juice
1 Tbsp. butter
1 1/2 oz. amber rum
1/2 oz. creme de cacao
1 pt. coffee ice cream**

Peel bananas. Cut in halves lengthwise, then crosswise into 1 inch pieces. Place with honey, pineapple juice and butter in a saucepan or chafing dish. Heat over a low flame, turning frequently, until bananas are soft, but not mushy, and liquid in pan has been reduced to a thick syrup. Add the rum and creme de cacao. Ignite the liquors. When flames subside, spoon bananas and sauce over the ice cream   in serving dishes.

The best way to flame any liquor is to pour out a tablespoonful of the liquor, then warm it by placing a lighted match under the spoon until it catches fire. Add the tablespoonful of lighted liquor into the pan.

BLUEBERRY MUFFINS

**1/4 c. butter or
margarine, softened
1/2 c. sugar
1 egg
3/4 c. milk
1/4 tsp. vanilla
1 3/4 c. plus 1 Tbsp. flour
2 1/2 tsp. baking powder
1/2 tsp. salt
1 c. blueberries (fresh or
frozen), thawed and
drained**

In medium bowl, cream butter or margarine and sugar until light and fluffy. Beat in egg; add the milk and vanilla. Blend until smooth. Add 1 3/4 cups flour, baking powder and salt. Stir only until barely blended. Toss berries with 1 tablespoon flour; fold into batter. Spoon into 12 greased muffin cups. Bake in preheated 425° oven about 25 minutes, until lightly browned.

LEMON BLUEBERRY MUFFINS - EZ

1 c. fresh blueberries
1 egg, beaten
2 c. packaged biscuit mix
1/3 c. sugar
2 Tbsp. butter or
   margarine, softened
1 lemon
Milk
Melted butter or
   margarine
2 Tbsp. sugar

In mixing bowl, combine egg, biscuit mix, 1/3 cup sugar, and 2 tablespoons softened butter or margarine.   Finely shred enough peel from lemon to make 1 tablespoon; set aside. Squeeze lemon; add enough milk to lemon juice to make 2/3 cup liquid. Add to biscuit mix mixture; mix well. Gently fold in blueberries. Fill greased muffin cups 2/3 full. Bake in a 400° oven about 25 minutes.

While warm, dip muffin tops in melted butter or margarine, then in a mixture of 2 table-spoons sugar and the reserved lemon peel. Makes 12 muffins.

BLUEBERRY STREUSEL

1/4 c. butter, softened
3/4 c. sugar
1 egg
2 c. flour
1/2 tsp.salt
2 tsp. baking powder
1/2 c. milk
2 c. blueberries (fresh or
   frozen)

Topping:
1/2 c. packed light brown
   sugar
3 Tbsp. flour
2 tsp. ground cinnamon
3 Tbsp. butter
1/2 c. chopped pecans

Cream together butter, sugar and egg. Add flour, salt, baking powder, and milk, stirring until well blended.   Carefully fold in berries. Spoon into greased 10 inch springform pan.

Mix together topping ingredients of brown sugar, flour, cinnamon, butter, and chopped pecans, using a pastry cutter or fork to blend. Sprinkle topping mixture over batter. Bake at 375° for 40 to 50 minutes, until tested done. Bake on lowest possible shelf in oven.

NO BAKE BLUEBERRY PIE - HEALTHY/EZ

Everyone agrees - the best blueberry pie ever!

4 1/2 c. fresh blueberries
3/4 c. sugar
2 1/2 Tbsp. cornstarch
2 Tbsp. water
1 1/2 Tbsp. fresh lemon
juice
1/2 tsp. cinnamon
1 (9 inch) graham pie crust
or baked pie shell

Reserve 1 cup blueberries, place remaining berries in pie crust. Place reserved blueberries in small saucepan and crush. Add sugar and stir over medium heat until sugar is dissolved. Stir lemon juice, water and cornstarch together until smooth and add to berry mixture along with the cinnamon. Continue to cook and stir constantly until the mixture boils and thickens. Pour in pie shell over blueberries and chill at least 3 hours or overnight. When serving, top with whipped cream or vanilla ice cream.

BLUEBERRY CUSTARD PIE - HEALTHY

2 Tbsp. honey
2 Tbsp. cornstarch
1 c. milk
2 eggs, beaten
1 Tbsp. butter
1 tsp. vanilla
1 (9 inch) baked pie shell

Topping:
1/4 c. honey
1 Tbsp. cornstarch
1/4 c. water
1 tsp. lemon juice
1 1/2 c. blueberries

Using a wire whisk, combine honey, cornstarch and milk in top of a double boiler, but not over heat. Add eggs and cook, stirring constantly, over boiling water until thick, about 5 minutes. Remove from heat and add butter and vanilla. Cool and spread over pie crust. Add topping.

Topping: Combine honey and cornstarch in a large saucepan. Add 1/4 cup water and mix with wire whisk until smooth. Cook mixture over medium heat until slightly thick, then add lemon juice and berries. Stir and cook for 5 minutes more. Cool and spread over custard. Chill before serving.

RASPBERRY TORTE

1 1/4 c. flour
1/4 c. sugar
1/4 tsp. salt
1 c. butter or margarine
3 Tbsp. cornstarch
1 c. sugar
2 (10 oz.) pkg. frozen
   raspberries, thawed
   (undrained)
45 large marshmallows
1 c. milk
1 c. whipping cream,
   whipped

Combine flour, 1/4 cup sugar and salt in a bowl. Cut in chilled butter until mixture resembles coarse crumbs. Pat in bottom of a 13x9 inch cake pan. Bake at 350° until lightly browned, 15 to 20 minutes. Cool.

Combine cornstarch and 1 cup sugar in a saucepan. Add raspberries and cook, stirring constantly, until mixture comes to a boil and is clear. Cool slightly. Pour over cooled crust in pan. Chill.

Meanwhile, place marshmallows and milk in a saucepan; cook over low heat, stirring frequently, until marshmallows are melted. Cool. Fold whipped cream into marshmallow mixture. Spread over chilled raspberry filling. Chill. Makes 12 generous, beautiful and delicious servings.

FRESH RED RASPBERRY JAM - EZ

3 c. finely mashed
   raspberries
6 c. sugar
1 pkg. powdered fruit
   pectin
1 c. water

Combine berries and sugar. Let stand at room temperature about 20 minutes, stirring occasionally. Boil pectin and water rapidly for 1 minute, stirring constantly. Remove from heat. Add fruit and stir 2 minutes. Pour into containers; cover. Let stand at room temperature 24 hours. If jam does not set, refrigerate until it does. Store in freezer. Makes about 8 or 9 half pints.

STRAWBERRIES SMETANA - EZ

A very simple, very elegant dessert. You may eliminate the liquors and sugar and simply do a layer of berries. Top with half the sour cream, sprinkle brown sugar over the top and repeat again with the rest of the berries and sour cream. This is my very favorite way of eating fresh strawberries.

1 qt. fresh strawberries
2 jiggers maraschino
** liquor**
1 jigger Grand Marnier
** liquor**
Sugar
1 c. sour cream
Light brown sugar

Remove stems from strawberries. Wash, drain well and combine with both liquors. Add 2 tablespoons sugar or more to taste and let marinate for 3 or 4 hours in the refrigerator. Spoon strawberries into serving dishes. Top with sour cream and sprinkle heavily with brown sugar.

STRAWBERRY ANGEL CAKE DESSERT

Mom first made this cake for my oldest brother's prom. It is delicious and is a beautiful looking cake. I also made 3 of these for my brother's wedding, cutting whole, fresh strawberries in halves and placing next to each other resembling a heart for decorating.

1 angel food cake
1 (3 oz.) pkg. strawberry
** jello**
1 c. hot water
1 (12 oz.) pkg. frozen
** strawberries or 1 1/3 c.**
** fresh berries, crushed**
1 c. whipping cream,
** whipped**
1 Tbsp. sugar
1 c. whipping cream,
** whipped (second)**

Bake cake according to directions; cool. Remove from pan. Dissolve jello in hot water. Add strawberries. Chill until thick. Fold in 1 cup whipped cream. Chill until thick. Cut cake in 3 layers. Fill layers with strawberry mixture, returning layers to cake pan. Chill until firm. Unmold. Add sugar to the other cup of whipped cream. Swirl over cake.

CHOCOLATE BERRY ROLL

This is a very impressive dessert for any occasion and easy.

1/4 c. butter
4 large eggs (room
  temperature)
3/4 c. sugar
2/3 c. pancake mix
3 Tbsp. cocoa
1 tsp. vanilla

Filling:
3 c. sweetened whipped
  cream
1 1/2 pt. fresh
  strawberries, sliced
  (save about 10 of the
  nicer ones for top
  garnish)

Preheat oven to 400°. Grease a 10x15 inch jelly roll pan, then line with waxed paper. Reverse the paper, greased side up. Sprinkle with flour. Melt butter and set aside. Beat eggs in mixing bowl until light and foamy. Gradually beat in sugar. Combine pancake mix and cocoa. Fold into eggs alternately with melted butter and vanilla to make batter. Pour batter into pan. Bake 12 minutes, or just until puffed and set. Immediately turn out on a towel, well sprinkled with powdered sugar. Remove waxed paper. Roll cake carefully in towel to cool.

Filling: Unroll cake. Spread with whipped cream, more thickly on one half. Add berries to 2/3 of cake. Roll up cake, starting with berries. Place seam down on tray. Top with remaining cream. Cut reserved berries in halves and garnish top. Refrigerate until serving.

OLD-TIME STRAWBERRY CREAM PUFFS

Cream puffs are easy to make, *really!* Believe it or not!

1 c. water
1/2 c. butter or margarine
1 c. flour
4 eggs
2 pt. fresh strawberries,
  halved
1 c. whipping cream,
  whipped and sweetened

To make Choux Paste: Preheat oven to 400°. In medium size saucepan, combine water and butter; bring to boil. Add flour, stirring vigorously, over low heat about 1 minute, or until mixture forms a ball. Remove from heat. Beat in eggs, one at a time, beating until smooth. Drop rounded 1/4 cupful, 3 inches apart, on ungreased baking sheet. Bake 35 to 40 minutes or until golden brown. Cool away from draft. Cut off tops. Pull out filaments of soft dough if desired.

At serving time, fold half the berries into whipped cream. Fill puffs, replacing tops. Arrange in dessert dishes. Spoon remaining berries around puffs.

"Idea:" Fill with strawberries and top with hot fudge sauce'

STRAWBERRY CREAM PIE - EZ

1 small pkg. strawberry
  jello
1 1/4 c. boiling water
1 pt. vanilla ice cream
1 (8 inch) graham cracker
  crumb crust
1 c. sweetened, sliced fresh
  strawberries or 1 (10
  oz.) pkg. frozen
  strawberries, thawed
  and drained

Dissolve jello in boiling water in large bowl. Stir in ice cream until melted. Chill until very thick. Fold in strawberries and pour into pie shell. Chill for 3 hours before serving.

Note: Raspberry jello and raspberries can be used instead of strawberries

**FRESH STRAWBERRY PIE

Easy, delicious and a favorite of our neighbors; will be yours as well. This can be made the day before.

2 c. water
1 c. sugar
Red food coloring
1 qt. fresh strawberries
2 Tbsp. cornstarch
1/4 c. water
1 (3 oz.) pkg. strawberry
  jello
1 baked 9 inch pie shell

In small saucepan, combine 2 cups water, the sugar and a few drops red food coloring. Bring to a boil, stirring until sugar is dissolved. Stir cornstarch into remaining 1/4 cup water until dissolved and add mixture to pan. Bring once again to a boil. Remove from heat and stir in jello. Stir until well dissolved. Let cool until partially set. Slice strawberries into pie shell. Pour jello over strawberries and refrigerate until set. Serve topped with whipped cream if desired.

"Idea:" Try this with raspberries and raspberry jello, or how about fresh peaches, adding a few drops of lemon juice to peaches to keep them from darkening.

UPSIDE-DOWN STRAWBERRY MERINGUE PIE

2 egg whites
1/2 tsp. vinegar
1/4 tsp. salt
1/3 c. sugar
1/2 tsp. vanilla
1 (9 inch) baked pastry
  shell
3 c. fresh strawberries
1/3 c. sugar
3 Tbsp. cornstarch
1/2 c. water
Red food coloring
1 c. whipping cream

Beat egg whites with vinegar and salt to soft peaks. Gradually add the 1/2 cup sugar and vanilla, beating to stiff peaks. Spread on bottom and sides of baked pastry shell. Bake in a 325° oven for 12 minutes; cool.

Mash and sieve 2 cups of the strawberries. In saucepan, blend together the remaining sugar and cornstarch. Add water and mashed berries. Cook and stir until mixture thickens and boils. Cook 2 minutes. Tint with several drops red food coloring; cool slightly. Spread over meringue; chill until set. Whip cream; spread over all. Carefully slice remaining whole berries into fans for top of pie.

SUNDAY STRAWBERRY DESSERT

2 c. crushed pretzels
3/4 c. butter or
  margarine, melted
3 Tbsp. sugar
1 (8 oz.) pkg. cream
  cheese, softened
3/4 c. sugar
1 (8 oz.) container whipped
  topping
3 c. fresh strawberries,
  sliced
2 c. water
1 c. sugar
Red food coloring
2 Tbsp. cornstarch
1/4 c. cold water
1 (3 oz.) pkg. strawberry
  jello

Spread pretzels over bottom of 9x13 inch cake pan. Pour butter over top of pretzels and sprinkle with the 3 tablespoons sugar. Bake at 325° for 8 minutes; cool.

Cream together the cream cheese and 3/4 cup sugar until light and fluffy. Fold in whipped topping and spread over pretzel mixture. Wash and slice strawberries and place over cream cheese mixture.

Meanwhile, prepare glaze. Bring 2 cups water, 1 cup sugar and food coloring to a boil. Add cornstarch to 1/4 cup cold water and stir to dissolve. Add to mixture and once more, bring to a boil. Remove from heat and stir in strawberry jello. Stir until dissolved. Let cool until partially set and pour over all.

FREEZER STRAWBERRY TOPPING

**6 (8 oz.) freeze proof
containers and lids
1 qt. *ripe* strawberries,
mashed
4 c. sugar
2 Tbsp. orange juice (fresh)
1 (1 3/4 oz.) pkg. fruit
pectin
3/4 c. water**

Wash containers and lids in hot, sudsy water. Pour boiling water over and drain on towel. In large bowl, stir strawberries, sugar and orange juice together until thoroughly mixed; let stand 10 minutes. In small saucepan, heat water and pectin until boiling; boil 1 minute, stirring constantly. Stir pectin mixture into fruit; continue stirring for 3 minutes to blend well. Ladle mixture into containers to 1/2 inch from top; cover with lids. Let stand at room temperature for 24 hours. Label and put in freezer. Will last 1 year in freezer and 3 weeks in refrigerator.

This is delicious served with pound cake or angel food cake, ice cream, rice pudding, cheesecake, cooked rhubarb, or use as jam.

UNCOOKED JAM - EZ

Tastes like the fresh fruit. A family favorite!

**2 c. mashed strawberries
4 c. sugar
1 pkg. powdered fruit
pectin
1 c. water**

Combine fruit and sugar. Let stand 20 minutes, stirring occasionally. Boil pectin and water rapidly for 1 minute, stirring constantly. Remove from heat. Pour into berries and stir for 2 minutes. Pour into prepared containers and cover. Let stand at room temperature 1 hour. Refrigerate until set. Store in freezer Once opened, keep in refrigerator. Makes 5 to 6 half pints.

Apricot, Peach or Nectarine Jam: Add 3 tablespoons lemon juice to finely mashed or ground fresh fruit. Substitute for strawberries, following same directions.

Note: If jam doesn't set well, use straight from the freezer (it will be pliable enough), or use as a topping.

OAT DATE LOAF - HEALTHY

1 egg
1/3 c. honey
1/3 c. brown sugar
1/4 c. margarine, melted
3/4 c. rolled oats
1 1/2 c. flour
1 tsp. baking powder
1/2 tsp. baking soda
1/2 tsp. salt
1 c. buttermilk
1/3 c. toasted wheat germ
  or oat bran
1/3 c. chopped dates or
  raisins

Heat oven to 350°. Grease 9x5 inch loaf pan generously and set aside. In a large bowl, whisk together the egg, honey, brown sugar, and margarine. Stir in the oats. Sift in a mixture of the flour, baking powder, baking soda, and salt; add alternately with buttermilk. Stir in the wheat germ and dates. Turn batter into pan and bake for about 55 minutes or until tested done with a toothpick. Cool for 10 minutes in the pan, then remove to a rack.

DATE LOAF

1/2 c. butter flavored
  shortening
2 c. packed brown sugar
2 c. boiling water
1 1/2 tsp. baking water
2 c. chopped dates
2 eggs, beaten
1 tsp. baking powder
1/4 tsp. salt
1 tsp. vanilla
3 c. flour, sifted
1 c. chopped nuts

Sprinkle the baking soda over the chopped dates; add boiling water. Set aside and cool. Cream shortening and sugar together until light and fluffy. Add eggs, salt and vanilla; mix well. Stir in flour with baking powder until well blended. Stir in dates and nuts. Place in 2 well greased 9 1/2x5 1/2x3 inch loaf pans. Let rise 20 minutes. Bake 1 hour and 15 minutes at 275°.

LEMON AND BUTTERMILK SPICE CAKE

3 c. flour
2 tsp. grated lemon peel
1 1/2 tsp. baking powder
1/2 tsp. baking soda
1/2 tsp. grated nutmeg
1/2 tsp. cinnamon
1/4 tsp. ground ginger
1/4 tsp. ground allspice
Pinch of salt
1/8 tsp. ground cloves
1 c. unsalted butter,
   softened
2 1/4 c. firmly packed dark
   brown sugar
1 tsp. vanilla
5 eggs (room temperature)
1 c. buttermilk

Lemon Cream Cheese
   Icing:
1 (8 oz.) pkg. cream
   cheese, softened
1/4 c. unsalted butter,
   softened
5 c. (about) powdered
   sugar
2 Tbsp. grated lemon peel
8 tsp. fresh strained lemon
   juice
1 c. finely chopped
   walnuts

Preheat oven to 350°. Generously grease two 9 inch round cake pans. Line bottoms with parchment or wax paper. Grease paper. Mix first 10 ingredients in medium bowl. Cream butter with sugar and vanilla in large bowl until light and fluffy. Add eggs, one at a time, blending well after each addition. Mix in dry ingredients, alternating with buttermilk, in 3 additions each. Blend until smooth, scraping down sides of bowl.

Divide batter between prepared pans. Bake until tester inserted in center of cakes comes out clean, 25 to 30 minutes. Cool cakes completely on racks. Run small sharp knife around sides to loosen; unmold cakes. Freeze partially before continuing.

Lemon Cream Cheese Icing: Beat cream cheese and butter until fluffy. Gradually beat in enough sugar to form thick, spreadable icing. Stir in lemon peel. Save walnuts for garnish.

Using serrated knife, halve each cake horizontally. Set 1 cake layer, cut side up, on platter. Brush with 2 teaspoons lemon juice. Spread with scant 2/3 cup icing. Top with second cake layer, cut side up. Repeat with the next layer, cut side up. Top with fourth layer, cut side down. Brush with 2 teaspoons lemon juice. Spread top and sides of cake with remaining icing. Press all but 2 tablespoons walnuts onto sides of cake. Sprinkle remaining walnuts atop cake.

LEMON TORTE

One of the best lemon anythings you'll ever taste!

3 c. flour, sifted
1/2 tsp. salt
1/2 tsp. baking soda
1 c. unsalted butter (room
   temperature)
2 c. sugar
3 large eggs (room
   temperature)
1 c. buttermilk
3 Tbsp. fresh lemon juice
2 tsp. grated lemon peel

Glaze:
1 c. powdered sugar
1/4 c. fresh lemon juice
2 Tbsp. unsalted butter,
   melted

Frosting:
2 1/2 Tbsp. butter (room
   temperature)
2 oz. cream cheese (room
   temperature)
2 c. powdered sugar
2 Tbsp. lemon juice
1 tsp. (or more) whipping
   cream
1 tsp. grated lemon peel

Preheat oven to 325°. Grease 10 inch tube or Bundt pan. Sift first 3 ingredients into medium bowl. Using electric mixer, cream butter with sugar in large bowl until light. Add eggs, one at a time, beating well after each addition. Mix in dry ingredients alternately with buttermilk in 3 additions. Mix in lemon juice and peel. Pour batter into prepared pan and bake until tester inserted near center comes out clean, about 1 hour. Cool cake in pan on wire rack for 15 minutes before removing.

Meanwhile, prepare glaze: Stir all ingredients in small bowl until smooth. Remove cake onto serving plate. Brush glaze over warm cake. Cool completely. (Can be prepared one day ahead. Cover and let stand at room temperature.)

Frosting: Beat butter and cream cheese in medium bowl until light. Gradually beat in powdered sugar. Mix in lemon juice, whipping cream and lemon peel. Add more cream, if frosting is too thick, or more powdered sugar if frosting is too thin. Spread frosting over top and sides of cake, swirling with icing spatula. Cut into thin slices, using serrated knife.

LEMON GLAZED BUTTER COOKIES

1 c. unsalted butter,
   softened
1/3 c. powdered sugar
1 c. flour
2/3 c. cornstarch
2 1/2 c. powdered sugar
1/2 c. butter, melted
2 Tbsp. fresh lemon juice

Preheat oven to 350°. Beat the 1 cup butter and 1/3 cup powdered sugar on medium speed 1 minute. Sift together flour and cornstarch and add to butter mixture. Blend until dough is soft, about 1 minute. Drop by teaspoonfuls onto ungreased baking sheet. Bake until very lightly browned, about 15 minutes. Transfer cookies to racks to cool.

Meanwhile, combine the 2 1/2 cups powdered sugar, melted butter and lemon juice. While cookies are still warm, mound 1/2 tsp. Icing on each; icing will melt. Cool completely.

BEST EVER LEMON PIE

1 (9 inch) pie crust
(unbaked)
1 1/2 c. sugar
1/2 c. cornstarch
1/4 c. tsp. salt
4 eggs, separated (room
temperature)
2 1/2 c. water
3 Tbsp. butter or
margarine
1 Tbsp. grated lemon rind
1/2 c. fresh lemon juice
1/4 tsp. cream of tarter
1/2 c. sugar (for meringue)

Prepare pie crust:: Fit into a 9 inch pie plate, making a high stand up edge. Prick pie crust all over with fork. Bake in a 450° oven for about 5 minutes. If bubbles have formed, prick again. Bake another 10 minutes or until pastry is golden brown. Cool completely.

Meanwhile, combine 1 1/2 cups sugar, cornstarch and salt in large saucepan; gradually add water, stirring with wooden spoon. Cook over medium heat, stirring constantly, until mixture thickens and bubbles, about 12 minutes. Cook 1 more minute and remove from heat.

Beat egg yolks slightly in small bowl. Slowly blend in about 1/2 cup of the hot mixture and add back into remaining mixture in saucepan. Cook over low heat, stirring constantly, 2 minutes; remove from heat. Stir in butter, lemon rind and lemon juice. Pour into cooled pastry. Press a piece of plastic wrap directly on filling to prevent formation of skin. Refrigerate at least 4 hours.

Beat egg whites and cream of tartar until foamy white. Slowly add remaining 1/2 cup sugar, 1 tablespoon at a time, beating at high speed until the meringue forms stiff peaks. Grease and lightly flour small cookie sheet. Shape meringue into 6 or 8 small mounds on cookie sheet, swirling with back of a teaspoon to form peaks. Bake in a 350° oven for 15 minutes, until golden brown. Cool on cookie sheet. When puffs are cool, carefully place on chilled pie (remove plastic wrap first with a small spatula).

LEMON CREAM PIE WITH PINEAPPLE - EZ

1 (9 inch) baked pie shell
1/3 c. fresh lemon juice
1 (15 oz.) can sweetened
  condensed milk
2/3 c. well drained, canned
  crushed pineapple
1 Tbsp. grated lemon rind
1/4 tsp. salt

Combine sweetened condensed milk, lemon juice and rind, and salt. Stir until thickened. (Reaction between milk and lemon juice causes thickening without cooking or eggs.) Stir in pineapple. Pour into pie shell. Refrigerate at least 3 hours before serving.

"Idea:" Substitute lime juice and rind for lemon. This pie is also good with a graham cracker crumb crust.

EASY KEY LIME PIE

1 (8 or 9 inch) baked pastry
  shell
1 (14 oz.) can sweetened
  condensed milk
3 eggs, separated
1/2 c. lime juice (fresh)
1/2 tsp. cream of tartar
1/3 c. sugar
Few drops of green food
  coloring

Preheat oven to 350°. In medium bowl, beat egg yolks; stir in condensed milk, lime juice and food coloring. Turn into shell. In small bowl, beat egg whites and cream of tartar until soft peaks form; gradually add sugar until stiff. Spread on top of pie; seal carefully to edge of shell. Bake 12 to 15 minutes, until golden brown. Chill at least 2 hours before serving.

LIME PARFAIT PIE

2 (3 oz.) pkg. lime jello
2 c. boiling water
1 tsp. shredded lime peel
1/3 c. fresh lime juice
1 qt. vanilla ice cream
1 baked 10 inch pie crust

Dissolve jello in boiling water. Stir in lime peel and lime juice. Stir ice cream in by spoonfuls until melted. Chill until mixture thickens. Pile into pie shell and smooth top. Chill until firm. Top with whipped cream and maraschino cherry before serving.

"Idea:" Why not try with orange or lemon jello and juice or how about orange jello, orange juice and throw in a can of drained mandarin oranges or drained pineapple? Make a pina colada ice cream pie.

WHOLE WHEAT PEAR-CARROT MUFFINS - HEALTHY

2 eggs
1/2 c. sugar
2/3 c. vegetable oil
1 c. cored and chopped
    Bartlett pears
1/2 c. grated carrot
3/4 c. flour
3/4 c. whole wheat flour
1 tsp. baking powder
1 tsp. baking soda
3/4 tsp. cinnamon
1/4 tsp. ginger
1/4 tsp. salt
1/2 c. chopped nuts

Preheat oven to 400°. Beat together eggs, sugar and oil; add pear and carrot. Combine flours, baking powder, baking soda, cinnamon, ginger and salt; mix well. Add flour mixture and nuts to egg mixture; stir just until moistened. Spoon into 12 greased muffin cups. Bake at 400° for 18 to 20 minutes, or until wooden pick inserted near center comes out clean.

FRESH PEACH MUFFINS -HEALTHY

1 c. lowfat vanilla yogurt
3 Tbsp. butter or
    margarine, melted˙
1 egg, lightly beaten
1 3/4 c. flour
1/3 c. firmly packed brown
    sugar
1 Tbsp. baking powder
1/4 tsp. baking soda
1/4 tsp. salt
1/4 tsp. cinnamon
1/8 tsp. nutmeg
1 large peach, pared,
    pitted and chopped
1/3 c. chopped nuts

Preheat oven to 400°. Generously grease 12 muffin pan cups. In medium bowl, combine yogurt, butter and egg. In separate bowl, combine next 7 ingredients. Stir into yogurt mixture. Add peaches and nuts. Spoon batter into cups. Bake 25 to 30 minutes. Loosen muffins from cups; cool on wire rack.

PEACH TORTE - EZ

An excellent new way to serve uncooked fresh peaches.

1 1/2 c. flour
1 c. chopped nuts
1/2 c. butter or margarine
1 (8 oz.) pkg. cream
  cheese, softened
1 egg
1 c. powdered sugar
1/4 tsp. almond extract
3 1/2 c. (8 oz.) non-dairy
  whipped topping,
  thawed
4 c. sliced fresh peaches

Mix together flour, nuts and butter. Press into 13x9 inch pan. Bake at 350° for 15 minutes; cool.

Beat cream cheese with electric mixer until smooth. Beat in egg, sugar and extract. Fold in 1 cup of whipped topping. Spread over cooled layer. Chill 4 hours or overnight. Before serving, arrange peaches over cream cheese layer and garnish with remaining whipped topping. Serves 12.

PEACHES AND CREAM SHORTCAKE - EZ

Another take-off on the jello-cake combination. Once again, use your imaginations, using any kind of fruit and any flavor jello you wish, or even try a different flavor cake mix.

1 pkg. yellow cake mix
1 (3 oz.) pkg. peach jello
1/3 c. water
1 (8 oz.) ctn. plain or
  peach yogurt
3 eggs
1 c. hot water
1 (4 oz.) ctn. whipped
  topping, thawed
Peach slices (fresh)

Heat oven to 350°. Grease 13x9 inch pan. In large bowl, combine cake mix, 2 tablespoons jello, water, yogurt, and eggs at low speed until moistened. Beat 2 minutes at highest speed. Pour into prepared pan. Bake 40 minutes or until toothpick inserted in center comes out clean. Cool cake in pan on cooling rack 15 minutes.

Meanwhile, combine hot water and remaining gelatin. Using long-tined fork, prick cake at 1/2 inch intervals. Pour jello mixture evenly over cake; chill. Serve with dollops of whipped topping and peach slices.

YUMMY FRESH PEACH PIE

4 c. fresh peaches, peeled
3/4 c. sugar
4 Tbsp. flour
1/4 tsp. salt
1/4 tsp. cinnamon
1 (9 inch) pie shell
   (unbaked)
1/4 tsp. nutmeg
1 tsp. grated lemon rind
1 c. light cream
1 Tbsp. brown sugar
1/4 tsp. cinnamon

Place peaches in pastry shell. Mix sugar, flour, salt, cinnamon, nutmeg, and lemon rind together in a separate bowl. Blend in cream and pour over peaches. Mix the 1 tablespoon of brown sugar with the 1/4 teaspoon cinnamon and sprinkle over pie. Bake at 400° for 50 to 60 minutes.

OPEN-FACED CUSTARD PEACH PIE

1 c. sugar
2 Tbsp. cornstarch
1 (9 inch) unbaked pastry
   shell
3 fresh peaches, peeled
   and halved
2 to 3 fresh peaches,
   peeled and diced
1/2 pt. heavy cream

Mix sugar with cornstarch. Cover inside of pastry shell with 3/4 of this mixture, pressing it out to the sides. Arrange peeled halves of fresh peaches close together around the outside edge, with insides of peaches up. Fill in with other peaches (diced) until pan is full. Sprinkle remainder of sugar and cornstarch mixture over the peaches and then carefully pour the cream around the halves, putting a little cream into each peach center. Put into a 400° oven for 10 minutes. Reduce heat to 350° and continue baking until custard is clear and firm (about 40 minutes). Sprinkle a little nutmeg over the top.

PEACH COBBLER

Growing up in peach country, this has always been a very special treat for our family. We've always been spoiled with tree ripened peaches, straight out of the orchards of Paonia, Colorado. I remember Mom making this since before I can remember.

3 c. fresh peaches, peeled and sliced
1 c. sugar*
2 Tbsp. flour
1/2 tsp. nutmeg
1/4 tsp. salt
2 Tbsp. butter

Topping:
2 c. buttermilk baking mix
2 Tbsp. sugar
1/2 c. milk or light cream
2 Tbsp. butter, softened
4 Tbsp. bran cereal
1/4 tsp. cinnamon
2 Tbsp. sugar

Mix the first 6 ingredients and place in a 2 quart baking dish that has been buttered.

Topping: Combine milk and bran cereal in a small bowl and soak 5 minutes. Meanwhile, combine baking mix and sugar. Add the butter and cut with fork until mixture resembles coarse oatmeal. Stir in milk mixture and mix well until dough is formed. Drop dough by teaspoonfuls over top of peaches. Mix cinnamon and sugar together and sprinkle over the top. Bake in a 350° oven for 25 to 30 minutes, until topping is golden brown and fruit is bubbling.

*Note: If you are using tree ripened peaches, cut down on the sugar!

NECTARINE CRUNCH BARS -HEALTHY

1 lb. fresh nectarines (3 medium)
1/4 c. sugar
2 Tbsp. lemon juice
2 Tbsp. water
1 1/2 tsp. cornstarch
3/4 c. butter or margarine
1/4 tsp. almond extract
1 c. flour
1 c. quick cooking oats
1/2 c. wheat germ
1/4 c. packed brown sugar
1/2 tsp. salt
1/2 tsp. cinnamon
Sweetened whipped cream

Dice enough nectarines to make 2 cups. In saucepan, combine nectarines, sugar and lemon juice. Cook and stir over medium heat 3 minutes. Mix water into cornstarch; stir into nectarine mixture. Cook and stir until thickened, about 5 minutes. Remove from heat. Stir in 1 tablespoon butter and almond extract. Cool.

In large bowl, mix together next 6 ingredients. Cut in remaining butter until mixture resembles coarse meal. Turn 2/3 crumb mixture into greased 8 inch square baking pan; pack firmly. Bake in a 350° oven for 15 minutes. Spoon nectarine mixture over baked layer, then sprinkle with remaining crumb mixture. Return to oven for 25 to 30 minutes longer, until lightly browned. Cool on rack 15 minutes; cut into bars. Serve warm or at room temperature, topped with whipped cream and remaining nectarine slices.

PUMPKIN BREAD - EZ

This recipe is great, because it makes 3 loaves (small). Freezes nicely.

3 c. sugar
4 eggs, beaten
1 (16 oz.) can pumpkin
1 c. vegetable oil
1/2 c. water
1/2 tsp. baking powder
2 tsp. baking soda
1 1/2 tsp. salt
1 1/2 tsp. cloves
1 1/2 tsp. cinnamon
3 1/2 c. flour
1 c. chopped walnuts

Mix the first 5 ingredients together in large mixing bowl. Add remaining ingredients; mix well. Pour into 3 meduim sized, greased loaf pans (8x3 1/2x3 inches). Bake at 350° for 45 minutes.

GOLDEN DANISH TWISTS

1/4 c. butter or margarine
1 c. hot scalded milk
1/4 c. sugar
1 Tbsp. salt
1 c. cooked pumpkin
2 eggs
1/2 c. warm water
2 pkg. dry yeast
3 c. flour

Orange Icing:
1/4 c. butter
2 Tbsp. flour
1/4 c. orange juice
2 1/2 c. powdered sugar
1 Tbsp. grated orange peel

Place first 9 ingredients in mixing bowl in order listed. Beat at medium low for 3 minutes. Stir in 2 1/2 to 3 cups flour to make a stiff dough. Cover; let rest 15 minutes. Prepare Orange Icing.

Toss dough on well floured surface until no longer sticky. Roll out half to 18x12 inch rectangle. Spread 1/4 of the icing over half of the rectangle along the 18 inch side. Fold uncovered dough over icing. Cut crosswise into 1 inch strips. Twist 4 or 5 times. Coil onto well greased cookie sheet, keeping flat and tucking ends under. Repeat with remaining dough. Cover; let rise in warm place until very light or doubled in size, 45 to 60 minutes. Bake at 375° for 12 to 15 minutes, or until golden brown. Remove from sheet immediately. Frost warm with remaining icing. Makes 36.

Orange Icing: Melt butter in small saucepan. Stir in flour and orange juice. Cook, stirring constantly, until thick. Stir in powdered sugar and orange peel.

Hint: Line cookie sheet with foil for easier dishwashing.

PUMPKIN CAKE ROLL

3 eggs (room temperature)
1 c. sugar
2/3 c. pumpkin
3/4 c. flour
1 tsp. baking powder
2 tsp. cinnamon
1/2 tsp. nutmeg
1 tsp. ginger

Cream Cheese Filling:
8 oz. cream cheese,
  softened
4 tsp. butter, softened
1/2 tsp. vanilla
1 c. powdered sugar

Beat eggs on high speed in large mixing bowl 1 minute. Add sugar and continue 4 more minutes. Stir in rest of ingredients. Pour into jelly roll pan that has been lined with foil and then greased. Spread batter evenly. Bake in preheated 375° oven for 12 to 13 minutes, until cake springs back to the touch and starts to pull away from the edges. Remove from oven and cool in pan about 5 minutes. Turn out onto towel sprinkled with powdered sugar. Remove foil and roll up gently in towel, jelly roll style. Cool. When cool, unroll gently and fill with cream cheese filling, gently rolling back up. Refrigerate at least 2 hours before serving.

Cream Cheese Filling: Cream all of the ingredients together until smooth.

PUMPKIN WALNUT CHEESECAKE

1 (6 oz.) Zwieback
  crackers, crushed*
1/4 c. sugar
6 Tbsp. butter, melted
3 (8 oz.) pkg. cream
  cheese, softened
3/4 c. sugar
3/4 c. light brown sugar
5 eggs
1 3/4 tsp. pumpkin pie
  spice
1 (15 oz.) can pumpkin
1/4 c. heavy cream

Walnut Topping:
6 Tbsp. softened butter
1 c. firmly packed light
  brown sugar
1 c. coarsely chopped
  walnuts

Blend Zwieback crumbs, 1/4 cup sugar and the butter in a medium size bowl. Press firmly over bottom and up side of a lightly buttered 9 inch springform pan. Chill.

Beat cream cheese in a large bowl at medium speed until smooth. Add sugars gradually, beating until well mixed. Beat in eggs, one at a time, until mixture is light and fluffy. Beat in pumpkin, pumpkin pie spice and heavy cream at low speed. Pour into prepared pan. Bake in a slow oven (325°) for 1 hour and 35 minutes. Remove cake from oven; sprinkle with Walnut Topping. Bake an additional 10 minutes. Cool cake on wire rack; refrigerate several hours or overnight. Garnish with whipped cream and walnut halves if you wish.

Walnut Topping: Combine softened butter with brown sugar in a small bowl; mix well until crumbly. Blend in coarsely chopped walnuts.

*Zwieback crackers are found in supermarkets with baby food.

PUMPKIN RAISIN MUFFINS

1 extra large egg
1 c. plus 2 Tbsp. milk
1/4 c. cooking oil
2 c. flour
1 tsp. cinnamon
1/2 tsp. ginger
1/4 tsp. cloves
1/4 c. sugar
3 tsp. baking powder
1 tsp. salt
1/2 c. raisins
1/2 c. canned pumpkin
1/3 c. brown sugar, mixed
   with 1/2 tsp. cinnamon

Grease bottom only of 12 muffin cups. Heat oven to 400°. Beat egg slightly. Stir in milk and cooking oil. Sift together flour, cinnamon, ginger, cloves, sugar, baking powder, and salt. Stir in raisins. Add to egg mixture with pumpkin just until flour is moistened. Fill cups 2/3 full of batter. Sprinkle tops with brown sugar-cinnamon mixture and bake 20 to 25 minutes or until golden brown. Remove from pans immediately.

PUMPKIN MAPLE CAKE

2 c. cake flour
2 tsp. baking powder
1 1/2 tsp. cinnamon
1/2 tsp. ground cloves
1/2 tsp. baking soda
1/4 tsp. salt
3 eggs, separated (room
   temperature)
2 tsp. distilled white
   vinegar
1 1/2 c. sugar
3/4 c. unsalted butter
   (room temperature), cut
   into 6 pieces
1/2 c. maple syrup
3/4 c. solid pack pumpkin
1/2 tsp. maple flavoring
15 pecan halves

Pumpkin Cream Frosting:
1 (8oz.) pkg. cream
   cheese, softened
3/4 c. powdered sugar
1/4 c. solid pack pumpkin
1 1/2 tsp. vanilla

Position rack in center of oven and preheat to 350°. Line 9 inch springform pan with parchment or waxed paper; butter pan and paper. Sift together flour, baking powder, cinnamon, cloves, baking soda, and salt. Beat whites in separate bowl until foamy. Drizzle vinegar and continue whipping until whites hold shape. Transfer to large bowl; do not clean work bowl. Add butter and mix 1 minute. Add syrup, blending well. Add pumpkin and maple flavoring, stirring well. Stir in flour mixture, then fold in beaten whites. Spoon into prepared pan and bake until tester inserted in center comes out clean, 50 to 60 minutes. Cool cake in pan 5 minutes. Remove from pan and cool completely.

Using long serrated knife, cut cake horizontally into 2 layers. Set top layer, cut side up, on platter. Spread with about 1/2 cup frosting. Cover with second cake layer, cut side down. Spread top and sides with remaining frosting. Arrange pecan halves around edge of cake.

Pumpkin Cream Frosting: Cream all ingredients until smooth. Cover and refrigerate until spreadable, about 10 minutes.

RHUBARB COBBLECAKE

1 1/3 c. sugar
2 Tbsp. cornstarch
1/4 tsp. ground cloves
1/2 c. orange juice
1/2 c. butter or margarine
1 1/2 lb. rhubarb, washed,
  trimmed and cut into
  1/2 inch pieces (about
  5 c.)
2 c. sifted flour
3 tsp. baking powder
1 tsp salt
1 c. milk
1 Tbsp. grated orange rind

Combine 1 cup sugar, cornstarch and cloves in a large saucepan; stir in orange juice. Heat slowly, stirring until sugar dissolves. Stir in 2 tablespoons of the butter or margarine and rhubarb; heat to boiling. Spoon into an 8 cup baking dish.

Sift flour, baking powder, 1/4 cup of the remaining sugar, and salt into a large bowl; cut in remaining 6 tablespoons butter until mixture is crumbly. Add milk all at once; stir just until moist. (Dough will be soft.) Drop in 6 even mounds on top of rhubarb mixture. Mix remaining sugar and orange rind in a cup; sprinkle over biscuits. Bake in a 425° oven for 25 minutes, or until topping is puffed and golden. Serve warm with cream if you wish.

PENNSYLVANIA DUTCH MERINGUE PIE (RHUBARB)

1 c. sugar
2 Tbsp. cornstarch
1 c. water
2 c. rhubarb, washed and
  cup in pieces (about 1/2
  inch in size)
1 Tbsp. butter or
  margarine
1/2 tsp. vanilla
1/2 tsp. lemon extract
1/4 tsp salt
3 egg yolks, beaten
1 (9 inch) pie shell
  (unbaked)

Mix together sugar, cornstarch and water in a large saucepan and bring to a boil over medium high heat. Reduce heat and simmer, stirring constantly, 5 minutes. Remove from heat. Stir in rhubarb, butter, vanilla, lemon extract, and salt. Mix a small amount of rhubarb mixture with egg yolks and return to pan, stirring constantly, until heated through. Pour into pie crust. Bake in preheated 375° oven about 35 minutes or until set. Remove from oven and cover with meringue. Return to oven until meringue is golden brown, about 5 to 10 minutes. (Keep a close eye on it; it will burn fast.) Refrigerate until chilled.

Never Fail Meringue:
1 Tbsp. cornstarch
1/2 c. water
3 egg whites (room
  temperature)
6 Tbsp. sugar
1/8 tsp. salt
1 tsp. vanilla

Never Fail Meringue: Blend cornstarch and water in a small saucepan until smooth. Cook over moderate heat about 5 minutes or until thickened, stirring constantly. Cool to room temperature. In a separate bowl, beat egg whites until foamy. Add sugar, salt and vanilla. Continue to beat until stiff peaks form. Gradually add cornstarch mixture, beating at low speed of electric mixer. Beat again on high speed until meringue is stiff. Spread on hot pie. Bake at 375° until golden brown, about 5 to 10 minutes.

This is an excellent meringue for any cream pie.

STRAWBERRY BANANA FIZZ - HEALTHY

1 small pkg. sugar free
  jello
3/4 c. boiling water
1/2 c. cold water
 Ice cubes
1 large banana, sliced
1/2 c. sugarless frozen
  strawberries, thawed
  and drained, or fresh
  strawberries

Dissolve jello in boiling water. Combine cold water and ice cubes to make 1 1/4 cups; add to jello mixture, stirring until slightly thickened. Remove unmelted ice. Divide banana slices and strawberries evenly between 5 dessert glasses. Measure 1 1/3 cups of the jello and spoon over fruit. Whip remaining jello with electric mixer until fluffy, thick and about doubled in volume. Pour over top of jello. Chill until firm. Serves 5.

PEAR-RASPBERRY JAM

Mom puts her jam into pint or half pint jars and then seals them. Process the jars in boiling water bath for 5 minutes to be sure the jars seal.

**4 c. prepared fruit (about
2 lb. ripe pears and one
10 oz. pkg. frozen
raspberries)
1/4 c. lemon juice
(2 lemons)
6 c. sugar
1/2 bottle fruit pectin**

Put thawed raspberries in 4 cup measuring cup. Fill to the top with chopped and peeled ripe pears. Place in a very large saucepan. Squeeze juice from 2 lemons; measure 1/4 cup juice into the fruit. Add sugar to fruit; mix well. Place over high heat to bring to a full rolling boil. Boil hard for 1 minute, stirring constantly. Remove from heat; at once, add pectin. Stir in well. Skim off foam with metal spoon, then stir and skim for 5 minutes to cool slightly and prevent floating fruit. Ladle quickly into prepared jars. Cover at once with 1/8 inch hot paraffin. Makes about 10 half pint jars.

PEACH AND BERRY COBBLER - HEALTHY

**1 Tbsp. cornstarch
1/4 c. brown sugar
1/2 c. cold water
2 c. lightly sugared fresh
peaches
1 c. fresh or frozen
blueberries
1 Tbsp. butter or
margarine
1 Tbsp. fresh lemon juice
1 c. flour
1/2 c. sugar
1 1/2 tsp. baking powder
1/2 tsp. salt
1/2 c. milk
1/4 c. butter or
margarine, soltened**

Mix first 3 ingredients in large saucepan. Add fruit. Cook over medium heat, stirring constantly, until thickened. Add 1 tablespoon butter and the lemon juice. Pour into a 2 quart casserole dish. Sift dry ingredients. Add milk and butter, both at once; beat until smooth. Pour over fruit. Sprinkle 2 tablespoons sugar, mixed with 1/4 teaspoon nutmeg over batter. Bake at 350° for 30 minutes, until top is nicely browned. Serve warm with cream or ice cream. Serves 6.

If using frozen peaches, drain and use juice in place of water.

Lessons and Hints on Eating, Cooking and Living Better

LESSONS AND HINTS ON EATING, COOKING AND LIVING BETTER

EATING HEALTHY

1. A plate full of different colors is a good indication that you are eating a balanced meal, the key to eating healthy.
2. Avoiding fats is much more important than avoiding sugar. Cheese, for example, is on the list of 10 worst foods you can eat, because of the fat and sodium.
3. Avoid deep or pan-frying as much as possible, especially if what you are cooking is breaded, as breading absorbs oil.
4. Always buy lean meat and trim fat. Skin a chicken *before* cooking.
5. Broiling is healthier than frying. If you do fry, drain off the grease from time to time. If you're cooking hamburger to be used in a recipe, rinse the cooked meat off with hot water and drain before using.
6. Ground turkey may be substituted into almost any recipe in place of hamburger. You will have to add a little olive oil to the pan to fry it. Make sure when you buy ground turkey that is does not include ground skin; check the ingredients on the label.
7. Margarine may be substituted for butter. Do not substitute diet margarine or whipped butter in baking, however, as it will change the texture of the item.
8. Substitute nonfat yogurt (plain) for sour cream.
9. Substitute 2 egg whites for each egg.
10. Sugar is not unhealthy if eaten in the right proportions. It does not cause any disease nor hyperactivity, as myths would lead you to believe. It is believed, however, that sugar substitutes may actually increase the appetite.
11. If you are a diabetic and can't have sugar, we do have some sugarless recipes listed in the index under "sugarless". You can do a lot with the new varieties of unsweetened fruit juices to sweeten things and even make syrups for hot cakes by merely using the juice and adding a small amount of cold water with a small amount of cornstarch. Stir well and heat over medium heat until thickened.
12. Olive oil is the new miracle cure.

APPETIZERS

1. Cut up fresh fruits and vegetables and serve with cubed cheese, dips and crackers. Add peanut butter or cream cheese to celery for a popular item.
2. The best and easiest dip is to mix a pint of sour cream with a package of dry onion soup. Just stir and let set for about 1 hour.
3. You can also use any assorted crackers and top with cheese and small pieces of ham or pepperoni. I once even used rattlesnake meat.
4. Hot appetizers can include anything from a pizza cut into small pieces, cocktail wieners mixed with a barbecue sauce, to miniature barbecued beef or chicken sandwiches.

5. Small finger sandwiches can be made with anything that a regular sandwich can be made of.
6. Try topping a tortilla with cream cheese, dill and crab or shrimp. Roll up and slice in about 1/2 inch pieces, providing a salsa to dip it in.
7. Try miniature quiches or egg rolls for appetizers.
8. Make your own version of nachos. How about Italian, using Italian sausage, mozzarella cheese and a marinara sauce for dipping?

SOUPS

1. Soup is another way of using up leftovers. You might want to keep a "soup bag" in the freezer to throw in the leftover corn, beans, chicken, and bits of cheese. When it fills up, you have the makings for a soup. Throw it in a pot with seasonings and/or bouillon or add pasta or rice, and you have a nice soup.
2. Combine things like creamed corn, cooked and diced potatoes and crabmeat for a different fish soup or try chicken or beef with rice or pasta and vegetables.
3. Never throw out the carcass of any poultry, beef or pork. Simmer the bones or carcasses in about 3 cups of water for about 45 minutes. Cool and remove meat from the bones with your fingers. Save the broth. Strain the broth, if desired, and add the meat back into the liquid. With chicken or turkey, simply add a box of chicken Rice-A-Roni, a can of okra and crushed tomatoes for an easy version of chicken gumbo.
4. For cream soups, start with the basic "roux" (a 50-50 mixture of butter and flour, browned) and add to it as you desire, adding milk, water or bouillon along with cooked, pureed broccoli, spinach, asparagus, etc. You can always add a little grated cheese to anything and your choice of seasonings. A dash of nutmeg to any cream soup makes a world of difference.

SALADS

1. For a green salad, use what is in season. Try mixing 2 different types of lettuce, a light green and a dark green (dark greens are much more abundant in vitamins).
2. Add color with radishes, tomatoes, purple cabbage or grated carrots. Other things you might want to add are mushrooms, bacon bits, sunflower seeds, diced cheese or shredded parmesan. Make a Chef's Salad by adding julienne strips of ham and turkey, sliced hard-boiled eggs and your favorite dressing.
3. Fruit salads can be made from any fruit you desire, fresh or canned. For a dressing, try whipped cream, your favorite flavor of yogurt or pudding. Other things you can add include chopped nuts, coconut, maraschino cherries, or marshmallows.
4. A friend of mine made a salad using lettuce, chopped apples, raisins, and cut maraschino cherries with a 50-50 dressing mix of mayonnaise and honey. Sounds strange, but tasted great and it was colorful!

5. Pasta salads are always popular, especially in the summer. Cook your favorite pasta. Rinse and cool. Add whatever you want to from veggies to meat and cheese. Try pasta with ham or pepperoni and cheese, raw broccoli, cauliflower, and mushrooms. Add a vinaigrette dressing for a great salad. Good for picnics and potlucks. Use any bottled dressing or make up your own.

VEGETABLES

1. Although there are several ways to prepare fresh vegetables, my favorite is to steam and serve them with a light coat of butter or to stir-fry them in a couple tablespoons of olive or peanut oil, adding sliced almonds, trying 2 or 3 different colored vegetables.
2. What ever you do, *do not overcook*. Not only will you destroy them, you will lose most of the vitamins. You might want to add a touch of lemon juice. Fresh vegetables are a little more work, but healthier and taste much better.

A FEW HINTS

Tomatoes:
1. Don't every buy or keep tomatoes refrigerated unless they are overly ripe.
2. To ripen tomatoes, place them in a fruit bowl or brown paper sack with apples; you will get a lot more flavor out of them.
3. If you have tomatoes getting too ripe, skin them and simmer for about 30 minutes. Crush them and make your own fresh spaghetti sauce or chile. Freeze them for later use.

Squash:
1. Cut a buttercup or acorn squash in half. Remove seeds and place 1 tablespoon butter and 2 of brown sugar in cavity. Place in pie plate with about 1/2 inch water and bake in a 350° oven about 1 hour, until tender.
2. Fry zucchini. Simply slice, steam and butter. Sprinkle Parmesan or melt a thin slice of Provolone cheese over the top. You may also batter fry. Beat 1 egg with 2 tablespoons water and a dash of garlic powder. Dip sliced squash in egg mixture, then bread in finely ground saltine crackers. Fry in butter flavored shortening. Salt and pepper to taste.

Carrots:
1. Steam and butter. Sprinkle a little brown sugar and/or a fruit juice concentrate over them if you'd like.

Green beans:
1. Using cooked beans, stir in 1 can cream of mushroom soup and a small can of French fried onion rings. Bake in a casserole until thoroughly heated in a 350° oven, about 25 minutes.

MAIN DISHES

1. This is one category I rarely use a recipe, particularly living alone and cooking for just one or two. Use recipes, but don't restrict yourself. Feel free to leave out, substitute or add to a recipe.
2. If the recipe serves 8, cut down proportionately to what you need or divide the leftovers into individual casserole dishes, cover and freeze for a later day. Think of things to add to them so that they are different next time.
3. Making up your own recipes has several advantages. It's a great way to use up what is on hand and yet have something new and fresh each meal. It's also economical, because you can take advantage of sales. To save a lot of money, plan your meals around what is on sale; don't plan a menu first. Take time to go through your weekly newspaper ads. In just a weeks time, you will save enough money to pay for this book.
4. Buy ground beef, shrimp, crab, chicken, etc. when it is on sale and freeze it in individual packages for later use. The same with pastas, rice, baking goods, etc. Fresh fruit and vegetables are always best when they're least expensive. Not only do you always have food available, but your money is working for you a lot more than any investment could. Using coupons also saves a lot.
5. Creating a casserole, pasta dish or stir-fry is simple: You begin with a starch, be it rice, pasta or potatoes. Add meat, chicken or fish and/or vegetables. Now all you need is a sauce. You can make a Veloute sauce (see index), a simple butter or olive oil and herb sauce. You can buy pre-made ones as a marinara or Hollandaise sauce. Canned soups work well also. You can add onions, nuts, cheese, bread crumbs, or cream cheese.
6. Use your imagination. Experiment with seasonings. If you're intimidated, try one of the multi-spices, such as "Mrs. Dash". Add spice in tiny amounts and then taste. A little spice goes a long way. Be especially careful of salt. Think of the salt already in some of the ingredients, such as saltines, ham or chicken bouillon.

POULTRY

1. The easiest way to bake a chicken is to poke holes in a lemon and stuff it into the cavity, removing giblets first. Place the chicken in a baking dish with a little water. Cover lightly with a foil tent and bake at 350° about 1 1/2 hours until done.
2. To check if poultry is done, poke a fork into the joint between the leg and thigh. If no blood emerges, the bird is done.
3. It is not necessary to buy a "broiling hen". A fryer will do just as well at half the price and a lot less fat.
4. Buy a turkey breast (bone in). Slice off the meat and prepare in any way you would veal. Turkey piccata is great. Cook the bones for soups or other purposes (see next step).
5. Buy a whole chicken or chicken breast when on sale. Remove skin (healthier) and simmer in about 2 cups of water for 30 minutes. Cool and remove meat from bones, separating it into individual portions. Seal and freeze for later use.

The broth will freeze as well. Use later to make chicken and dumplings, creamed chicken, etc.

6. When roasting any type of bird, especially the smaller ones, place them breast side down. The juices are in the back and will flow through to give you a moist bird.

FISH

1. When purchasing fish, make sure that it doesn't have a "fishy smell". This is a sign that the fish is old. The fish should have a bright, fresh color to it.

2. The healthiest and easiest way to prepare fish is to either bake or poach it in a tiny bit of water. To bake it, coat a pan with vegetable spray. Add the fish, a sprinkle of lemon juice and a little dill, paprika or garlic powder. Cover with foil and bake at 375° for 10 minutes. Uncover and bake an additional 10 minutes. *Do not overcook fish!*

3. Try making a light citrus or raspberry sauce for fish. Stir in 1 teaspoon cornstarch with 2 tablespoons cold water. Add to 3 tablespoons juice and heat slowly, stirring constantly, until thickened. Pour over top of broiled fish. Don't add dill, garlic or salt, instead try maybe a dash of nutmeg or cinnamon.

PASTA

1. Use amount of water directed on package, about 6 cups for every 8 ounces, lightly salted with a few drops of vegetable oil. Bring to a rapid boil. Cook, stirring for 3 minutes. Drain, rinse with hot water and use immediately.

2. If used in salads, rinse with cold water. *Do not overcook pasta!* If you have to save pasta after cooked, toss with butter or shortening before cooling. Stir pasta with a fork a couple of minutes into cooking to keep it from sticking together.

GENERAL

1. For making smoother gravies and sauces, use a small whisk for stirring. Also, after you've browned the flour with the butter or drippings, add the water or milk slowly, stirring constantly. Bring to a boil, reduce heat and simmer until thickened.

2. If gravy or sauce is too thin, mix a couple tablespoons cornstarch with about 1/4 cup cold water. Stir well and add to sauce or gravy.

3. When breading meat or vegetables to fry, dip meat or vegetables in coating and place on waxed paper. Refrigerate for 2 hours. The coating will stay on better and will save time when preparing a meal.

BAKING

General:

1. *Read recipe all the way through before starting.* Place all ingredients in front of you. Separate eggs, crush nuts, grease pans, etc. before starting.

2. When batter is mixed, recheck recipe to make sure you put everything in before you pour it into the pan.

3. Invest in heavy metal baking pans, high quality. You will be amazed at the difference it will make in the product. They're easy to clean and well worth the investment.
4. Make sure oven is preheated. Check out your oven with an oven thermometer periodically to make sure you have a true reading.
5. Plan your recipes at least a couple hours in advance. When butter or margarine is an ingredient, it has to be softened to cream. All ingredients should be room temperature, especially eggs.
6. Butter and margarine may be interchangeable. I usually use a 50-50 mixture. Don't ever use a diet or whipped margarine. It will change the texture.
7. When whipping cream, use a chilled metal bowl and beaters. For stability, sprinkle some dry milk crystals over the cream before beating. Also use powdered sugar instead of regular sugar.
8. Separate eggs while chilled, then bring whites to room temperature before beating. Use a metal bowl and make sure it is free of any oils.
9. The easiest way to break nuts or chocolate chunks is to place them in a heavy freezer bang and pound them with the side of a heavy mallet.
10. Soak raisins in warm water about 1 hour before using, then drain them. They will be soft and plump.
11. When creaming butter and sugar together, rinse the bowl with boiling water first. They'll cream faster.
12. Dust chips or dried fruit with flour before adding to breads or cakes. It will keep them from sinking.

EGG TIPS

See our special section "What do I do with the rest of it?" For ideas when you have extra egg yolks or whites left.

1. To test for freshness, place eggs in water; they should sink if fresh.
2. Keep eggs in carton in refrigerator. This will keep them fresher than if you remove them and place them in the door.
3. If you wish to center the yolk for purposes as hard boiling for deviled eggs, store them large end up.
4. You may store yolks by: (a) Placing them in a plastic container with a lid. Lightly cover them with water. Drain off water before using. (b) The yolks may also be frozen. Gently stir in 1/2 teaspoon salt or 1 teaspoon sugar for every 6 yolks (adjust sugar or salt accordingly when you use later). Freeze together or individually in an ice cube container. Pop out and store in freezer bag. Bring to room temperature before using.
5. You may store extra whites by keeping them covered in a plastic container in the refrigerator for up to 2 weeks. If you keep them longer, rotate them by using the saved ones up and separating new ones. I once had to do this for a wedding, requiring 3 angel food cakes. What do you do with 36 egg yolks? If you're worried about cholesterol, use 2 egg whites in place of 1 egg in baking. It will make little difference in texture.

Boiled Eggs:
1. Poke a hole with a straight pin in the large end of the eggs.
2. Place eggs in a saucepan with enough warm water to cover the eggs. Add 1/2 teaspoon salt and 1 tablespoon vinegar. Let set about 10 minutes. Cover saucepan and bring water to a boil. Turn off heat and let pan set on burner for 21 minutes (9 for a soft boiled egg). Remove eggs from water and place them in ice water. Bring pan of water back to a boil and place eggs back in for only 1 minute. Remove them and return them to the ice water to finish cooling.

BREAD

1. Put a small dish of water in the oven if you like a soft crust on your bread.
2. *Never* overheat the water when adding to yeast. It should be 120° maximum or warm to the touch. If the yeast doesn't react (get foamy), throw it away. You will only be wasting time and ingredients.
3. Always use the lowest possible rack in the oven when baking loaves of bread. Otherwise, the bottoms of your loaves will turn out moist. This is also advisable with muffins and fruit breads.
4. You can tell when a loaf of bread is done by thumping the crust. You should hear a hollow thump.
5. Put a piece of paper towel in with bread that you freeze. This will prevent it from getting soggy.
6. If you need a warm place for your dough to rise, turn your oven on for about 5 minutes. Turn it off and let your dough rise in the oven.
7. When baking with whole wheat flour, the dough should be just a little sticky after kneading. This is a secret to keep the bread from being too dry. If substituting whole wheat flour for white in a recipe, it is better to do it 50-50 with white flour.

Muffins and Pancakes:
1. Stir dry ingredients into liquid, only until barely moistened. I like to use only a wire whisk. You may use a spray vegetable coating for muffin tins.

CAKES

1. When using an angel food cake mix, add 1 fresh egg white with the water.
2. In several of the recipes for cakes and fruit breads, you will find the term, "until tested done", meaning that the cake should spring back when touched lightly and that a toothpick inserted into the cake or bread should come out clean.
3. Make sure cake pans don't touch each other or the side of the oven when baking.

COOKIES

1. For a soft, chewy texture, remove cookies from oven as soon as the sides are lightly browned. If you like a harder cookie, leave them in the oven longer.

2. Should cookies get hard, place them in a plastic bag with a piece of bread. Seal and let set for 24 hours. Cookies will soften up.
3. All cookies should be baked near the center of the oven.
4. Unless the recipe indicates otherwise, cookie should remain on cookie sheets 3 or 4 minutes after removing from the oven to allow them to set, so they may be easily removed without breaking.
5. If you have trouble with the dough spreading out, chill the dough first and never put cookies on a warm cookie sheet.
6. Dough *must* be thoroughly chilled before rolling out for sugar cookies. Flour cookie cutters well before using. I prefer the metal, open-face cookie cutters overplastic. They don't stick!
7. Toast oatmeal in a 350° oven for about 10 minutes before adding to cookies. It makes a nutty flavor.

PIES

Pie crusts are probably the most important part of the pie. Here are some hints for a good flaky crust:

1. Use *ice cold water* when making the dough.
2. Handle dough as little as possible. *Do not knead.*
3. Loosely wrap dough around pin once it is rolled out to move the crust from the board to the pie plate.
4. Don't throw away the scraps, instead roll them out. Add some melted butter and sugar cinnamon. Roll up and slice like you would miniature cinnamon rolls. Place on ungreased pan and bake in a 400° oven about 15 minutes.
5. Place foil around outside edges of crust to keep them from burning. This is especially true of any pie needing more than 30 minutes baking time.

FRESH FRUIT

All of our recipes using fresh fruit in a separate section in alphabetical order.

1. Bananas: Peel and slice into a bowl. Add a little powdered sugar, a couple of tablespoons orange juice concentrate, milk, and some sunflower seeds. If bananas get too ripe, they're perfect for cake or bread.
2. Peaches 'n Cream: Nothing like a couple of peaches, peeled and lightly sprinkled with sugar. Add cream or milk for an anytime treat.
3. Cereal: What's cereal without fresh fruit. One of my favorite breakfasts is hot oatmeal with a mashed banana, brown sugar, butter, and milk with a dash of cinnamon.
4. Fruit and Cheese: Try serving apples or grapes with cheese. Add a little wine and crackers and you have a table fit for entertaining.

Lemon:
1. Lemon peel, twist or zest all refer to the yellow part of the skin. Use only the outer yellow part. You may grate it off, or cut it off with a knife or vegetable peeler, if using it for decoration. Peel the lemon peel just prior to serving or cover peels with a slightly dampened napkin.

2. Room temperature lemons will yield more juice than a cold one. You may microwave on HIGH for about 30 seconds. Rolling them on the counter with the palm of your hand will also increase yield. However, if you're grating a lemon peel, it works better chilled.
3. Lemon juice may be refrigerated up to 3 days in a tightly sealed container. It also freezes nicely. The best way to freeze is to do it in ice cube trays. Once frozen, remove and place in plastic bag and secure. They are convenient and will last up to 4 months. For a little zest, try adding them to iced tea or mineral water.

WHAT DO I DO WITH THE REST OF IT?

There are some recipes that leave you with extra egg yolks or whites, sour cream or buttermilk that you don't know what to do with. Pumpkin is another thing where the recipe uses 1 cup and then, what do you do with the rest of it? Pumpkin has its own section and here are some recipes for the others. Refer to the index for page number.

Egg Yolks (number implies the number of egg yolks or whites): German Gold Pound Cake (6), Eclairs (6), Cheesecake Supreme (3), German Chocolate Cake (3), Special Banana Cake (2), Danish Apple Bars (1), Party Butter Cookies (1), Cream Cheese Sugar Cookies (1).

Egg Whites: Swans Down Angel Food Cake (12), Poppy Seed Cake with Cream Cheese Frosting (3), Oat Bran Muffins (3), Old-Fashioned Divinity (3), Ritz Cracker Torte (3), Upside-Down Strawberry Pie (3), Banana Pudding with Fruit Sauce (3), Surprise Meringue Cookies (2), Perfect White Cake (2), Strawberry Banana Pie (2).

You may also substitute 2 whites in place of 1 egg in any baking if you wish to make it healthier. Of course, you can always feed the extra egg parts to your dog or cat. It's great for their fur!

Sour Cream: Orange Frosted Cocoa Bundt Cake, Sour Cream Chocolate Cake, Frosted Cashew Cookies, Fruit 'N Philly Pancake, Dropped Sugar Cookies, Easy Does It Cookies.

Buttermilk: Wheat Cakes, Savory Hot Cakes, Coca-Coca Cake, Black Forest Cake, German Chocolate Cake, Lemon Torte, Lemon and Buttermilk Spice Cake, Goldie Cookies (Raisin Filled), Whole Wheat Bread.

Cream Cheese: Cold Appetizer Pizza, Stuffed French Toast, Chocolate Cheesecake Squares, German Chocolate Cheesecake Squares, Caramel Pecan Cheesecake, Cheesecake Supreme, Pumpkin Walnut Cheesecake, Black Forest Cheesecake, Grape Crepes, Fruit 'N "Philly" Pancake, Orange or Apricot Sparkle, Cherry Pretzel Salad or Dessert, Pistachio Dessert, Pumpkin Cake Roll. Also cream cheese is always great in an omelet or to use as a spread on muffins or bagels.

Index

Sour Cream Enchiladas....58
Sourdough French Toast....83
Spaghetti Pie....53
Special Banana Cream Pie....172
Speedy Lasagna....54
Spicy Beef Sandwich....19
Spinach Salad....12
Strawberries Smetana....177
Strawberry Angel Cake Dessert....177
Strawberry Banana Fizz....195
Strawberry Banana Pie....120
Strawberry Cream Pie....179
Strawberry Pineapple Cooler....4
Stuffed French Toast....84
Stuffed Turkey Patties with Tomato
    Sauce....36
Stuffing for Turkey....34
Sugarless Apple Pie....167
Sugarless Cupcakes....102
Sunday Strawberry Dessert....180
Super Lasagna....55
Surprise Meringue Cookies....104
Swans Down Angel Food....89
Swedish Rosettes....117
Sweet and Sour Spam....51
Sweet Dough....78
Swiss Steak....41

Taco Beef Soup....5
Taco Style Potato and Turkey Skil-
    let....35
Tangerine Snowballs....157
Tangy Orange Drops....112
Tempura Batter....1
The $10,000 Oatmeal Cookies....109
The Best Gingerbread....99
Toasted Coconut Pecan Pie....120
Toll House Cake....135
Tomato Juice Cocktail....25
Turkey Burgers....37
Turkey Loaf....38
Turkey or Chicken Stew....63
Turkey Reuben Sandwich....18
Turkey Spaghetti....53
Turkey Stock....5
Turkey Stroganoff....36
Turkey Tacos....35
Turkey-Poppy Seed Casserole....39

Twenty-Four Hour Slaw....11

Uncooked Jam....181
Upside-Down Strawberry Meringue
    Pie....180

Vanilla Pudding Pecan Pie....119
Veal Parmigiana....40
Vegetable Pasta Toss....60

Wheat and Raisin Chocolate Chip
    Cookies....104
Whole Wheat Applesauce Coffee
    Cake....163
Whole Wheat Biscuits....84
Whole Wheat Bread....69
Whole Wheat Carrot-Banana
    Bread....170
Whole Wheat Cinnamon Rolls....77
Whole Wheat Pear-Carrot Muf-
    fins...187
Wholesome Wheat and Oat Rolls....72
Winnie's Lime or Lemon Party
    Salad....15

Yellow Cake....98
Yummy Fresh Peach Pie....189

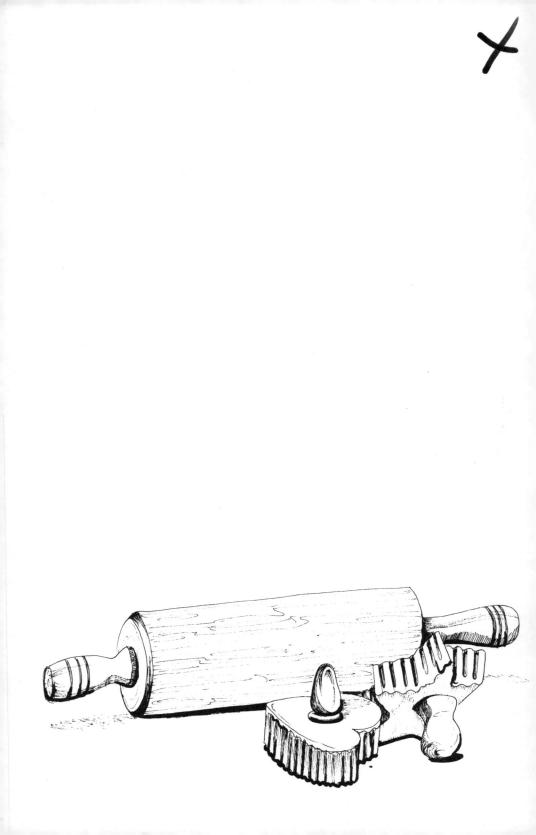

Name _____

Address _____

City/State/Zip _____

Telephone (_____) _____

Please send best-selling Colorado Collection cookbooks as indicated below:

	QUANTITY	PRICE	TAX (Colorado residents only)	TOTAL
COLORADO COOKIE COLLECTION	_____	$12.95	$ .39 per book	$ _____
NOTHIN' BUT MUFFINS	_____	$ 9.95	$ .30 per book	$ _____
101 WAYS TO MAKE RAMEN NOODLES	_____	$ 9.95	$ .30 per book	$ _____
MYSTIC MOUNTAIN MEMORIES	_____	$14.95	$ .45 per book	$ _____
	_____		Plus $2.00 each for shipping and handling	$ _____
			TOTAL ENCLOSED	$ _____

SEND A GIFT TO SOMEONE SPECIAL

Name _____

Address _____

City/State/Zip _____

Message _____

_____

_____

Please make checks payable to:

C & G Publishing, Inc.
2702 19th Street Road
Greeley, CO 80631
1-800-925-3172

Name _____

Address _____

City/State/Zip _____

Telephone (_____) _____

Please send best-selling Colorado Collection cookbooks as indicated below:

	QUANTITY	PRICE	TAX (Colorado residents only)	TOTAL
COLORADO COOKIE COLLECTION	_____	$12.95	$ .39 per book	$ _____
NOTHIN' BUT MUFFINS	_____	$ 9.95	$ .30 per book	$ _____
101 WAYS TO MAKE RAMEN NOODLES	_____	$ 9.95	$ .30 per book	$ _____
MYSTIC MOUNTAIN MEMORIES	_____	$14.95	$ .45 per book	$ _____
	_____		Plus $2.00 each for shipping and handling	$ _____
			TOTAL ENCLOSED	$ _____

SEND A GIFT TO SOMEONE SPECIAL

Name _____

Address _____

City/State/Zip _____

Message _____

_____

_____

Please make checks payable to:

C & G Publishing, Inc.
2702 19th Street Road
Greeley, CO 80631
1-800-925-3172

Applesauce Cake

- ½ short
- 2 c sugar
- 2 eggs
- 1½ c apple sauce - blend
- 2 t into ½ c boiling H²O
  (baking soda)
- 2½ c flour
- ½ t salt
- ½ t cin
- ½ t. cloves
- ½ t allspice

- 1 c· walnuts
- 1 c raisins

350° for ~~the~~ 40-45 min
9 x 13

Frosting -

- ½ c butter melt
- 1 c brown sugar
- ¼ c milk

stir till boil - cool (5 mins)
add powdered sugar (1½ c)